Developing Vocational Expertise

Principles and issues in vocational education

Edited by John Stevenson

LONDON AND NEW YORK

First published 2003 by Allen & Unwin

Published 2020 by Routledge
2 Park Square, Milton Park, Abingdon, Oxon OX14 4RN
605 Third Avenue, New York, NY 10017

Routledge is an imprint of the Taylor & Francis Group, an informa business

Copyright © this collection John Stevenson, 2003
Copyright © in individual chapters remains with the contributors, 2003

All rights reserved. No part of this book may be reprinted or reproduced or utilised in any form or by any electronic, mechanical, or other means, now known or hereafter invented, including photocopying and recording, or in any information storage or retrieval system, without permission in writing from the publishers.

Notice:
Product or corporate names may be trademarks or registered trademarks, and are used only for identification and explanation without intent to infringe.

National Library of Australia
Cataloguing-in-Publication entry:

Developing vocational expertise:
Principles and issues in vocational education.

Includes index

ISBN 1 86508 9792.

1. Vocational education. 2. Occupational training.
3. Technical education. I. Stevenson, John C.

370.113

Index compiled by Russell Brooks

Typeset in 10.5/12pt Sabon by Midland Typesetters, Maryborough, Victoria

ISBN-13: 9781865089195 (pbk)

Contents

List of figures	vii
List of tables	viii
Acknowledgments	x
Contributors	xii
Introduction	xiii

PART I: VOCATIONAL EXPERTISE AND ITS DEVELOPMENT

1 Expertise for the workplace — 3
John Stevenson
- Introduction — 3
- Concepts of expertise — 4
- Expertise as facility with meaning — 5
- Relationships of meaning — 7
- Psychological concepts of expertise — 11
- Summary of ideas about expertise — 20
- Introducing some common abstractions — 23

2 Vocational teaching and learning in context — 26
John Stevenson
- Introduction — 26
- Curriculum sources for vocational teaching and learning — 27
- Teaching and learning assumptions — 28

Curriculum theories	31
Economic press for codification of meaning	33
Some bases for planning teaching and learning	37
Generating teaching and learning principles	40
Conclusion	43

PART II: Developing Vocational Expertise for Key Pursuits

3 Developing literacy — 51
Jean Searle

Introduction	51
What is literacy?	52
Literacy theories, research and practice	55
Literacy in the workplace	64
Implications for teaching and learning	71
Conclusion	75

4 Developing numeracy — 81
Clive Kanes

Introduction	81
Numerical practices	82
The theme of visibility	84
The theme of useability	86
The theme of constructibility	92
Dilemmas and conflicts	95
Numeracy curriculum development	100
Implications for practice	104
Conclusion	105

5 Developing information literacy — 110
Fred Beven

Background	110
Work in the knowledge economy	111
Information literacy for work	114
Research	119
Implications for curriculum development	130
Recommendations for teaching	131

6 Developing problem-solving skills — 135
Howard Middleton

Introduction	135
Problems	136
Problems as challenges	140
What makes problems difficult?	141
Representing problems	143
Problem-solving	147
Developing problem-solving skills: implications for teaching and learning	149

CONTENTS

7 Developing creativity	**153**
Irena Yashin-Shaw	
Introduction	153
Creative thinking in vocational settings	153
What is creativity?	154
Models of creative problem-solving	156
The hierarchical view of thinking	159
The knowledge base	159
Second-order procedures	161
Third-order procedures	165
Other features of the model	166
Creative problem-solving in graphic design: a case study	166
Implications for teaching and learning in vocational settings	168
Conclusion	179
8 Working values	**183**
John Stevenson	
Introduction	183
Values	184
Social origins of values	185
Cognitive treatment of values in relation to knowledge	186
Values in settings and communities of practice	187
Recent research on workplace values	189
Implications for curriculum development	190
Implications for teaching and learning	193
Conclusion	196
PART III: EMERGING CHALLENGES IN INSTRUCTIONAL DELIVERY	
9 Strategies for developing flexible learning	**203**
Clive Kanes	
Introduction	203
What is flexible learning?	204
What is the rationale for flexible learning?	206
Three frameworks for developing flexible learning	209
Flexible learning as a learning activity	212
Developing a flexible learning curriculum	217
Flexible learning principles and teaching methods	219
Conclusion	222
10 Guiding vocational learning	**226**
Stephen Billett	
Guided learning	226
Intersubjectivity, appropriation or mastery: outcomes of guided learning	228
Conceptual bases of guided learning	231
Curriculum and guided learning	235

Implications for instruction	238
Conclusion	242

11 Integrating approaches to developing vocational expertise — 247
John Stevenson

Introduction	247
Teaching and learning as an activity system	248
Sample actions illustrating teaching and learning principles	250
Instantiations of principles and sample actions in approaching vocational teaching and learning	254
Conclusion	258

Index   266

List of figures

1.1	Relationships of expertise and meaning	22
2.1	The structure of a human activity system	38
2.2	Relationships of expertise, meaning and learning	41
4.1	Model of numeracy as a cultural-historical activity system	102
5.1	Main menu at Site A	121
5.2	Main menu at Site C	122
5.3	Main menu at Site D	122
6.1	Revised concept of a problem space	138
7.1	The synthesised model for creative problem-solving	160
7.2	Simplified version of the creative problem-solving model	175
9.1	Model of flexible delivery as a cultural-historical activity system	214
11.1	Teaching and learning as an activity system	249
11.2	Relationships of expertise, meaning, learning principles, sample actions and instantiations	259

List of tables

3.1	Definitions of literacy	53
3.2	Reading, writing and literacy theory and practice	56
3.3	Workplace activities	70
4.1	Strands and strand organisers for *Mathematics—A Curriculum Profile for Australian Schools*	85
4.2	Principles for the learning and teaching of numeracy and indicative teaching methods	96
4.3	Cluster analysis of overall strand site ranks	98
5.1	Generic (key) workplace skills frameworks	116
5.2	Comparison of key skills	117
5.3	Extract from the summary of the key competency 'Collecting, analysing and organising ideas and information'	118
5.4	Extract from the summary of the key competency 'Using technology'	119
5.5	Comparison of mnemonics used in generic context 5 of Event 'Issuing Ticket'	125
7.1	Generation procedures and definitions	162
7.2	Exploration procedures and definitions	163
7.3	Evaluation procedures and definitions	164
7.4	Executive control procedures and definitions	165

LIST OF TABLES

7.5	Extract of protocols showing presence of all categories of thinking	168
7.6	Extract of protocols showing greater relative frequency of executive control and generation at the beginning of the problem-solving process	169
7.7	Extract of protocols showing greater relative frequency of evaluation towards the end of the problem-solving process	171
8.1	Illustrative values found in hospitality and airline work sites	191
9.1	Facets and indicators of flexible learning practice	205
9.2	Flexible learning principles and flexible teaching principles and methods	220
11.1	Sample actions flowing from the principle: *Proceeding from learners' sense of vocation*	251
11.2	Sample actions flowing from the principle: *Contextualising learning and making functions and purposes explicit*	252
11.3	Sample actions flowing from the principle: *Focusing learning primarily on the capacity-to-do*	252
11.4	Sample actions flowing from the principle: *Making setting element relationships clear*	253
11.5	Sample actions flowing from the principle: *Sharing meanings*	253
11.6	Sample actions flowing from the principle: *Relating one learning setting meanings with those of other settings*	254
11.7	Sample actions flowing from the principle: *Building connections among different meanings and their renditions*	255
11.8	Instantiations of *proceeding from learners' sense of vocation*	256
11.9	Instantiations of *contextualising learning and making functions and purposes explicit*	257
11.10	Instantiations of *focusing learning primarily on the capacity-to-do*	260
11.11	Instantiations of *making setting element relationships clear*	261
11.12	Instantiations of *sharing meanings*	262
11.13	Instantiations of *relating one learning setting meanings with those of other settings*	263
11.14	Instantiations of *building connections among different meanings and their renditions*	264

Acknowledgments

The authors gratefully acknowledge permissions given to reproduce material from the following sources. These include:

FIGURES

Chapter 2, Figure 2.1: The structure of a human activity system, reproduced with permission from Figure 2, p. 15, in Y. Engeström, 1999, 'Expansive learning at work: toward an activity-theoretical reconceptualization', keynote address, *Changing Practice through Research: Changing Research through Practice*, 7th Annual International Conference of the Centre for Learning and Work Research, Griffith University, Brisbane.

ACKNOWLEDGMENTS

TABLES

Chapter 3, Table 3.3: Workplace activities, reproduced with permission from Table 4: Workplace activities in J. Searle, & A. Kelly, 2002, *Acting Smart: An Investigation of Assumptions and Principles which Underpin Training and Assessment Within One Civil Construction Company*, Language Australia, Melbourne.

Chapter 5, Table 5.2: Comparison of key skills in Australia, Britain, the United States and New Zealand, reproduced with permission from Table 1, p. 15, P. Kearns, 2001, *Review of Research: Generic Skills for the New Economy*, National Centre for Vocational Education Research, Adelaide.

Contributors

Fred Beven is Deputy Director, Centre for Learning and Work Research, Griffith University, Queensland, Australia.

Stephen Billett is Associate Professor, Centre for Learning and Work Research, Griffith University, Queensland, Australia.

Clive Kanes is Director, Centre for Learning and Work Research, Griffith University, Queensland, Australia.

Howard Middleton is Director, Centre for Technology Education Research, Griffith University, Queensland, Australia.

Jean Searle is Director, Queensland Centre of Adult Literacy and Numeracy, Australian Research Consortium, Queensland, Australia.

John Stevenson is Professor of Post-compulsory Education and Training, Centre for Learning and Work Research, Griffith University, Queensland, Australia.

Irena Yashin-Shaw is a Research Fellow, Centre for Learning and Work Research, Griffith University, Queensland, Australia.

Introduction

John Stevenson

The purpose of this book is to synthesise approaches that might be taken to developing vocational expertise. The various chapters discuss and report research relevant to establishing an understanding of the nature of vocational expertise and synthesising principles to guide instruction. The book is aimed at researchers in the field of vocational education and training, teachers and trainers seeking to understand and improve teaching and learning practices, and policy-makers seeking to improve the quality of vocational education and training. The book replaces an earlier work which is now out of print, *Cognition at Work: The Development of Vocational Expertise*, published by the National Centre for Vocational Education Research, from 1994 to 2000.

The book explores what should be the subject of the education that seeks to develop individuals for the workplace—vocational education. What kind of knowledge should be the subject of vocational education and how should it relate to the kinds of expertise that we see in the workplace? Chapter 1 provides an extensive analysis of what constitutes expertise in everyday and vocational contexts. It is assumed that the idea of expertise developed in this book will be applicable to many fields of human endeavour outside of the subject areas explicitly examined here.

The book does not seek to advance a singular theoretical perspective for understanding issues and synthesising teaching and learning principles. Rather, each chapter of the book draws upon a variety of theoretical perspectives to examine the issues and then synthesise a position about how to approach teaching and learning for the relevant subject area. Some of these perspectives are cognitive psychology, discourse theory and activity theory.

The book's primary focus, then, is on synthesising approaches to teaching and learning in vocational education, rather than on developing policy *per se*, or giving advice to researchers about issues such as gaining access to workplace premises. Nor does the book seek to compare and contrast the various qualification/certification provisions of the systems across various countries; there is not the space needed to examine them meaningfully. Rather, it is the knowledge and meanings currently being targeted in vocational courses that are being examined, and the teaching and learning approaches needed to develop such meanings.

Moreover, the book cannot hope to cover the myriad of occupations that are the subject of vocational education, and so the main subjects have been chosen from the Key competencies/Core Skills/ Necessary Skills identified in various countries as generic and important across occupations. This choice is discussed further in Chapter 1. Accordingly, the chapters focus explicitly on these subject areas and examine their claims for genericity. If even these sets of skills are not really generic, then the specific skills of the multitude of occupational areas will certainly not be generic. It is in responding to the challenges of these examinations that we can synthesise curricular, teaching and learning approaches.

The contributors take a structured approach to the development of vocational expertise generally, and the development of core sets of knowledge for work. Within each area of expertise, the various chapters outline recent theoretical and research developments, then apply these ideas in advancing a range of approaches to curriculum development, teaching and learning.

The book is divided into three parts. Part I discusses the nature of expertise for the workplace. Part II examines the nature of expertise in various topic areas—literacy, numeracy, information literacy, problem-solving skills, creativity, and values—and advances possible approaches to instruction in these areas. Part III examines challenges in instructional delivery, including flexible delivery and guiding learning. Chapter 11 integrates the contributions of the other chapters in the book.

Chapter 1 examines important characteristics of workplace capacities, developed through experience and commonly called expertise. Limitations of commonly used words and their underlying dualistic constructions (such as academic/vocational, theoretical/practical) in capturing these capacities are outlined. It is argued that vocational expertise involves a meaningfulness that connects problems encountered in workplaces and in other individual and societal pursuits, and that it consists of a facility with situated, normative meanings that

INTRODUCTION

include both propositional and procedural knowledge. The chapter provides a basis for exploring curriculum development and educational delivery implications, which are discussed in Chapter 2.

Chapter 2 adopts the ideas of expertise developed in Chapter 1 and analyses the policy idea of competence as a basis for designing teaching and learning in vocational education and training. It unpacks this idea in terms of the various capacities that are involved (Chapter 1) and the kinds of approaches that can be taken to their development through learning. On this basis, the challenges to, and approaches available for, curriculum designers and teachers/trainers are examined. The chapter advances a set of teaching and learning principles for developing vocational knowledge.

Chapter 3 examines how psycholinguistic and socio-cultural theories of literacy have been drawn upon to promote different discourses (definitions) of literacy, as decontextualised skills or as socially situated practices. The author shows how these discourses have led to the development of very different approaches to the teaching and assessment of reading and writing. She demonstrates how the strengths of each approach can be utilised in providing a holistic approach to literacy teaching practice.

Chapter 4 examines how different theoretical approaches give rise to different ideas of what constitutes numeracy and different approaches to the development of numerical knowledge. Drawing on activity theory, the author outlines the important contributions of different characteristics of the instructional situation in which learners engage. These ideas are used to advance approaches that can be taken to the teaching and learning of numerical knowledge for vocational purposes.

Chapter 5 examines what constitutes information literacy by drawing upon recent examinations of its workplace use. This includes ideas about information literacy as a fundamental competency, ideas of how computer literacy should be developed for work and an examination of computing literacy in workplace practice. The chapter then discusses how approaches to teaching and learning might be fashioned as a consequence.

Chapter 6 examines the importance of various kinds of problem-solving in contemporary vocations. It draws on cognitive theory to outline and examine models of problem-solving for well-defined and ill-defined problems. On the basis of these models, approaches are outlined for the teaching and learning of the knowledge needed for solving the kinds of problems that will constitute contemporary and future work.

Chapter 7 examines the reasons why the development of creative thinking is important in vocational education and training, and examines various models of creative thinking. It draws on cognitive theory and theories of creative thinking to integrate different ideas about creative thinking processes. The chapter illustrates these processes with examples of creative thinking cognitive procedures. The chapter outlines approaches that can be taken in the development of creative thinking for learners in vocational education and explores the implications for curriculum design.

Chapter 8 examines relevant research on the kinds of values that have been found to be operating in workplaces. The involvement of values in the personal and collective meanings that enable competent and expert performance is examined.

In Chapter 9, elements of flexibility in learning and models of flexible delivery are explained and their strengths and limitations examined. Based on these ideas, and on research on the use of flexible delivery in vocational education and training, the chapter advances important considerations for instructional designers seeking to make vocational learning more flexible.

In Chapter 10, the nature of the learning processes that are involved in guided learning, and the factors that affect successful learning guidance, are examined. These ideas are used to suggest ways in which successful approaches to learning guidance can be designed and implemented.

Chapter 11 takes up the challenges of Chapters 1 and 2, and the problems and approaches advanced in Chapters 3–10, to synthesise an integrated approach to the development of vocational knowledge. It adopts a stance that practical knowledge is situated, normative and concrete, related directly to its functionality. The chapter brings together, into an integrated framework, suggestions for teaching such essential knowledge as literacy, numeracy, problem-solving, information literacy, creativity and the capacity for complex problem-solving, as well as suggestions for approaching flexible delivery and learning guidance.

Together, the various chapters examine the idea of expertise from a variety of theoretical perspectives, outline recent research in the various areas and synthesise approaches that can be taken to understanding various aspects of expertise, fashioning instructional strategies and improving teaching and learning.

Part I

Vocational Expertise and its Development

1

Expertise for the workplace

John Stevenson

INTRODUCTION

This chapter explains important characteristics of human capacities, developed through experience and commonly called expertise. It is argued that vocational expertise:

- arises socially and consists of a contextualised, normative capacity-to-do;
- constructs and draws upon a meaningfulness that connects such doing with other kinds of individually constructed and shared meanings;
- connects problems encountered in workplaces with other individual and societal pursuits; and
- transforms itself in response to engagement and experience.

The chapter is structured as follows. Firstly, concepts of expertise are examined, followed by an outline of how different kinds of knowing can be differentiated. Secondly, the range of different kinds of meaning and their interrelationships are examined. Meaning is seen to be related to doing, the field of activity, practice, vocation and others' constructions of meaning. Thirdly, these ideas of expertise as facility with meaning are examined in relation to various psychological concepts of expertise. Finally, the various ideas advanced in the chapter are brought together in a summary of the nature of expertise.

The chapter provides a basis for addressing economic and vocational education challenges and for exploring curriculum development and educational delivery implications for contemporary vocational education in Chapter 2. It also provides an introduction to the examination of various abstractions of important kinds of capacities in Part II of the book: literacy, numeracy, problem-solving, creativity, computer literacy and values.

CONCEPTS OF EXPERTISE

I will call *expertise*, at the outset, the ability to do something well—better than others just starting out on the undertaking. What constitutes doing something well is a social construct. Firstly, expertise is relative to others—one is regarded as expert if one can do things better than others can. Secondly, it is determined by what people in various groups would judge as expert. Expertise can refer to all walks of life. For instance, it can refer to occupational undertakings or undertakings in life more generally—for example, an expert plumber, gardener, public speaker or bike-rider. When referring to work, expertise sometimes refers to whole occupations such as an expert lawyer, motor mechanic or politician. It is also used to refer to aspects of occupations—for example an expert decision-maker or negotiator.

In all these cases, what counts as expertise is socially determined. Thus, in the building industry, there would be a consensus on what constituted good carpentry, and this would vary somewhat across communities, depending on the histories of the communities, their locations, the kinds of homes being built and the equipment and materials being used. This would also apply to undertaking medical surgery, playing the piano and solving physics problems. In everyday language, various terms are used for expertise. For instance, some homeless people are seen to be 'street-smart'. People can be seen in positive terms like efficient, skilled, capable, gifted, clever or excellent. At the same time, a progression in expertise is usually apparent with practice. So an expert car driver can drive a car much better than someone just learning can—the car is driven automatically, fluidly, with confidence, without attention to all the sub-skills involved, and with precision; and unexpected problems that arise can be handled. An expert architect can design a new building better than a new architect can—quickly, without recourse to multiple schematics, taking the various factors into account, overcoming design problems and complexities in the brief with ease, and creating an original design. Often expertise is so automated that it cannot easily be described.

Thus various ideas of expertise are culturally and historically situated. At different times and in different places, acknowledgment of expertise has consisted of acknowledging capacities as varied as:

- having superior memory;
- being able to execute an action skilfully;
- being able to generate convincing arguments;
- being able to solve new problems;
- being able to innovate;
- being able to make good judgements;
- having higher status in a community, and so on.

The focus on one or more of the various characteristics of expertise has depended on the culture (e.g. modern or indigenous), the setting (e.g. in the workplace or in school), and the time (e.g. during times of economic crisis or times of plenty).

Various theoretical ideas about expertise are aimed at elaborating such questions as:

- What do we mean by doing something well?
- What enables an individual to do something well?
- Why does this capacity improve with practice?
- Is this capacity confined to a specific field, or is it general?
- Can the capacity be learned, and how?
- Where is the capacity located?

In this chapter, the capacity to do something well, or expertise, is seen as being derived from meaning. That is, an expert is regarded as someone who has considerable facility with meanings and their interconnections. An expert derives this facility from many experiences, connecting the various meanings that the experiences offer, as well as meanings that others construct on those experiences. Expertise is being able to access and utilise the rich connections among meanings that enable an expert to perform well on routine tasks and to work out ways to solve creative and other problems.

EXPERTISE AS FACILITY WITH MEANING

In understanding what constitutes expertise, it is important to recognise what constitutes meaning. Here the Deweyan (Dewey 1966 [1916]) idea of meaning as the understanding derived from personally significant experience is taken as the primary idea of meaning. In his work, Dewey saw the object of learning as developing the capacity to engage in appropriate practice based on experience—where appropriate practice was practice seen by the individual as related to intention in pursuit of vocation. That is, Dewey connected meaningfulness to the extent to which knowing grows out of some question of concern to the learner, adds meaning and enables accomplishment of purposes. He regarded experience as the basis for constructing meaning and learning how to interpret new situations. For Dewey, experiences in pursuit of vocation provided the richest source of meaning, where vocation was seen as any calling of personal significance, irrespective of whether it was paid work. This idea of meaning combines the concepts of *sense* and *meaning* used in Russian psychology (Leont'ev 1981 [1959]; Wertsch 1981), where sense denotes personal significance to the individual, and meaning denotes comprehension of the shared collective historical understanding captured in language and in other social artefacts.

According to Ryle (1949), meaning can be of two forms: knowing-that (knowing that something is the case, such as that the sky is blue) and knowing-how (knowing how to secure a goal—for example, how to juggle, ride a bike, swim or make jokes). According to Ryle, the meaning involved in being able to do things does not rely on some counterpart knowledge-that. Rather, it is a distinctly different kind of meaning in itself. We simply know how to do things, deriving this capacity from experience, with practice. While subsequent authors have drawn upon this distinction, they have usually focused on knowledge-that, as though it were more fundamental or important than knowledge-how . For instance, the theoretical work in universities, expressed as knowledge-that, is often seen to be higher—or more important or fundamental—than the knowledge-how of skilled trades. Indeed, the knowledge-how of skilled trades is often put down in verbal descriptions in order for it to be accredited.

Moreover, meaningful experience seems to be of many kinds (Phenix 1964), and the meanings may not all lend themselves to expression in terms of language or in other symbolic forms. Following Phenix, the ways in which we construct meaning—how we understand our experiences—can be thought of in six main ways. Firstly, meaning may be in the form of symbolics—language, mathematics, gestures and rituals. Symbolic meaning is especially important in itself and in communicating other kinds of meaning. It is also important in opening up meaning constructed in other ways to inspection and evaluation (Polanyi 1969a). A second realm of meaning is empirics, scientific ways of understanding experience—for example, in terms of factual descriptions, generalisations and theoretical formulations. The meaning of scientific academic work, over centuries, has been captured in the language of texts and mathematical formulae. A third realm is esthetics, the various arts including literature: these are also powerful in communicating meaning. A fourth is ethics, or moral meanings. A fifth is synoetics, which is sometimes called personal knowing or tacit knowing (Polanyi 1969a, 1969b [1958], 1983). It is direct awareness of concrete experience. The direct, personal significance of synoetic meaning is like Leont'ev' s idea of sense. The sixth area of meaning is synoptics, referring to meanings that are comprehensively integrated, such as history, religion and philosophy. According to Phenix, one can try to connect different kinds of meaning—for instance, through symbolics.

There are other views of the distinctive forms that meaning can take. For instance, Hirst (1974) separates forms of knowing differently (as Mathematics, Physical Sciences, History, Religion, Literature and the Fine Arts, Philosophy and Morals). A more recent work (Gardner 1983) distinguishes multiple intelligences: linguistic, musical, logical-mathematical, spatial, bodily kinaesthetic and personal. This work is based on reviewing evidence from studies of 'prodigies, gifted individuals, brain-damaged patients, *idiots savants*, normal children, normal adults, experts in different lines of work, and individuals from different cultures' (Gardner 1983, p. 9). Gardner argues more for the multiplicity of intelligences than for the particular set that he advances.

Another important work on understanding the nature of meaning is that of Polanyi, who conceptualised tacit knowledge. This idea that not all meaning can be made explicit in language corresponds with Phenix's synoetic meaning. However, Polanyi makes the important point that we afford legitimacy tacitly to language and to other ways of constructing and communicating meaning. In this way, Polanyi's tacit knowledge is like Leont'ev's sense. Phenomena become meaningful when we extend ourselves into them and dwell in them, using physical and other tools to understand them. For Polanyi, the physical and other tools become subsidiary as we focus on the whole and derive meaning tacitly. These processes are like Leont'ev's (1981 [1959]) idea of the need for activity in understanding socially constructed meanings, as in language. Such tools may in fact be our 'frameworks' of anticipation (Polanyi 1969a, p. 108) (e.g. theoretical frameworks—symbolic frameworks of anticipation). Polanyi called judgement the reconciliation of different ways of knowing—for example, reconciling explicit (codified or symbolic) meaning, the ideas suggested by those codes and direct experience.

Thus both Phenix (1964) and Polanyi (1969a, 1983 [1966]; Polanyi & Prosch 1975) have elaborated the ways in which we can seek to connect meaning and reconcile these different ways of knowing. As for Leont'ev, this involves activity—active engagement which is adequate to making the necessary connections. However, it needs to be remembered that, while we can recognise different kinds of meaning, we should not confuse one with the other, or give more value to one over the other. In the end, according to Polanyi (1969a, 1983) [1966], all legitimacy comes from tacit meaning.

RELATIONSHIPS OF MEANING

If expertise is facility with meanings and their interconnections, then we need to know more about the relationships of meanings. Meanings here are seen to be related to their function and purpose; to one's sense of vocation; to the experience/situation from which they were derived; to other meanings that one can derive from that and similar experiences/situations, and to the meanings that others can derive from/contribute to that experience/situation. These relationships are outlined below.

Meaning and doing

Firstly, meaning is related to doing, where doing refers to direct experience—for example, in undertaking a task (hammering a nail, building a house, feeding a child, writing a journal article, playing chess, balancing a budget), which may or may not involve solving a problem (in any field, such as personal, chess, physics, planning, composition, managerial, financial). Doing involves subjective and intersubjective engagement, overcoming the detached separation of one from what one is experiencing. Meaning in doing is concrete rather than abstract, and specific rather than general. Dewey gave primacy to active doing as the cornerstone of meaning:

> The knowledge that comes first to persons, and that remains most deeply ingrained is knowledge of *how to do*; how to walk, talk, read, write, skate, ride a bicycle, manage a machine, calculate, drive a horse, sell goods, manage people, and so on indefinitely ... When education ... fails to recognize that primary or initial subject matter always exists as matter of an active doing, involving the use of the body and the handling of material, the subject matter of instruction is isolated from the needs and purposes of the learner, and so becomes just a something to be memorized and reproduced upon demand (Dewey 1966 [1916], p.184).

Dewey saw meaning as arising from and residing in the capacity to do things. This relation of meaning to doing applies to activity whether it is generative or reproductive—one has a capacity-to-do whether it be the routine teaching of a class or the design of a new building. We seek to understand experience in order to handle new experiences. He saw meaning as conscious and continuous with doing, morality, intention, judgement of worth and criticality. He regarded various organised bodies of information (e.g. theory) as arbitrary vehicles for representing and communicating meaning. Thus the meaning is in the capacity-to-do. But such meaning may well have connections to other ways of rendering this meaning. For instance, one might be able to use language to state the kind of problem or ways of going about solving certain classes of problems, but these are conversions of the synoetic understanding into these other forms, not the capacity itself. These connections may be reconciled or not, relying on judgement based on experience (doing).

Meaning can be in, and arise from, doing or can be manifested in other ways, but the rendition in doing is seen to be primary. When one can do something, the meaning that is involved is direct (synoetic). It does not consist in some other separate kind of meaning outside the direct experience.

The meaning in the capacity-to-do may well be relatable to other ways of constructing meaning, such as language and other symbolic representations in the form of diagrams and equations, and these other kinds of meanings may well be drawn upon. But the various ways of rendering meaning are not hierarchical or isomorphic.

Meaning and fields of activity

Meaning is connected across being, living and working. That is, we construct and represent meaning for work purposes in the same way that we construct meaning for other life purposes. The capacities we draw upon for engaging directly in work practice (e.g. working in a team or producing new artefacts) are the same capacities we draw upon to advance civic matters (e.g. marshalling support or producing flyers) and to pursue our vocations as family members (e.g. negotiating, cooperating, producing, caring, saving and consuming).

We may relate these meanings to other kinds of meanings, such as symbolics, and we transform our meanings as a result of experience in any activity. However, the relating and transforming of meaning from any one kind of experience in any field of activity will have pervasive implications for all meaning. Humans do not like cognitive dissonance, and seek to reconcile different constructions of meaning. So, for instance, if we find new ways of seeing and pursuing our relationships with family members, these are likely to affect how we engage in co-construction of new protocols in the workplace.

Meaning and practice

The construction of meaning is situated in practice. Because each setting (Barker 1978) has its own characteristics, we construct meaning for each new situation that we operate in. We may see apparently similar contexts differently because of the different, historically derived artefacts, and the meanings immanent in them, and because of the community of the practice (consisting of people and their interrelationships, also historically derived) (Lave & Wenger 1991). Thus the way in which meaning is constructed on work in a busy office in one setting may be different in another busy office, even in the same industry. This may be because of differences in systems, information flow, processes, goals, rules, norms and responsibilities. So knowing how to process a guest arriving in a country hotel may require different capacities-to-do than knowing how to process a guest arriving in a city hotel (Stevenson 1996). Knowing what is appropriate in solving an airline passenger problem for one airline in a large international airport may be different from what is appropriate for different passengers travelling on another airline from a small provincial city (Beven 1997). These differences may be compounded by different divisions of responsibilities, different layouts of the facilities, different expectations of the owners and different computer systems or software. In a community of practice, individual constructions of meaning will be reconciled by the individual with other constructions that are already held and with various ways in which the meaning can be rendered. It needs to be remembered, too, that practice is situated in wider society, its culture and its economy, because of the physical relationships as well as the fact that the individuals working together in a setting relate to wider cultures and economic realities. The drive for profit in an organisation will, for instance, be moderated by law, taxation and social responsibilities.

Meaning and vocation, purpose and function

An openness and will to understand experience are necessary in order to understand it, learn from it and use these meanings to understand future experiences. This openness will come from vocation—an impulse or calling to pursue things of personal significance. Thus the purpose and function of meaning comes from engagement in activity directed at a personally important purpose or goal (which may also have social significance—with a shared motive) (Dewey 1966 [1916]; Leont'ev 1981 [1959]). Unless the function of the activity is apparent, related to some important purpose, it is unlikely to be seen as meaningful and meaning will not be derived from it (see also Pea 1987). The meaningfulness derived from experiencing the planning and undertaking of a task will be associated with features of that task as they relate to the goals being pursued and their meaning in relation to vocation. So, for example, the goal of becoming an accountant will influence the way in which idea of balance is constructed, which may be different from the construction of balance in pursuit of engineering vocations.

Shared and co-constructed meaning

Individuals bring their own set of meanings (related to own vocations, purposes and culture, and immanent in their previous experiences of doing) to new tasks. Working in concert with others, there are bound to be differences in the (personal) meanings that are involved. Groups are commonly pursuing an object (motive) (Engeström 1999) through working together. It is collective activity in relation to an object situated in practice that is used to create the beginnings of a scaffolding for meaning to be shared. Individuals share an object (motive), even though they may also have their own individual goals to achieve in relation to the shared motive, and different goals in relation to still other objects.

For instance, in town planning, the outcome of interactions of groups of architects trained in the same university, transforming an existing plan to a new one, would be different from the outcome if the architects had different training and experiences, or if the team also included people from social welfare agencies, environmental groups, transport experts, and so on. Each would construct different meanings on the purposes of the existing plan; each could seek to share these constructions in a way that was accessible to others so that they could relate these meanings to their own. The communicated meaning would be experienced variously by different participants in the setting, related to their own goals and existing meanings. The outcome of working together and of constructing a shared object may well be qualitatively different. So too for the construction of a new product for a firm, when designers, marketers, experts in new systems and so on come together.

In order to share meanings, individuals communicate about and through the object. Much of this communication is in language or other symbolic form as well as in gestures and other body language. Some may be in the form of direct collective activity in relation to the object and be supported also by operations undertaken in relation to various artefacts and technologies in the setting. As each person shares and seeks to apprehend different meanings, individual meanings change and new meanings are created. Objects may initially be seen differently, but a new, shared construction may arise through interaction, and the outcomes may well be creative.

Facility with meanings and their interconnections, then, involves the capacity to understand experience in meaningful ways, connect these meanings, appraise these meanings and share them with others in order to reconsider and transform them further.

PSYCHOLOGICAL CONCEPTS OF EXPERTISE

Considerable psychological research has been conducted into explanations of expert action. Generally, these explanations have abstracted from the idea of meaning, and have posited various cognitive representations in the mind—for example, schemas upon which the expert draws to accomplish goals. These representations are thought to consist of rich networks of concepts enabling experts to see problems at a deep level, associated automated procedures that enable experts to accomplish familiar goals efficiently and smoothly, and of general problem-solving procedures to handle new and unfamiliar situations. The quest in educational and psychological literature to define cognitive representations has been to depict this expertise in a form that would guide the educational development of such expertise.

Major psychological ideas of what constitutes expertise are outlined in the following paragraphs, and each is related to the idea advanced here that *expertise is facility with meanings*. This is followed by a summary of the idea of expertise advanced in this chapter. Some common contemporary abstractions of important areas of key expertise are then introduced in the final section, for discussion in subsequent chapters.

Expertise as memory and knowledge

Older ideas of expertise were that experts appeared to have superior memory. For instance, it was thought that expert chess players must possess superior memories for pieces on the board, as they could remember the individual positions of pieces in actual chess games better than could novices. However, when further research showed that chess players in fact had memories equivalent to novices when the pieces were randomly placed on a chessboard, it was understood that it was not the pieces that were being remembered, but the position of the pieces in relation to whole games (Chase & Simon 1973; de Groot 1965). That is, meaningful chunks (chunked in relation to personally significant intentions—chunked to make sense) were being remembered. In contemporary society, however, expertise is still afforded people with good memories—those who are good at game shows, crosswords and recalling theories. Memory, of course, does assist in doing things well. However, what is remembered will be meaningful only if it is relevant to the capacity-to-do things, and perceived as relevant by the individual engaged in purposeful action.

A related view is that expertise consists of possessing a large stock of propositional knowledge—that is, knowledge of verbal or other concepts held in memory at various degrees of abstractions. (This cognitive view posits mental representations to explain meaning.) The best example of this kind of knowledge is theoretical knowledge. Such knowledge represents collective cultural meanings, derived historically by the relevant community. For instance, an expert in teaching would be able to think of teaching in terms of various theoretical concepts concerned with such matters as the learner, learning, the curriculum, classrooms, psychology, sociology, and so on. There would be concepts at a more specific level, such as for learning and reinforcement. An expert teacher would have acquired the ability to see problems in terms of *reinforcement* if that is appropriate; or at a higher level—for example, in terms of *learning*; or at a higher level still—for example, *development* if the problem turns out not to be a reinforcement one, or a learning one, but one related to development as a whole.

Much of the expertise-as-knowledge view has been derived from studies of computer simulations of human thinking as a basis for supposing the architecture of cognition (Durso 1999; Newell 1990). Computer simulations of thinking are often based on the premise that knowledge can be divided into two kinds: knowledge-that and knowledge-how.

Considerable research has been conducted into determining the knowledge of propositions that experts possess, and building these into artificial computerised expert systems. These propositions are combined with 'production' systems consisting of rules in the form 'If X, then do Y' (Anderson 1982) to mirror the supposed knowledge of experts. In this case, the knowledge is not necessarily that of theoretical disciplines, but is more functionally conceived and represented.

One of the limitations of this conception of expertise is that the propositional knowledge which is the subject of theoretical disciplines of knowledge often does not transfer to practice. Individuals do not always apply the theorised propositional representations even when they seem relevant. Moreover, expertise can be recognised in individuals accomplished in sporting, artistic, surgical and other skilful pursuits without their being able to articulate in propositional terms what constitutes their expertise.

Despite the overwhelming focus in cognitive psychology on propositional representations, the idea of expertise as knowledge in the form of plural, qualitatively different kinds of cognitive representations has long been proposed. These include plural representational encoding and memory systems (Martin 1993; Paivio 1979; Tulving 1984), multiple intelligences (Gardner 1983) and 'non-traditional intelligences' (Sternberg 1985).

In relation to the idea of expertise as facility with meaning, expertise can be seen as memory and knowledge only if we see such 'knowledge' as contributing to a facility with meanings. That is, an expert chess player can construct meaning on chess pieces in relation to the meaning of whole games. For this facility to develop, the individual needs to be able to make sense of that kind of knowledge. An expert problem-solver can construct a problem at a deeper level of abstraction if that person can relate direct experience of the problem to other kinds of ways in which the meaning can be rendered—for example, as principles from physics—and even then a solution will result only if the problem-solver can relate these meanings to ways of proceeding and to a sense that it is appropriate to do so.

Expertise as performance and as language

A considerable amount of cognitive research focuses on knowledge-that, especially as it is expressed in language. However, from his Madagascar studies, Bloch concluded that language appears to play only a small role in the transmission of complex, everyday and practical meaning. Bloch argued that 'under certain circumstances, this non-linguistic knowledge can be rendered into language and thus take the form of explicit discourse, but changing its character in the process' (Bloch 1998, p. 7). He concluded that practical skills are better transmitted non-linguistically to save double transformation into and out of language. For him, the nature and form of expert knowledge for everyday purposes appears to be more related to how the knowledge is used than how it may be elaborated as semantic conceptual schemata like those found in scientific texts: 'Concepts involve implicit networks of meanings which are formed through the experience of, and practice in, the external world' (Bloch 1998, p. 7).

One of the clearest manifestations of expertise is the demonstration of that ability in undertaking tasks. This capacity improves over time with practice. It becomes more unitary, less clumsy, more fluid, less verbally mediated and more automatic. These features can be seen clearly in skilful performances in sport, music, trade work, solving particular classes of maths and physics problems and so on. Based on Fitts' 1964 work on the development of physical skills, Anderson (1982) developed a comprehensive theory of how propositional knowledge (knowledge-that) is gradually proceduralised (into knowledge-how) with practice over time. He theorised that general procedures interpret new situations, draw upon and utilise productions (specific procedures) to generate a performance and then combine (compose) and proceduralise sequences of procedures until performance is smooth and the propositional knowledge disappears.

Being literate or proficient in the technical use of a language is often seen as a mark of expertise. Certainly mastery of language is important in assessment undertaken in educational institutions, aimed at measuring the degree of mastery over an area of theoretical knowledge. Often verbal statements about performance are taken to indicate the ability for performance. For instance, the capacity to solve a physics problem on paper is taken as a good indicator that situations in practice requiring the application of physics principles will be solved successfully. Unfortunately, such apparent knowledge often does not get 'transferred' to everyday situations where it would appear to be appropriate. The appropriation of the meanings conveyed in language requires active engagement (Leont'ev 1981 [1959]) in order to make personal sense of the meanings.

More sophisticated analyses of the capacity to use language view expertise not just as technical mastery of the given meaning of words and sentences and their generation in response to different kinds of situations. They also recognise as expertise the understanding of the power relations (ideologies, discourses) in communication and how these power relations position those involved, as well as the capacity to take 'right' action in redressing injustices.

In relation to the idea of expertise as facility with meaning, expertise can be seen as performance, where the performer engages in activity that achieves a goal and, through practice, smooths out that performance and is able to execute that performance when warranted. The meaning is in the performance itself—it is synoetic. It is direct, not detached or impersonal. In order to undertake the performance when appropriate, the performer must connect a number of meanings—meaning immanent in the performance itself, meanings in relation to the tools that are used, meaning in relation to the characteristics of the setting, meanings about what constitutes appropriateness in the setting, and meanings about the goals that are being achieved and their relation to vocation. Being able to relate these meanings to those conveyed through language also contributes to a facility with meanings or expertise. The analysis for facility in the use of language itself is analogous, where the performance is in the utterances and the relations to other meanings can also be comprehensive in the case of experts. In the case of understanding through language, though, the meaning is symbolic.

Expertise as problem-solving and transfer

In contradistinction to skilled action and verbal statements of principles and theories, expertise is often seen as the capacity to solve new problems. This view is that experts see problems in different ways from novices because of their experience in the particular domain (Chi et al. 1981). They may be capable of seeing the problem at various levels of abstraction (more deeply than novices) and may be able to work with a level of abstraction that leads them to a solution (Glaser 1989; Gott 1989). On the other hand, novices see the problem in terms of its surface features and use weak problem-solving methods such as means–end analysis to develop a solution. The idea is that experts work through a problem space starting with a problem-state and generating operators to move forwards towards the goal state (Newell & Simon 1972). Novices are seen to be working backwards from the goal state. In this view of expertise, some kinds of knowledge-how are seen as specific procedures for achieving familiar goals, while others are seen to be more general or higher order, used to deal with new problems, monitor cognition as a whole, and switch attention.

In a related way, expertise is sometimes seen as transfer: the capacity to utilise past experience in interpreting and dealing with new experiences (Kimball & Holyoak 2000). Novices are seen as capable of 'near' transfer as they are able to apply procedures directly. Experts are seen as capable of 'far' transfer, in being able to 'read' the nature of a problem, context, culture, setting or environment in such a way that new procedures are generated for dealing with it. This capacity is seen to arise from conceptualising the problem at higher levels of abstraction. However, apparent expertise in one setting often does not transfer to situations where it would seem to be appropriate.

In relation to the idea of expertise as facility with meaning, expertise as problem-solving and transfer can be seen as the construction of meaning on new experience. In problem-solving and in transfer, meanings derived from previous experiences are used to try to understand the problem in relation to experiences of other problems. If the problem is identical to a previous one, previous meanings are applicable and the problem can be solved. If not, then attempts will be made to find meanings in any realm that have some correspondence with features of the problem. Fluency in connecting different kinds of meanings is helpful in generating a course of action. Success in problem-solving suggests that doing in relation to solving is highly connected to the meaning attributed to the problem—that is, the ways in which it makes sense or is personally meaningful to the problem-solver. As for performance, meaning in problem-solving is connected to meanings in relation to the setting and what is appropriate in the setting.

Expertise as creativity/innovation

While problem-solving is seen to be a hallmark of expertise and the capacity to solve problems has been the subject of a great deal of cognitive research, the problems selected for study are often well structured with clear criteria for a successful solution. Many problems, however, do not have a clear goal state or problem state (Middleton, this volume). The problem may not be well structured and what constitutes a solution may not be known in advance. Problems of innovation, design and creativity in general have these characteristics (Middleton, Yashin-Shaw, this volume). An expert designer, then, is one who can generate original solutions to problems. It involves a working forward and a generation of new artefacts. So it involves drawing upon existing meaning, but in new ways. From the work of Middleton and Yashin-Shaw, it seems that various procedures and the use of imagery assist creativity, but that these devices are not fixed items of knowledge.

In relation to the idea of expertise as facility with meaning, expertise as creativity and innovation appears to involve the capacity to make shifts in meaning—to see things in new ways. For this, one needs the capacity to interrelate alternative ways of constructing meaning on phenomena, and interconnectedness amongst realms of meaning would be facilitative.

Expertise as conceptual change

The recent conceptual change literature (e.g. Schnotz et al. 1999) reinforces the idea that concepts originate in human practice, bringing together such findings as the following:

- People know in a variety of ways, none of which is intrinsically superior.
- Verbal concepts are but one kind of symbolisation and conceptual change involves changes in systems of signs.
- Concepts are intrinsically linked to practical and physical skills.

> - Conceptual change depends on ontological and epistemological beliefs. Conceptual change does not necessarily replace everyday constructions of meaning, and may well result in syntheses of different kinds of representations. Different representations appear to compete for activation in different situations and for different tasks.
> - *Thinking, concepts, mental models, representations* and *schemas* are not synonymous terms.

In relation to the idea of expertise as facility with meaning, expertise as conceptual change usually deals with one kind of meaning: that which is symbolic. However, this literature is now moving towards recognition that symbolically mediated forms of meaning are arbitrarily devised and linked to other kinds of meaning, including beliefs and practical capacities. Moreover, for conceptual change ideas to include various kinds of meaning, the idea of concepts needs to be transformed into one that is less reliant on symbolic kinds of meaning or representation.

Expertise as schemas

Cognitive psychology has traditionally separated knowledge into two types: knowledge-that and knowledge-how . This equates roughly with a separation of conceptual understanding and the capacity to do things. Sometimes schemas are represented by researchers in purely propositional terms—for instance, a schema for furniture would include the concept of a chair. However, the idea of schema in cognitive psychology may also bring knowledge-how and knowledge-that together. It is sometimes assumed that we have schemas for doing things—that is, our understanding of a situation may include both concepts and ways of handling the situation. For instance, experts may have schemas for fixing roofs to houses. Different schemas may relate to different kinds of roofs for different kinds of houses, but each would include the capacity to proceed with the work that is involved, as well as for recognising and dealing with the various kinds of problems that might arise. Moreover, schemas may be normative, involving ethical and other judgements of appropriateness. Schemas may also be specific or general. So we may have a general schema for creative work, but the specific form of the schema may vary across settings and tasks. This broader idea of schemas, beyond symbolic representations of knowledge-that, is more useful in understanding meaning, facility with meaning and interconnections among meanings.

While some of the schema literature still gives a special place to language—in the labelling of categories, which explain regularities in the world; in the expression of concepts; and in communicating knowledge—verbalised concepts are now being recognised as just propositional representations alongside other kinds of representations. The interaction between meaning as language and meaning as action, in expertise and its development, has been exemplified and detailed in Hutchins' (1995) detailed examination of the collective nature of cognition when a crew overcomes the failure of navigational equipment as a ship enters a harbour. Other recent cognitive research on expertise confirms that expertise does not consist in the kinds of structured representations found in theoretical texts. For instance, Boshuizen and his colleagues (1995) found that discipline-based verbalisable medical knowledge is transformed qualitatively in practice.

The cognitive research literature now also gives more attention to multiple forms of meaning, assumed to be represented as cognitive structures, including implicit knowledge (see Buchner et al. 1995; Long 1995), multiple intelligences (Gardner 1983), non-traditional intelligence (Sternberg 1985) and multiple encoding and memory systems (Martin 1993; Paivio 1979; Tulving 1984).

In relation to the idea of expertise as facility with meaning, the concept of schemas is a theoretical construct about how meanings and their interconnections are represented in the mind. It connects meaning as knowing-that and knowing-how, but is often seen as value- and emotion-free. It often ignores the idea of vocation and the functionality of knowledge in respect of vocation, and the normative aspects of this pursuit. However, it could be argued that the theoretical idea of schemas should contain such features, and then schemas may well be considered as cognitive representations of meaning consisting in rich interconnections among different ways of knowing in relation to vocation and situated activity. Nevertheless, it needs to be remembered that schemas are theoretical constructs removed from activity itself, and are merely a theoretical device for thinking about how such activity may be mediated.

Expertise as judgement and appropriate practice

Being expert involves making good judgements. Indeed, the fact that school knowledge does not readily transfer to everyday practice is sometimes seen as appropriate (Pea 1987) where the person does not see it as appropriate to draw upon or utilise that kind of meaning. As outlined earlier, recognising that meaningfulness may be in verbal or other (e.g. tacit) form, Polanyi argues that judgement consists in reconciling the *text*, the *conception* suggested by the text and *experience*.

Expert action does not occur in a vacuum, drawing solely upon cognitive structures in the mind. Rather, expert action occurs in a setting conceptualised in various ways—for instance, as a community of practice (Lave & Wenger 1991) or as an activity system (Engeström 1999; Leont'ev 1981 [1959]). Socio-cultural studies have indicated that various features of these settings are important for expertise. For instance, in activity theory, what is appropriate practice is seen to be culturally and historically derived, mediated by artefacts in the system, and mediated by community, rules and the division of labour.

In relation to the idea of expertise as facility with meaning, this conception of expertise as judgement and appropriate practice places a primary emphasis on the meaning that comes from concrete experience (activity) in a community of practice. Experts relate ethical, symbolic, scientific, synoetic and other meanings. In constructing meaning in a setting, the norms of the setting are taken into account, and related to wider societal norms and personal mores. Meaning does not consist just in knowing-that and knowing-how, but also in understanding what is appropriate and being able to render this in doing.

Expertise as shared meaning and as activity

In activity theory (Engeström 1999; Leont'ev 1981 [1959]), expert action is often seen as co-constructed. Scaffolding is provided through intersubjective sharing of meaning as people work together in seeking to achieve an outcome.

In seeking a view of expertise that incorporates many of the insights from different theoretical positions, activity theory is particularly helpful. Firstly, it enables expertise to be seen as the capacity to pursue an object situated in practice. What one is able to do in one situation does not automatically transfer to other situations. These other situations have to be 'read' as similar and transfer has to be seen as appropriate. Moreover, expertise may relate to the artefacts or instruments utilised in a particular setting and new artefacts and instruments may pose problems for the expert. Activity theory also enables expertise to be seen as normative. Activity systems exist in a community with its own rules and division of labour. As for a community of practice, expertise is derived from constructing meaning on activity that one engages in, in the setting. One may be permitted to take on more complex or important tasks and construct meaning on them as expertise develops (Lave & Wenger 1991).

All activity systems represent an historically derived set of tensions and conflicts, and what is appropriate and permissible over time will evolve as these tensions and conflicts are played out. Moreover, in activity systems tasks can be shared and, through the tasks and communication about the tasks, meaning can also be shared. So when expertise is conceptualised in relation to activity, it can be seen as normative, situated, mediated, functional, shared and cultural, as well as related to motive. Moreover, it can be seen as historically constructed. As the tensions and contradictions in an activity system lead to new forms of activity, so too what counts as expertise changes. In seeking to come to a conclusion about what constitutes expertise, then, the concept of an activity system has considerable power.

In relation to the idea of expertise as facility with meaning, activity theory acquits itself well and extends meaning-making to the co-construction of meaning in pursuit of a collective object. However, it must be remembered that the meanings that individuals construct on an activity are not the activity itself. Meaning is in how the activity is understood by the individuals who are involved. This meaning can be rendered in doing (as activity), but there are other realms of meaning as well, and experts have facility in interconnecting various ways in which experience is meaningful: in doing; in symbolic representations of the activity; in scientific ways of viewing the activity; ethically, and so on. Particular experiences may not be meaningful in all of these ways, but facility in interconnecting relevant realms of meaning contributes to expertise.

SUMMARY OF IDEAS ABOUT EXPERTISE

In summary, the following ideas about expertise can be advanced:

1. Expertise consists in doing something well, better than and differently from others new to the undertaking.
2. The ability to do something well (the 'capacity-to-do') can be thought of as:
   a facility with meaning, derived from experience; and
   b facility in connecting meaning derived from particular experiences with other meanings, such as:
      (i)   meanings derived from other experiences;
      (ii) meanings in relation to other purposes;
      (iii) meanings rendered in other ways;
      (iv) social meanings found in language; and
      (v)   meaning as understood by others.
3. An important primary understanding of experience as meaning (sense) is direct, personal and concrete.
4. Expertise involves normative judgement in culturally and historically situated practice, relating meaning derived from previous experience to new situations.
5. The capacity-to-do improves with experience, becoming more fluid, efficient and automatic for familiar situations.
6. Personally significant meaningfulness is just one way in which experience can be understood—different individuals will understand (make sense of) the same experience differently and will communicate about it differently. Experts can make sense of new experiences, drawing upon meanings rendered in a way that is relevant to the new situation.
7. An expert is likely to understand experience in more than one

way, to be able to connect direct concrete experience with other renditions of that meaning. For instance, an expert may be able to relate engineering principles to skilful action in a trade, economics to accounting practice, or interpersonal relationship principles to working in a team.

8 In new situations where the problems appear to be different from those routinely handled, experts are able to draw on various ways of seeing the problem, finding different ways of constructing meaning on the problem and of drawing on existing meanings in its solution. These different ways of constructing meaning may be derived from various kinds of sources—for example, communications with others about the meanings they construct on experiences, understandings of the tools and technologies in the setting, relating new goals to senses of vocation and purpose, and considering how the new tasks, goals or purposes relate to previous activity.

9 Meanings derived historically by a community can be rendered in language. As with all meaning, individuals need to engage in activity to apprehend these meanings and connect them with personally significant meanings. Experts have considerable facility with such interconnections.

10 Abstractions about experiences can be coded in many ways—for instance, in language as theoretical and ethical principles or in terms of mathematical or other symbols.

11 Meaning can be co-constructed with others, constructed in relation to artefacts and technologies in the setting, constructed in relation to other known ways of reading the problems and its situation (e.g. theories), and so on. Of course, one of these ways may be in terms of theoretical principles that connect different kinds of problems and go beyond immediately apparent features of a particular problem. While such latter principles may be propositionally known and meaningfully related to personal experience, they may also be tacit.

The characteristics of expertise and the kinds of meaning upon which experts draw and which they interrelate in expert action are depicted in Figure 1.1.

This view of expertise makes it difficult to adopt many inadequate propositions from cognitive psychology. That is, theoretical constructs for the supposed representation in the mind of expertise as the capacity-to-do need to be considered critically, with some caution. Firstly, the idea of concepts needs to extend beyond propositional representation of verbalisable principles. Secondly, the idea of understanding should not be confined to the ability to state propositions. Thirdly, the idea of doing should not be explained in terms of knowledge-that. Fourthly,

DEVELOPING VOCATIONAL EXPERTISE

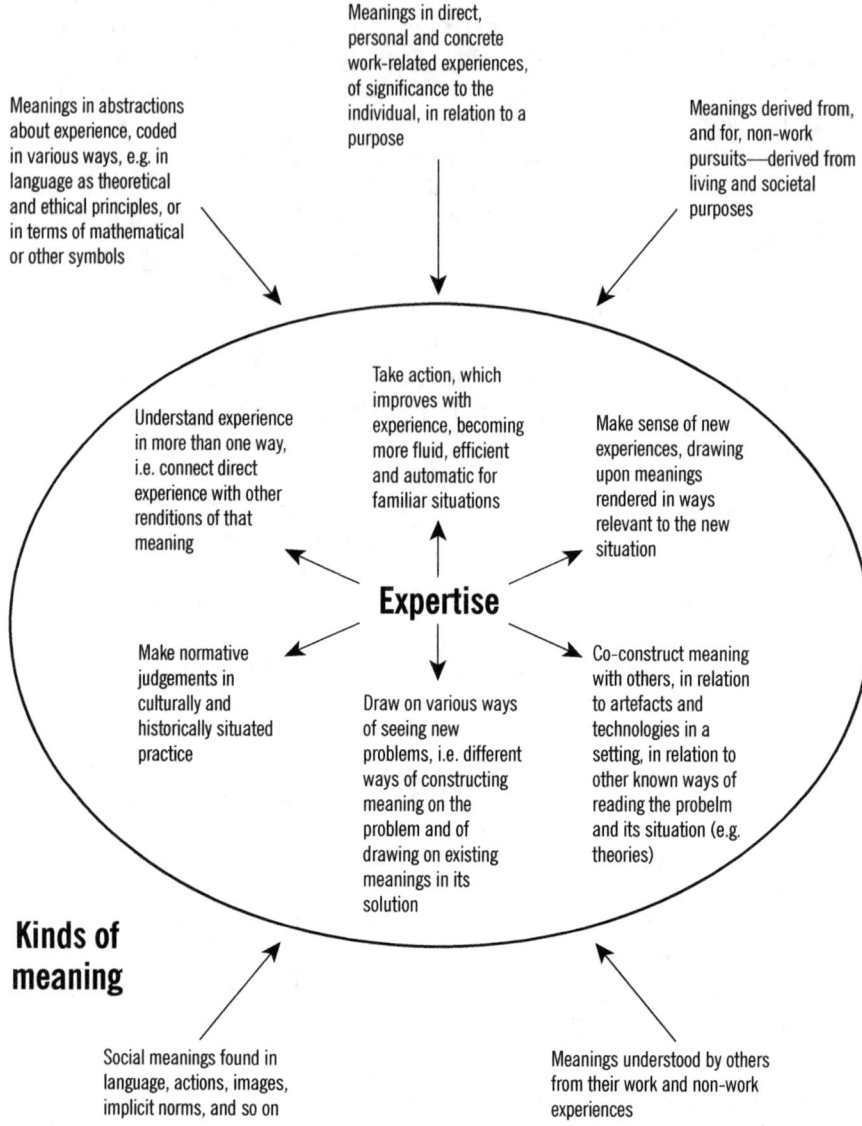

Figure 1.1 Relationships of expertise and meaning

the kinds of understanding, represented as schemas, need to be plural and interconnected. Fifthly, thinking and acting should not be confounded with artificial constructs theorised as cognitive representations.

INTRODUCING SOME COMMON ABSTRACTIONS

Part II of this book deals at length with some common abstractions of ideas of vocational capacities. These include literacy, numeracy, problem-solving, creativity, information literacy and values. These have been chosen as, in various guises, they have surfaced in economic constructions of what constitutes transferable vocational competence. The importance attached to these abstract ideas of competence is expressed in many ways. Literacy is sometimes called communication or is regarded as a personal, interpersonal or social skill. Numeracy goes by a number of terms including mathematical ideas and techniques, working with numbers and working with information. Problem-solving can also be subsumed in thinking skills, or ability to transfer, or to work with information and systems. Computer literacy is seen as basic to, and involved in, working with information and using technology. Creativity is sometimes included in thinking skills or called innovation or design, and seen to be especially important in globalising economies. Values are taken up because they are usually omitted from economically derived lists of competence, or are stated in very conforming ways, or are assumed not to warrant attention because they are thought to be covered in specified behaviours.

As argued in this chapter, it is a mistake to proceed from such generic labels as these to a view that such denoted capacities can be taught as such. Rather, each is a label pointing to individuals constructing and utilising normative meanings in highly situated functional activities and in concrete situations, and the nature of each varies across these activities and situations. These matters are taken up in detail in Chapters 3 to 8.

In Chapter 2, the context of developing expertise in vocational education and the ways in which teaching and learning can be approached are discussed.

REFERENCES

Anderson, J.R. 1982, 'Acquisition of cognitive skill', *Psychological Review*, vol. 89, no. 4, pp. 369–406
—— 1993, 'Problem-solving and learning', *American Psychologist*, vol. 48, no. 1, pp. 35–44
Barker, R.G. 1978, 'Theory of behaviour settings' in *Habitats, Environments and Human Behaviour*, ed. R.A. Barker and Associates, Jossey Bass, San Francisco
Beven, F. ed. 1997, *Learning in the Workplace: Airline Customer Service—A Further Examination of Critical Aspects of Practice of the Tourism and Hospitality Industry,* Centre for Learning and Work Research, Griffith University, Brisbane

Bloch, M.E.F 1998, *How We Think They Think: Anthropological Approaches to Cognition, Memory, and Literacy*, Westview Press, Boulder, COL

Boshuizen, H.P.A., Schmidt, H.G., Custers, E.J. & Van De Wiel, M.W. 1995, 'Knowledge development and restructuring in the domain of medicine, the role of theory and practice', *Learning and Instruction*, vol. 5, pp. 269–85

Buchner, A., Funke, J. & Berry, D. 1995, 'Negative correlations between control performance and verbalizable knowledge indicators for implicit learning in process control tasks', *Quarterly Journal of Experimental Psychology*, vol. 48A, pp. 166–87

Chase, W.G. & Simon H.A. 1973, 'The mind's eye in chess', in *Visual Information Processing*, ed. W.G. Chase, Academic Press, New York

Chi, M.T.H, Feltovich, P.J. & Glaser, R. 1981, 'Categorization and representation of physics problems by experts and novices', *Cognitive Science*, vol. 5, pp. 121–25

de Groot, A.D. 1965, *Thought and Choice in Chess*, Mouton, The Hague

Dewey, J. 1966 (1916), *Democracy and Education*, Collier-Macmillan, Toronto

Durso, F.T. 1999, *Handbook of Applied Cognition*, Wiley, Chichester

Engeström, Y. 1999, 'Expansive visibilization of work: an activity-theoretical perspective', *Computer Supported Cooperative Work*, vol. 8, pp. 63–93

Fitts, P.M. 1964, 'Perceptual-motor skill learning', in *Categories of Human Learning*, ed. A.W. Melton, Academic Press, New York

Gardner, H. 1983, *Frames of Mind*, Basic Books, New York

Glaser, R. 1989, 'Expertise and learning: how do we think about instructional processes now that we have discovered knowledge structures?', in *Complex Information Processing*, eds D. Klahr & K. Kotovsky, Erlbaum, Hillsdale, NJ

Gott, S. 1989, 'Apprenticeship instruction for real-world tasks: the coordination of procedures, mental models, and strategies', *Review of Research in Education*, vol. 15, pp. 97–169

Hirst, P.H. 1974, *Knowledge and the Curriculum: A Collection of Philosophical Papers*, International Library of the Philosophy of Reason, Routledge & Kegan Paul, London

Hutchins, E. 1995, *Cognition in the Wild*, MIT Press, Cambridge, MA

Kimball, D.R. & Holyoak, K.J. 2000, 'Transfer and expertise', in *The Oxford Handbook on Memory*, eds E. Tulving & F.P.M. Craik, Oxford University Press, Oxford

Lave, J. & Wenger, E. 1991, *Situated Learning: Legitimate Peripheral Participation*, Cambridge University Press, Cambridge

Leont'ev, A.N. 1981 (1959), *Problems of the Development of the Mind*, Progress Publishers, Moscow

Long, J. 1995, 'Commemorating Donald Broadbent's contribution to the field of applied cognitive psychology. A discussion of the special issues papers', *Applied Cognitive Psychology*, vol. 9, pp. S197–S215

Martin, J. 1993, 'Episodic memory: a neglected phenomenon in the psychology of education', *Educational Psychologist*, vol. 28, no. 2, pp. 169–83

Newell, A. 1990, *Unified Theories of Cognition*, Harvard University Press, Cambridge, MA

Newell, A. & Simon, H.A. 1972, *Human Problem Solving*, Prentice-Hall, Englewood Cliffs, NJ

Paivio, A. 1979, *Imagery and Verbal Processes*, Holt, Rinehart & Winston, New York

Pea, R. 1987, 'Socializing the knowledge transfer problem', *International Journal of Educational Research*, vol. 11, no. 6, pp. 639–63

Phenix, P.H. 1964, *Realms of Meaning: A Philosophy of the Curriculum for General Education*, McGraw-Hill, New York

Polanyi, M. 1969a, *Knowing and Being: Essays by Michael Polanyi*, ed. M. Green, Routledge & Kegan Paul, London

—— 1969b (1958), *Personal Knowledge: Towards a Post-Critical Philosophy*, 3rd impression, Routledge & Kegan Paul, London

—— 1983 (1966), *The Tacit Dimension*, Peter Smith, Gloucester, MA (reprint, originally published by Doubleday)

Polanyi, M. & Prosch, H. 1975, *Meaning*, University of Chicago Press, Chicago and London

Ryle, G. 1949, *The Concept of Mind*, Hutchinson, London

Schnotz, W., Vosniadou, S. & Carrereto, M. eds 1999, *New Perspectives on Conceptual Change*, Pergamon, Amsterdam

Sternberg, R.J. 1985, *Beyond IQ: A Triarchic Theory of Human Intelligence*, Cambridge University Press, New York

Stevenson, J.C. ed. 1996, *Learning in the Workplace: Tourism and Hospitality—A Report on an Initial Exploratory Examination of Critical Aspects of Small Businesses in the Tourism and Hospitality Industry*, Centre for Skill Formation Research and Development, Griffith University, Brisbane

Tulving, E. 1984, 'How many memory systems are there?', *American Psychologist*, vol. 40, no. 4, pp. 385–98

von Krogh, G., Nonaka, I. & Nishiguchi, T. eds 2000, *Knowledge Creation: A Source of Value*, Macmillan, London

Wertsch, J.V. trans. and ed. 1981, *The Concept of Activity in Soviet Psychology*, Armonk, New York

2

Vocational teaching and learning in context

John Stevenson

INTRODUCTION

This chapter examines possible sources for the curricular decisions that have to be taken when designing and engaging in vocational teaching and learning activities. An examination of these sources reveals that decision-makers make assumptions about:

- desirable learning processes and products;
- the relative value of individual, economic and societal ends; and
- the nature of knowledge (meaning) and its acquisition.

Each of these sets of assumptions and the various positions that can be adopted with respect to it are examined. The range of curriculum theories available for tackling these same issues is then outlined, and it is concluded that the planning of teaching and learning should occur in the context of actual practice, cognisant of, but not drawing directly from, a single 'grand universal theory' for curriculum development or instructional design. Secondly, the various ways in which the economic press for codifying meaning manifests itself are outlined, and the underlying assumptions identified. Using cultural-historical activity theory

(Engeström 1987, 1999; Leont'ev 1981 [1959]) as a basis for conceptualising contextual teaching and learning practice, approaches for planning teaching and learning for vocational education are then developed, and teaching and learning principles advanced.

CURRICULUM SOURCES FOR VOCATIONAL TEACHING AND LEARNING

In Chapter 1, various dimensions of expertise are identified and it is argued that experts draw upon, and inter-connect, different kinds of meaning in expert action (Figure 1.1). The question for vocational educators is how to design instruction to develop learners towards expertise. There are numerous possible starting points for planning teaching and learning in vocational education. For instance, Tyler (1950) identified as sources for the curriculum, considerations of the *learner*, of contemporary *society* and of the *subject* matter.

Thus, for instance, one could start with the individual *learners*, their aspirations and their previous experiences and capacities. These analyses would enable one to devise learning experiences that connected previously developed meanings with the new capacities needed to pursue new goals. For instance, some learners may aspire to work in commercial kitchens, but have quite different previous experiences in cooking or working with foods and their ingredients, and quite different ideas about nutrition and health practices; or they may aspire to be mechanics and have quite different personal experiences with the maintenance and driving of cars and different ideas about pollution and safety.

Another place to start is with analyses of contemporary *society*, asking questions about what kinds of activities are needed to improve society at the local, national and global levels. Using frameworks like those developed by Campbell et al. (1992) and by Parker et al. (1999) (see Chapter 8), one might seek to develop learning experiences which would enable learners to develop normative capacities for activities involving, for instance, cooperation, mutual respect and tolerance, non-violent behaviour, critical consumption, environmental protection and productive and generative work. These themes would assume considerable importance and be seen as integral to, rather than separate from, developing expertise for pursuing occupations and careers in various industries—for instance, in hospitality (e.g. as a chef), construction (e.g. as a carpenter) and engineering (e.g. as a mechanic) industries.

Still further, one could begin with an analysis of the *subject matter*. This might involve examining kinds of activities in which the learners might engage as preparation for the kinds of work to which they aspire. For instance, one could analyse the work as it is currently being performed, the ways in which that kind of work may change in the future and the kinds of capacities that are involved. This may involve interviews, surveys and meetings, and these methods may seek information from those undertaking various relevant work activities, those involved in supervising such work activities, those who have had experiences with critical incidents at work, those researching future directions of relevant industries and careers, and so on. It might also involve perusal of any statements of industrial standards that exist. For a discussion of various techniques, see Finch & Crunkilton (1993, Chapter 6) and Harris et al. (1995, Chapter 11).

Irrespective of these kinds of elemental sources for possible curriculum content, there is a wide range of relevant curriculum considerations for vocational learning in the particular socio-political, economic and historic context. These may be collected together as relevant *factors* or concerns (Laird & Stevenson 1993). For instance, one could start with notions of change, the kinds of capacities utilised in generating and dealing with change, and the histories of emphases in curriculum development in different economic times (Stevenson 1996a). Or one could consider such ideas as those of thinking skills, working with information and symbols, problem-solving abilities, working in teams and creativity, found in statements of key competencies, core skills and necessary skills (Green 1997; Mayer 1992; US Department of Labor Secretary's Commission on Achieving Necessary Skills 1992).

Looking at further examples of contemporary concerns, one could consider the problems of codifying knowledge in times of rapid knowledge transformation—for example, the codes assigned to engineering and scientific knowledge in texts and research journals versus the ways in which new information, processes and systems are developed and known in innovative workplaces (Gibbons et al. 1994; Lundvall & Borrás 1997). Similarly, one could look at ways in which careers and career education are structured—as in the sixteen career education clusters used by the US Department of Education (Riley 2000) where, for example, mechanics is found in the Scientific, Research, Engineering and Technical Services cluster; and commercial cookery in the Hospitality and Tourism cluster.

TEACHING AND LEARNING ASSUMPTIONS

Each of the above examples makes assumptions about the value or emphasis that should be placed on various approaches to teaching and learning. Some of the major categories of assumptions can be clustered as:

(i) learning processes and products;
(ii) the relative value and responsibilities for individual, economic and societal ends; and
(iii) the nature of knowledge and how it is acquired.

These clusters of underlying assumptions are examined in the following paragraphs. The various curriculum development approaches that have been taken with respect to (i)–(iii) are then examined in the following section.

Learning processes and products

With respect to (i), there has been a long debate in the literature about setting different kinds of educational objectives—for example, behavioural, expressive, process, instructional and cognitive objectives (e.g. Eisner 1969; Gronlund 1970; Mager 1962; Posner 1982; Stenhouse 1978). Some of these (e.g. *behavioural objectives*) focus on aiming instruction at pre-specified performances or behaviours which are assessable—for instance, being able to prepare a particular kind of food to a pre-stated standard; being able to use a certain tool in a particular way; being able to describe a diagnosis of a particular problem (or class of problems) and its solution; or being able to describe models of teamwork or cultural values. They depend on a belief that desirable ends can be pre-specified.

Similarly, *cognitive objectives* focus on the kinds of knowledge to be targeted in instruction. These are also pre-specified (e.g. being able to solve unfamiliar problems requiring the concept of momentum), and help in selecting learning experiences that will hopefully lead to these capacities—developing the idea of adhesion in welding; solving some adhesion problems; considering the classes of problems to which the idea of adhesion might apply. Some cognitive objectives are designated as metacognitive, referring to the capacity to monitor, reflect upon and modify one's own cognitive processes, especially in problem-solving.

For *process, instructional and expressive objectives*, on the other hand, the experiences of learning are thought to be more important than pre-specification of educational or learning ends, with individuals constructing their own meanings from experiences. For instance, visiting a workplace, engaging in those work activities that are attractive and accessible, and making judgements about that kind of work might be seen as more important than being able to describe ten prescribed characteristics of the workplace. Similarly, the experiences of working cooperatively with people from other cultures on an unfamiliar problem might be seen to be more valuable than being able to state abstract principles about stereotyping.

These various emphases seem to come in cycles, responsive to various social and economic crises such as returns to product emphases; seeking to develop 'given' knowledge; in times of war; and economic depression (Stevenson 1996a).

Individual, economic and societal ends

With respect to (ii), one set of assumptions is that the purpose of vocational education is to meet the *needs of industry*, meaning that the 'client' or 'customer' is industry and that industrial standards for work activity should be used as the primary (even exclusive) basis for curricular statements and teaching. Alternatively, it might be thought that there are wider *societal issues* and stakes in vocational education: what kinds of buildings are appropriate in city landscapes; what effects of industrial activity on the environment are socially desirable; what place should work have in social life; what justifies company profit in a community; and what kinds of consumption should be encouraged in marketing?

Still further, it may be thought that there are primary obligations towards individual *learners* seeking to acquire capacities for working. The following might also be taken into account in deciding what should be learned or what learning experiences are appropriate: learners' individual capacities and work-related needs; individuals' aspirations, needs and concerns beyond work; the relationships of work with identity and non-work pursuits; possibilities that careers will undergo massive qualitative changes in an individual person's life; the likelihood of periods of unemployment; the possibility that capacities developed now may not be adequate for that individual's future work and non-work activities; and the problematic relationships among employees, employers and society.

The reconciliation of purposes in vocational education curriculum development is problematic, but recognising that there are different purposes, making them explicit, and engaging in instructional design activity directed at reconciliation, rather than leaving them implicit, is more likely to achieve better links among different interests, and between curriculum planning and implementation (Stevenson 1998).

Nature of knowledge and its acquisition

With respect to (iii), one view that might be taken on knowledge is that it has an *essential nature*—it is given, timeless, accessible and transmissible. For example, what constitutes being a mechanic can be determined, written down and learned as such by transmission from one who has that knowledge to a learner. This transmission may be through demonstration, oral instruction or communicating in other verbal ways.

Another view is that vocational knowledge (e.g. that of mechanics) is an application of *scientific or engineering knowledge* to a limited set of problems. Learning involves the inculcation of scientific and engineering theory and problem-solving procedures and their application to examples of the set of problems to be found in practice. (Some practical experiences in acquiring the acquisition of 'technical skills' would also be called for.)

Another view is that knowledge is *constructed* meaningfully and differently by individuals through personally significant experience. From this view, learning to be a mechanic is more problematic. A learner needs to engage in mechanics' work directly and seek to make sense of that experience through connecting it with understandings of previous experience; with other renditions of mechanics' knowledge (e.g. in manuals and texts); and with meanings developed through wider life experiences. A related view is that being a mechanic is not a single phenomenon—it means different things to different mechanics in different settings; and mechanical knowledge is not universal, static or given, but constructed afresh in changing circumstances. Moreover, mechanical knowledge may not be organised as engineering knowledge, but functionally in relation to experience, and this functional organisation itself undergoes change through experience.

Another dimension of differences in views about knowledge and its acquisition is that understanding and *values* are recognised by some as immanent in any capacity-to-do, while others separate them—usually focusing exclusively on knowledge-that or knowledge-how.

CURRICULUM THEORIES

Many researchers have tackled these issues, seeking to develop curriculum principles for guiding the planning and activities of teaching and learning. Various theoretical approaches take different stances with respect to (i)–(iii) above.

These theoretical approaches to curricula and their development can be used to orient those involved in practice. They can be summarised in various ways. For instance, drawing on Reid (1981), Marsh and Willis (1995) divide curriculum theorists into *system-oriented a priorists* (prescribing means and ends of education), *system-supportive explorers* (concerned about ethical decision-making in context), *system-opposing a priorists* (who have alternative prescriptions to overcome injustices) and *system-indifferent explorers* (concerned with individuals and their growth). These different clusters take on board different combinations of the assumptions in (i)–(iii) outlined above, with different value stances, different emphases on what are seen to be desirable processes and products and different orientations with regard to the kinds of knowing seen to be legitimate.

Approaches to curriculum planning, teaching and learning can also be differentiated in other ways. For instance, they can be differentiated (Vallance 1999) as those which identify important *procedures* (e.g. identifying objectives, selecting learning experiences, organising learning experiences and evaluating learning experiences—Tyler 1950), those which identify points or '*commonplaces*' (i.e. the teacher, learner, subject matter, milieu) around which decisions need to be made (e.g. Schwab 1969), those which advance sets of *concerns* to be addressed (e.g. Eisner & Vallance 1974), and those which offer *'perspectives from which educational activity can be valued'* (Vallance 1999, p. 57) (e.g. Huebner 1966). Each of these approaches seeks to incorporate important elements in curriculum decision-making processes, covering the range of possible concerns, ensuring a logically related set of decisions is made and taking account of the range of values that stakeholders can have.

Each of these possible manifold approaches offers a starting point in addressing the tensions, conflicts and problems that are involved in planning teaching and learning. At the same time, an enduring problem is that, given the diverse range of expectations, pressures and interests shaping contemporary curriculum practice (Stevenson 1998), various theoretical frameworks often lead to the privileging of certain views and the marginalisation of others (Garrick & Usher 2000). That is, coherence of activity is often purchased at the cost of unduly limiting the range of curricular concerns and stakeholder interests actively expressed in contemporary curriculum practice.

Moreover, each approach has its own limitations. As Wraga writes in his review of Slattery's (1995) work, curriculum theory has been undergoing considerable reconceptualisation in response to 'diverse forms of enquiry that draw from hermeneutics, critical theory, phenomenology, poststructuralism, aesthetic inquiry, autobiographical enquiry, theological theory, gender studies, racial theory and even chaos theory' (Wraga 1996, p. 463).

What is clear is the need to consider the planning of teaching and learning in any field (including vocational education and training) in the context of actual practice, rather than developing grand universal theories. To avoid the privileging that can come from so-called general theories, the particulars of situations and the local, variant views on what is relevant and desirable need to be addressed, rather than 'averaged' or marginalised. An important context for vocational teaching and learning is competency-based training and economic pressures on the development of vocational knowledge. Thus the fact of competency-based training policy cannot be ignored by, say, focusing solely on a 'process'-based approach to curriculum development. Similarly, the actual concerns of teachers and learners under competency-based training policies, of employers taking on graduates of competency-based courses or of communities protesting the irrelevance of specific or generalised competences cannot be ignored by just taking the policy line. Nor can we ignore the needs of industry to flourish in a changing globalising and competitive environment where the nature and structure of work and productivity are being transformed, or of communities resisting the concomitant effects of such change on society.

The contemporary realities of economic presses on the codification of meaning are examined in the following sections.

ECONOMIC PRESS FOR CODIFICATION OF MEANING

An important vocation for many is work in the economy. While, as argued above, economic considerations are not the only important bases for vocational expertise, they are nevertheless relevant and pervasive. In work, meaning is directed at work functions, motivated by one's role in the organisation. In order to ensure that education prepares people adequately for their roles in work, there are often calls from industry for changes in emphasis or for certain kinds of learning. In this section, these various calls are clustered into those to do with performance on predicted tasks, those for adaptability to change, and those preparing people for effectiveness in transforming globalising economies. These calls are examined in terms of the kinds of meaning that are involved (see Chapter 1).

Calls for outcomes

Calls for learning to prepare people for various job functions are usually calls for learning outcomes. These outcomes are expressed in various ways—for example, as literacy, as specific work skills or as attitudes to work. Often they are related to mappings of occupations undertaken by industry and called *industry standards*. The codes used for this kind of knowledge are sometimes expressed as *outcomes*, *behavioural objectives* or *competencies*. In each case, they seek to describe a target performance.

Contemporary governmental policies for the practice of vocational education and training centre around a call for outcomes in the form of competence. The word *competence* when used in policy statements represents a discourse aimed at a particular kind of codification of the meanings, which advocates think that individuals should derive, draw upon and utilise in work. According to Swanchek and Campbell (1981), the current competency movement can be traced back to the 1960s when the US Office of Education gave grants for the development of model training programs for elementary school teachers. These models included 'the precise specification of competences or behaviors to be learned, the modularisation of instruction, evaluation and feedback, personalization, and field experience' (1981, cited in Tuxworth 1989, p. 11). For descriptions of the contexts and processes of deriving competences, see Burke (1989, 1995) and Harris et al. (1995).

In terms of the clusters of assumptions (i)–(iii) outlined earlier, this focus on pre-specified demonstrable abilities constitutes a product or outcome approach to instruction. The focus is not on learning processes, cognitive processes or learning experiences. The value is for economic objectives, especially those of the industry representatives who have been able to participate in the processes of setting industrial standards. This value is not on individuals, with their plural aspirations and needs, or on wider societal concerns. The assumptions about knowledge are that it is unproblematic, codifiable, unchanging and able to be transmitted to individuals.

The assumptions underlying competency-based training are historically situated, and have been extensively analysed (e.g. Hyland 1994; Jackson 1993; Stevenson 1992, 1993). Competency-based training represents a technicist approach to instruction, with confidence that workplace capacities can be specified in advance, to be acquired by learners through instruction. Different competency-based approaches to pre-specifying capacities as competence differ in terms of the extent to which the target capacities are specific or general, disaggregated or holistic, behavioural or cognitive. However, in all cases they exert control through the codification of meaning. Other important assumptions are about the essentialist nature of vocational knowledge, and the movement's reading of economically relevant capacities.

Sometimes, in competency-based training, the descriptions are quite elaborate, referring to conditions under which the performance is to be executed and the criteria used for judging the performance to be acceptable. These criteria are expressed as learning outcomes, performance criteria, evidence guides and range of variables statements.

A focus on prescribed outcomes for learning may be seen as a new kind of behaviourism in the form of managerialism. That is, it may be interpreted as attempts to exert control over what is taught in vocational education for managerial purposes. Pre-specification of learning outcomes towards which learners are to be shaped is a neat way of confining what is learned. It deals efficiently with removing what industry may see as irrelevant content in vocational curricula. Only the essential skills, relevant to immediate industrial needs, are usually captured in vocational curricula of this type.

Flowing from a consideration of Figure 1.1 in Chapter 1, there are three main disadvantageous effects of outcomes approaches on the development of meaning. Firstly, the relationship between the pre-specified material to be taught and the individual's sense of vocation may not be apparent to the learner, and the learning experiences may not be seen by them as meaningful. Sense (personal significance) and meaning (apprehension of the collective construction, as reflected in the competency statement) may be alienated because the individual may not be able to connect individual goals and aspirations (and the meanings needed in pursuing them) with motives underlying the codified statements. The learner may not even be aware of these latter motives. Try as the learner may to acquire the content, mastery may be elusive because of the difficulty of constructing meaning. Secondly, the scope for connecting meaning between what is done on the job and what else happens in everyday living may also be obscure. This may be because the learning is atomised into small bits and the whole is not seen. It may also be because societal, industrial and individual goals are in conflict, and there is no space to reconcile them. The resultant cognitive dissonance will probably lead to assimilation rather than accommodation of meaning—isolating the 'knowledge' from what the individual sees as personally meaningful. Thirdly, because the emphasis, in this kind of learning, is largely on demonstrating how to do things without there necessarily being any consideration of why or how this doing relates to other meanings in the experiences, rich connections among meanings are not developed, affecting capacities for developing a sense of appropriateness, an understanding of why things are done and a capacity for relating meaning to new and different challenges.

Calls for adaptability

Calls for specific competences in the 1980s gradually became supplemented with calls for what have variously been called key, core or necessary competences or skills. This move is one aimed at securing 'transfer' of knowledge in changing circumstances—that is, adaptability—despite the substantial body of literature that sees the idea of such transfer as misplaced (see, for example, the special edition of *Review of Research in Education* (Iran-Nejad & Pearson 1999) and the special edition of the *International Journal of Education Research*, 1999, vol. 31).

These 'generic' codes are labels for capacities that the advocates believe are common to many different kinds of work, and even apply across work and other life pursuits. For instance they include abilities to collect, analyse and organise information; to use technology; to use mathematical ideas and techniques; to work with others and in teams; to plan and organise activities; and to communicate ideas and information (Mayer 1992). They may be expressed as basic skills, thinking skills and personal qualities in terms of being able to productively use resources, interpersonal skills, information, systems and technology (US Department of Labor Secretary's Commission on Achieving Necessary Skills 1992). Similarly, some commentators refer to horizontal skills, transversal and personal skills, social skills and metacompetence (Sellin 1999). We also have labels such as intellective and connective skills, mobile knowledge workers and symbolic analysts (Harvey 1989; Young 1993).

While these kinds of labels can be seen to point to capacities, which can be abstracted from analyses of various kinds of work, it is a mistake to believe that they can be learned as such. Rather, as outlined in Chapter 1, learning consists of constructing meaning on direct experience, where such activity is situated. That is, it is a mistake to think that being able to communicate adequately in one situation for one set of purposes will apply to another situation and purpose; or that to be able to engage in an activity which achieves solution of one kind of problem connotes the capacity to solve all kinds of workplace problems. Certainly these labels are interesting ways of articulating some of the challenges for vocational education, but care must be taken not to confuse the verbal labels with the kinds of meaning that individuals derive from intentional, functional, purposive, situated, concrete practice (see Chapter 1, Figure 1.1; Beven 1997; Stasz 1997; Stevenson 1996b). Similarly, they may be helpful labels for learners seeking to derive meaning from different kinds of experiences, but they are no substitute for the experiences themselves.

Calls for explicit innovative capacities

In economies transforming in the face of globalisation, there have been further additions to what are regarded as economically important capacities. For example, there has been the claim that 'Mode 2' knowledge is more important than 'Mode 1' knowledge (Gibbons et al. 1994), where Mode 2 knowledge is transdisciplinary and localised, arising from the context of application, rather than disciplinary and general, arising from codified academic knowledge. (It is like Phenix's synoetic meaning—see this volume, Chapter 1.) A recent European Report (Lundvall & Borrás 1997) argues the importance of tacit meaning in globalising economies, where the tacit meaning is both that of procedural skills as well as more general managerial capacities. These authors argue that this meaning is socially embedded in the organisation and in organisational networks, and that there are problems in making it explicit and sharing it. They argue that competitive businesses in globalising economies need to find ways of sharing these meanings. Others also argue that knowledge creation in contemporary economies involves both tacit and explicit knowledge and that these are complementary (Nonaka et al. 2001), with continuous conversions among tacit and explicit ways of understanding, as new meaning is constructed, externalised, shared and re-combined, by individuals and in concert with others. In terms of Figure 1.1 (Chapter 1), these calls recognise the significance of those kinds of meaning that are difficult to render in language as well as meanings which do not fit easily into the structures of academic disciplines.

Summary

Thus economic presses for the codification of meaning as explicit knowledge can take a variety of forms, depending on whether the focus is on meaning required (managed and controlled) for the routine execution of predicted skills, for 'transfer' in times of economic change or for innovation for competitive activity in globalising economies. These various economic agendas take the form of restating what is considered to be legitimate vocational knowledge, by assigning new codes to that meaning which they consider relevant. Unfortunately, this quest for control through the legitimisation of codes can get in the way of individual construction of meaning, which itself is derived from meaningful (personally relevant—functional, purposeful, related-to-vocation) experience. Unless these economically coded meanings are explicitly related by the individuals to other ways in which they construct meaning (Chapter 1, Figure 1.1), then the knowledge will be inert. For individuals to cope with new situations, they do not rely on having acquired knowledge coded as 'problem-solving', 'creativity' or the like. Moreover, there is a problem that the codes can be confused with meaning itself, and assumptions made that they can be 'taught'.

Rather, it needs to be understood that individuals use personally relevant meanings that they have derived from previous experience to understand and deal with new situations. This meaning may well be able to be given an abstract title such as 'problem-solving skills' or 'creativity', but it is not known to the individual as such and is not acquired as such. The individual may come to know in these ways, but only if the codes become connected with existing, personally significant meanings. Rather, the individual knows how to proceed because of the various ways in which they can construct meaning on the new situation, drawing upon relevant realms of meaning and their interconnections. The individual will not assign meaning to the learning of detached problem-solving (or other key/core skills) unless the experiences are seen to be functional and personally relevant, related to senses of vocation. Moreover, different individuals will not 'know' problem-solving in the same way, as they will have constructed meanings, their interconnections and their own facility with them and their interrelationships differently.

SOME BASES FOR PLANNING TEACHING AND LEARNING

Given the various possible curricular theories and approaches, the need for teaching and learning to be contextualised and the various possibilities for incorporating different kinds of meaning in vocational instruction, it is important to have a conceptual basis from which to make instructional decisions. Drawing from the nature of expertise and how meaning is acquired, there are several possible starting points in developing such a basis for teaching and learning in vocational education and training. Two such bases are advanced here.

Firstly, the planning of teaching and learning can be thought of as constructing/engaging in an activity system (Engeström 1999; Leont'ev 1981 [1959]). In an activity system, there is a *subject* (or several subjects) interacting collectively in a *community* with a shared *object* (motive) leading to certain *outcomes* (Figure 2.1). In the case of teaching and learning, there are learners and teachers (and possibly others) working together towards the motive of deriving meaning—the outcome is the meanings that individuals construct. In an activity system, there are *instruments* or artefacts that mediate the activity. In this case, they can be thought of as all of the resources that are used—tools, technologies, manuals, equipment, texts and other physical features of the setting as well as conceptual tools such as theories of teaching and learning. In an activity system, there exists a community (e.g. teachers, learners, co-workers, aides—all with connections to society more widely) and a division of labour (e.g. the teacher as source of knowledge, or facilitator, or resource; the learner as proactive or receptive taking more or less responsibility for what, where and how they learn) (see Stevenson & McKavanagh 1994). Activity systems also have explicit and implicit *rules* for activity in the system (e.g. what is appropriate behaviour). Each of these features of activity systems is historically situated, developed in response to tensions and contradictions in the system, within and between all these elements and with other activity systems. The artefacts—in particular, language and resources that use language—embody the cultural-historical meanings derived by the community over time.

In approaching teaching and learning, then, important features to consider are the elements of the contextualised activity system and their cultural-historical nature. Learners, of course, also operate within other

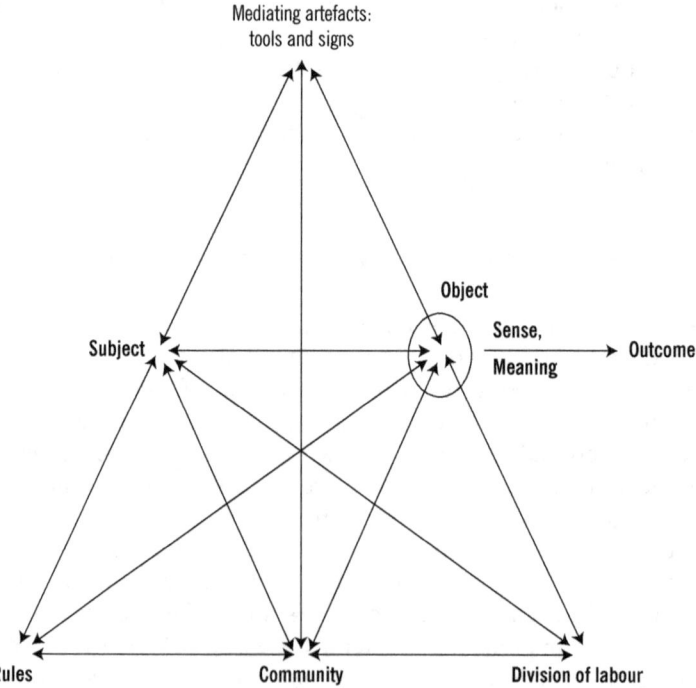

Figure 2.1 The structure of a human activity system
Source: Engerström 1999, p. 2, derived from Engeström 1987, p. 78

activity systems—for example, in relation to their homes, their friends and their involvement in society more widely. These other activity systems have other objects, such as caring for children, achieving a just society and protecting the environment. The role of teaching and learning experiences is to assist in deriving meaning and connecting it with meanings derived and rendered in other ways and in other activity systems.

Secondly, the planning of teaching and learning can be thought of in terms of developing supposed cognitive representations of meaning. A framework developed by de Jong and Ferguson-Hessler (1996) (although developed for the field of physics) is based on functional experiences, and therefore has promise for developing teaching and learning principles for vocational education. Their taxonomy separates categories of representations from the variety of qualities that they may have. Separation of various kinds of theorised *types* of representation have a long history in cognitive psychology, although the strengths of each approach will not be dealt with here (see Chapter 1); and the four-fold set of types used by de Jong and Ferguson-Hessler is taken to be as good as any other set of types. That is, as for other taxonomies, each type needs to be seen in terms broader than those that can be conveyed in language. For example, conceptual knowledge may be found not only in scientific theory, but in other realms of meaning; procedural knowledge may be found not only in physical action and be expressible not only as Anderson's (1982) productions, but may also be found in problem-solving processes and be rendered in forms appropriate for other realms of meaning. The main focus here is on qualities.

Ignoring the separation of different *types* of supposed cognitive representations, the strength of this taxonomy is that it does not confine hierarchical terms for different *qualities* (e.g. 'deep', 'structured', 'general') to one class of posited representations. That is, supposed cognitive representations for the capacity-to-do can be theorised in terms ranging from deep, structured, compiled and general to surface, elemental, declarative and verbal, without confining these terms to such ideas as that of 'concepts'. The set of different kinds of meaning can therefore have the full range of qualities.

Moreover, it is interesting to examine the range of differences in qualities across the set of supposed knowledge *types*, examining indicators of meaningfulness. For instance, depth is seen to relate to meaningful action as opposed to rules and recipes, and to analysis and planning as opposed to symbol-driven searches; structure is seen to relate to meaningfulness as opposed to independent concepts and laws, and to groups of features and actions; compiled meaning is seen to involve intuitive tacit understanding as opposed to verbalisable principles, and automatic action as opposed to step-by-step choices, planning and execution; and non-verbal modes are seen to be important ways of understanding.

In the next section, ideas drawn from activity theory and qualities of knowledge are used to generate teaching and learning principles for vocational education in the context which has been examined in this chapter.

GENERATING TEACHING AND LEARNING PRINCIPLES

Based on the nature of expertise advanced in Chapter 1, the kinds of meaning that experts interconnect and draw upon (Chapter 1, Figure 1.1), the idea of teaching and learning as a contextualised activity system and the recognition that knowledge can be viewed in terms of both types and qualities, the following principles are advanced (see Figure 2.2).

In order to build facility with meanings and their interconnections, learners need to be engaged in appropriate activity that makes meanings apparent, related to clear functions and purposes, related to their own senses of vocation, and related to alternative ways of constructing meaning. Thus:

- *Learning should proceed from the learner's sense of vocation*—needs, aspirations and intentions, previous experiences and the meanings extracted from them, existing capacities-to-do, relationships among the learner's work and non-work goals and meanings. Then learning can be based on what is already understood and can readily be connected with it. Differences between new and old meanings can be made explicit and reconsidered; attempts to develop new meaning should not be disconnected from the self.
- *Learning should occur in settings or activity systems where the function and purposes of the learning are clear and explicit, related to vocation; and collective motives and personal goals should be related.* The tasks in which learners engage should be tasks with an explicit relationship to tasks that constitute current or future work or other vocations. Then the learner will be able to relate doing with purpose and function, and with instructions and other ways of rendering meaning. Motivation to learn and interest in learning will be high, and the outcomes of learning and doing will be transparent, fleshing out the meanings in the capacity-to-do. No 'transfer' will be necessary in order to relate 'knowledge' with application or practice. Learners then can make personal sense of the activity and relate it to collective meaning.
- *Learning should focus primarily on developing the capacity-to-do, where learners seek to accomplish goals.* This involves

VOCATIONAL TEACHING AND LEARNING IN CONTEXT

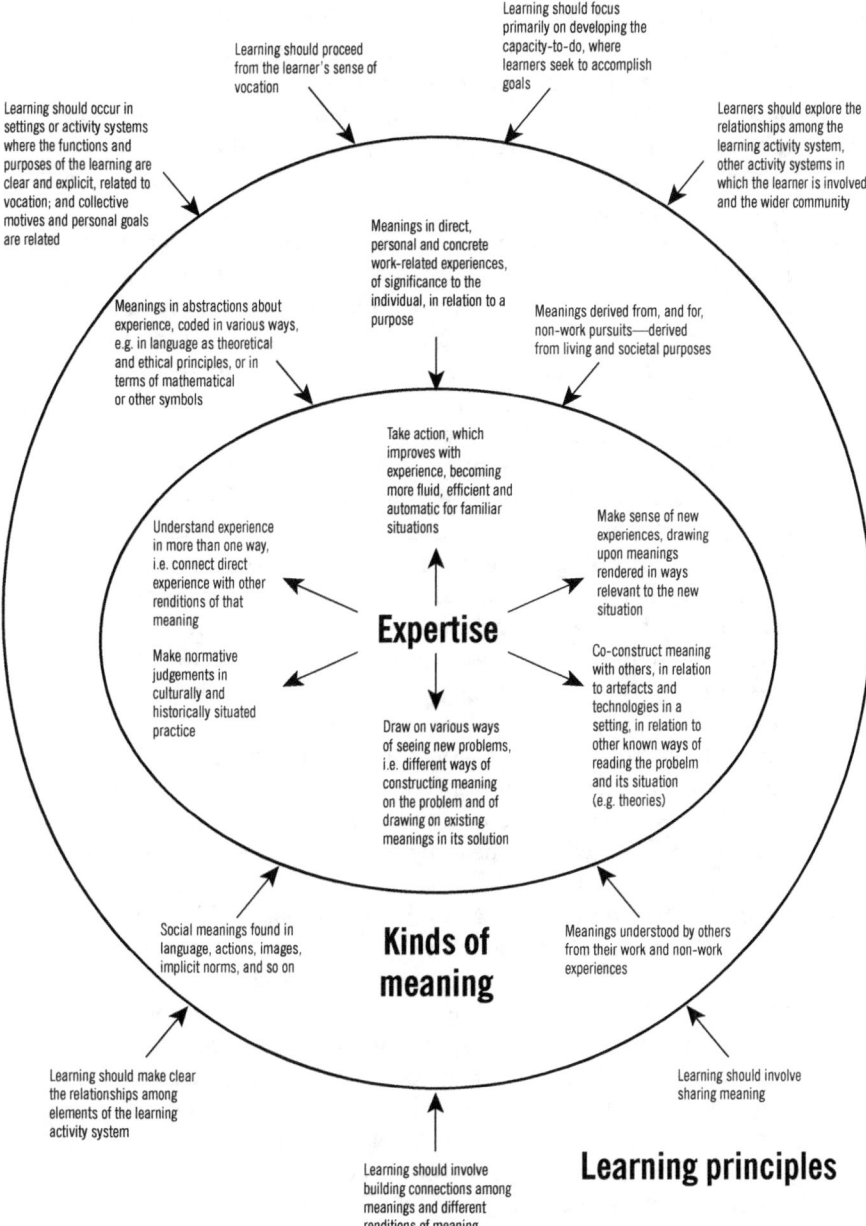

Figure 2.2 Relationships of expertise, meaning and learning

trying things out, being shown, watching and discussing with others and receiving feedback—all involving direct, concrete experience with real artefacts in activity systems. Learners need to be proactive rather than reactive; involved rather than passive; taking responsibility rather than relying on others for initiative; taking a personal stake rather than feeling marginalised.

- *The relationships among elements of the learning activity system should be made clear*—the implicit and explicit rules and the normative nature of meaning in the setting; the tools, technologies, processes, equipment and materials and tensions in their histories; the ways in which subjects share objects in achieving outcomes and how these are represented in the setting; who constitutes the community and the nature of the division of responsibilities. This includes power relationships in the setting and how the learner is positioned with respect to them. Then the learner can seek to make sense of given ways of doing things, the possible reasons why activities are undertaken in a particular way, and tensions and contradictions in the system, within and between elements. This will involve watching and discussing with others, forming and appraising opinions, putting ideas forward, and exploring the boundaries of what is possible. Learners need opportunities to connect meaning and activity, understand the culturally situated and historically transient nature of meaning at a point in time in a setting, and come to terms with the personal and shared ways in which meaning is constructed in relation to doing in a context.
- *Learning should involve sharing meaning.* This involves making aspects of the activity system visible for inspection; showing and demonstrating, discussing and sharing alternative different ways of reading tasks, the setting, problems and various ways forward; and finding ways of cooperating that improve practice. It also involves reconciling capacities-to-do, other intuitive and tacit meanings, theories, principles, other symbolic representations of meaning and other relevant realms of meaning. Such learning should proceed from direct concrete experience rather than verbalised propositional statements. It also involves building connections with manuals, instructions and texts.
- *The relationships among the learning activity system, other activity systems in which the learner is involved and the wider community should be explored* so that the learner can seek to connect meanings across systems and tensions and contradictions among them. This will involve discussion, reading,

formulation of views, and reconciling tensions and contradictions. It will also involve reconciling the individual's plural vocations in work, personal life and society. Learners will have the opportunity to discern the interrelationships among society, its economy and personal and community welfare and quality of life; the forces and pressures involved and their own position and responsibilities in relation to them.

- *Learning should involve building connection among meanings and different renditions of meaning.* This involves making explicit the connections outlined in other points here—meaning and doing; others' meanings; knowledge codified in manuals, instructions and texts; connections within and among elements and systems, and with broader society; meanings across plural vocational pursuits; old and new meanings; old and new work, technologies, tools, equipment and materials. It involves experiences in discerning the connections among different renditions of meaning in words, diagrams, pictures, gestures, action and images. It also involves developing a facility in operating upon such interconnections as are needed in different situations. Drawing upon de Jong and Ferguson-Hessler (1996), this involves seeking to understand the qualities of meaning derived from practice and relate them to other qualities that meaning can have—for example, relating verbal renditions of meaning to imaginal ones; rules to embodied action; step by step frameworks for action and planning to automatic action; compiled meaning to verbal propositions. Experiences in connecting the primary sources of meaning (derived from practice) with other renditions involve explicit communication about these meanings.

CONCLUSION

Various assumptions can underpin approaches that are taken to planning curricula and designing teaching and learning experiences in vocational education and training. Important assumptions are those to do with emphases on learning processes and products; relative weights given to the needs and aspirations of individuals, industry and society as a whole; and perspectives on the nature of meaning and its acquisition. Approaches to curriculum development that adopt various combinations of underpinning beliefs each have their own limitations. Local curriculum and teaching and learning decision-making is warranted, taking account of the various kinds of assumptions that can be made and the socio-politic and historic context. The current economic press for knowledge codification is examined in terms of calls for outcomes, calls for adaptability and calls for innovative capacities. The particular case of competency-based training and its assumptions is examined and found wanting.

Economic presses for codification of meaning can get in the way of individual construction of meaning for economic challenges, by developing abstracted codes, confusing the codes with meaning itself and assuming that the codes can be taught.

Activity theory and research on the qualities of supposed cognitive representations of meaning are outlined and used to derive principles that might guide teaching and learning in vocational education so that learners are developed towards expertise. In summary these principles are:

- to proceed from the learner's sense of vocation;
- to situate learning in concrete, functional, purposive settings;
- to focus primarily on developing the capacity-to-do;
- to engage in understanding interrelationships in learning/working activity systems;
- to share meaning;
- to relate meanings so derived to other activity systems and the wider community; and
- To build connections among meanings and different renditions of meaning, together with a facility of operating upon such interconnections.

REFERENCES

Anderson, J.R. 1982, 'Acquisition of cognitive skill', *Psychological Review*, vol. 89, no. 4, pp. 369–406

Beven, F. ed. 1997, *Learning in the Workplace: Airline Customer Service*, Centre for Learning and Work Research, Griffith University, Brisbane

Burke, J.W. ed. 1989, *Competency Based Education and Training*, Falmer, London

de Jong T. & Ferguson-Hessler, M.G.M. 1996, 'Types and qualities of knowledge', *Educational Psychologist*, vol. 31, no. 2, pp. 105–13

Eisner, E.W. 1969, 'Instructional and expressive objectives: their formulation and use in curriculum', in *Instructional Objectives* vol. 3, ed. R.E. Stake, AERA monograph series on curriculum evaluation, Rand McNally, Chicago

Engeström, Y. 1987, *Learning by Expanding: An Activity-Theoretical Approach to Developmental Research*, Orienta-Konsultit Oy, Helsinki

—— 1999, 'Expansive learning at work: toward an activity-theoretical reconceptualization', keynote address, *Changing Practice through Research: Changing Research through Practice*, 7th Annual International Conference of the Centre for Learning and Work Research, Griffith University, Brisbane

Finch, C.R. & Crunkilton, J.R. 1993, *Curriculum Development in Vocational and Technical Education: Planning Content and Implementation*, 4th edn, Allyn & Bacon, Boston

Gibbons, M., Limoges, C., Nowotny, H., Schwartzman, S., Scott, P. & Trow, M. 1994, *The New Production of Knowledge: The Dynamics of Science and Research in Contemporary Societies*, Sage, London

Green, A. 1997, 'Core skills general education and unification in post-16 education', in *Dearing and Beyond 14–9 Qualification Frameworks and Systems*, eds A. Hodgson & K. Spours, Kogan Page, London.

Gronlund, N.E. 1970, *Stating Behavioural Objectives for Classroom Instruction*, Collier-Macmillan, London

Harris, R., Guthrie, H., Hobart, B. & Lundberg D. 1995, *Competency-Based Education and Training: Between a Rock and a Whirlpool*, Macmillan, Melbourne

Harvey, D. 1989, *The Condition of Postmodernity: An Enquiry into the Origins of Cultural Change*, Blackwell, Oxford

Hyland, T. 1994, *Competence Education and The NVQs: Dissenting Perspectives*, Cassell, London

Iran-Nejad, A. & Pearson, P.D. eds 1999, *Review of Research in Education*, vol. 24, AERA, Washington DC

Jackson, N. 1993, 'If competence is the answer what is the question?', *Australian and New Zealand Journal of Vocational Education Research*, vol. 1, no. 1, pp. 46–60

Laird, D. & Stevenson, J. 1993, 'A curriculum development framework for vocational education', *Australian and New Zealand Journal of Vocational Education Research*, vol. 1, no. 2, pp. 71–92

Leont'ev, A.N. 1981 (1959), *Problems of the Development of the Mind*, Progress Publishers, Moscow

Lundvall, B.-Å. & Borrás, S. 1997, *The Globalising Learning Economy: Implications for Innovation Policy, Report Based on Contributions from Seven Projects under the TSER Programme DG XII*, Commission of the European Union, Brussels

Mager, R.F. 1962, *Preparing Objectives for Programmed Instruction*, Fearon, San Francisco

Marsh, C. & Willis, G. 1995, *Curriculum Alternative Approaches: Ongoing Issues*, Merrill, Englewood Cliffs, NJ

Mayer, E. Chair 1992, *Putting General Education to Work: The Key Competencies Report*, The Australian Education Council and Ministers for Vocational Education Employment and Training, Canberra

Nonaka, I. & Nishiguchi, T. 2001, *Knowledge Emergence: Social Technical and Evolutionary Dimensions of Knowledge Creation*, Oxford University Press, Oxford

Parker, W.C., Nonomiya, A. & Cogan, J. 1999, 'Educating world citizens: toward multinational curriculum development', *American Educational Research Journal*, vol. 36, no. 2, pp. 117–46

Posner, G.A. 1982, 'A cognitive science conception of curriculum and instruction', *Journal of Curriculum Studies*, vol. 14, no. 4, pp. 343–51

Reid, E. 1981, 'Core curriculum: precepts or processes?', *Curriculum Perspectives*, vol. 1, no. 2, pp. 25–32

Riley, R.W. 2000, *Career Clusters: Adding Relevancy to Education*, Brochure, US Department of Education, 400 Maryland Avenue SW, Washington DC

Schwab, J.J. 1969, 'The practical: a language for curriculum', *School Review*, vol. 78, pp. 1–23

Sellin, B. 1999, *European Trends in the Development of Occupations and Qualifications*, vol. 1, CEDEFOP—European Centre for the Development of Vocational Training, Thessalonika

Slattery, P. 1995, *Curriculum Development in the Postmodern Era*, Garland Publishing, New York

Stasz, C. 1997, 'Do employers need the skills they want? Evidence from technical work', *Journal of Education and Work*, vol. 10, no. 3, pp. 205–23

Stevenson, J.C. 1992, 'Australian Vocational Education: learning from past mistakes?', *The Vocational Aspect of Education*, vol. 44, no. 2, pp. 233–44

—— 1993, 'Competency-based education in Australia: an analysis of assumptions', *Australian and New Zealand Journal of Vocational Education Research*, vol. 1, no. 1, pp. 87–104

—— 1996a, 'The metamorphosis of the construction of competence', *Studies in Continuing Education*, vol. 18, no. 1, pp. 24–42

—— ed. 1996b, *Learning in the Workplace: Tourism and Hospitality. A Report on an Initial Exploratory Examination of Critical Aspects of Small Businesses in the Tourism and Hospitality Industry*, Centre for Skill Formation Research and Development, Griffith University, Brisbane

—— 1998, 'Finding a basis for reconciling perspectives on vocational education and training', *Australian and New Zealand Journal of Vocational Education Research*, vol. 6, no. 2, pp. 134–65

Stevenson, J.C. & McKavanagh, C. 1994, 'Development of student expertise in TAFE colleges', in *Cognition at Work: The Development of Vocational Expertise*, ed. J.C. Stevenson, National Centre for Vocational Education Research, Adelaide

Swanchek, J. & Campbell, J. 1981, 'Competence/performance based teacher education: the unfulfilled promise', *Educational Technology*, June, pp. 5–10

Tuxworth, E. 1989, 'Competency based education and training: background and origins', in *Competency Based Education and Training*, ed. J.W. Burke, Falmer, London

Tyler, R.W. 1950, *Basic Principles of Curriculum and Instruction*, University of Chicago Press, Chicago, ILL

US Department of Labor Secretary's Commission on Achieving Necessary Skills 1992, *Learning a Living: A Blueprint for High Performance. A SCAN's Report for America 2000*, US Department of Labor, Washington DC

Vallance, E. 1999, 'Ways of knowing and curricular conceptions: implications for program planning', in *Issues in Curriculum: A Selection of Chapters from Past NSSE Yearbooks*, eds. M.J. Early & K.J. Rehage, University of Chicago Press, Chicago, ILL

Wraga, W.G. 1996, 'Toward a curriculum theory for the new century: essay review of Patrick Slattery's Curriculum development in the postmodern era', *Journal of Curriculum Studies*, vol. 28, no. 4, pp. 463–74

Young, M.F.D. 1993, 'A curriculum for the 21st Century?', *British Journal of Educational Studies*, vol. 31, no. 3, pp. 202–22

Part II

Developing vocational expertise for key pursuits

3

Developing literacy

Jean Searle

INTRODUCTION

This chapter argues that literacy is not simply a set of decontextualised skills which can be codified, measured and audited. Rather, literacy refers to a range of highly contextualised social practices in which people engage. As these practices vary according to events or aspects of people's lives, so do the 'literacies' they require. In order to unpack what this means, this chapter has been subdivided into a number of sections. In the first section, 'What is literacy?', some assumptions or master myths about literacy are examined in order to problematise what literacy is and what literacy can do. This section is followed by a review of what psycholinguistic, socio-cultural and critical theories, and research about literacy have to say about literacy and learning, the literate practices of individuals in society and literacy and power—or social transformation. In this section, four different discourses of literacy—as decontextualised skills, as a technology, as socially situated practices and as multiliteracies—are introduced to show the relationships among ideology, theory and practice. The third section presents cases drawn from recent research in several workplaces in order to exemplify these relationships. Finally, elements of each of these sections are synthesised in order to suggest principles for curriculum design, instruction and assessment in vocational education and training.

WHAT IS LITERACY?
Everyday concepts of literacy

If you were to ask a range of people what they think literacy is, they would probably respond in a number of different ways. They may equate literacy with being able to read and write—but read and write what? To a child, reading might involve sitting in a circle and taking turns reading a story at school, or being at home and listening to a bedtime story. To an adult, reading might be checking the sports results in the newspaper, or using a technical manual at work. Each of these definitions suggests that reading is purposeful, involves a text and implies a context. However, other people will talk about literacy in terms of newspaper headlines such as, 'Literacy standards fall' or 'Learn to read or lose the dole'. From this viewpoint, literacy is perceived to be a set of desirable skills or technologies. The problem with this 'autonomous' point of view is that it assumes that there is a defined set of skills which, once learnt in lower primary school, will fit a person for the rest of their lives. Further, should this person have difficulties later, then he or she is to blame. But who decides what the standards should be? Do they change through time? And why is literacy perceived to be a 'social good'? The purpose of this chapter is to expose some literacy myths, to demonstrate how autonomous views of literacy lead to inappropriate and sometimes punitive practices, and to propose a more socially just approach. The starting point is to outline some definitions of literacy and then to discuss some of the theories and models of literacy in relation to learning or meaning-making.

Definitions of literacy

The concept of literacy is not value-free—it has social, cultural, political, economic and educational implications. As a result, what is regarded as being literate depends on the definition of literacy that is adopted at a particular time in history and in a particular context. Further, there is no universally accepted definition of literacy. In fact, literacy may be viewed in relation to learning—as a cognitive or thinking skill, as a social practice or, in relation to power struggles, as an emancipatory act. Each of these positions is outlined in Table 3.1.

In summary, although Table 3.1 presents a limited number of definitions, they represent some of the major theories which have informed school literacy practices as well as those in adult, vocational and workplace contexts. Later in this chapter, it will be shown that the basic skills (autonomous) model of literacy has been updated as a technological model to suit government and industry economic imperatives to codify knowledge and make individuals more accountable for their actions. However, as examples from the workplace will show, this is a very limited view of actual social practices and does not address power

Table 3.1 Definitions of literacy

Functional literacy	'A person is functionally literate when he [sic] has acquired the knowledge and skills in reading and writing which enable him to engage effectively in all those activities in which literacy is normally assumed in his culture and group' (Grey 1956, cited in Oxenham 1980, p. 86).
Basic literacy (autonomous model)	Literacy acquisition is the development of a series of decontextualised basic skills. It assumes unidimensional progress from illiterate to literate, or indeed towards civilisation or economic take-off (Street 1984).
Social literacies (ideological model)	Social literacies refer to 'both behaviour and conceptualisation related to the uses of reading and/or writing. "Literacy practices" incorporate not only "literacy events" as empirical occasions to which literacy is integral, but also folk models of those events and the ideological preconceptions that underpin them' (Street 1992, p. 13).
Critical literacy	Literacy may lead to social transformation. Literacy is about 'reading the world' not just 'the word' (Freire & Macedo 1987).
Vocational/workplace literacy (technological model)	Literacy is the ability to perform competently a number of literacy and numeracy tasks, covering a range of skill levels from one to five within prose, document and quantitative literacy domains (Wickert 1989, building on the work of Kirsch & Jungeblut 1986).
Multiliteracies	Multiliteracies relate to 'the increasing multiplicity and integration of significant modes of meaning-making, where textual is also related to the visual, the audio, the spatial, the behavioural . . . "multimedia" and in electronic "hypermedia" . . . to focus on the realities of increasing local diversity and global connectedness' (Cope & Kalantzis 1995, p. 6).

relations within organisations. In the next section, some of the historical relationships between literacy and power are introduced and some myths are exposed.

Discourses of literacy

Historically, literacy has been used as a means to maintain the power and control of certain vested interests, whether these are religious, government, bureaucratic or trading groups. More recently, governments and agencies have been at pains to quantify, explain and remedy the problem of 'illiteracy'. For example, UNESCO and the World Bank have focused on measuring the extent of adult 'illiteracy' by gathering statistics on access to schooling, and implementing mass literacy campaigns in developing and underdeveloped countries. However, while not denying that increasing an individual's literacy may make the person more productive, the assumption that this would ultimately lead to improved national economic development, growth and progress is a myth that is both limiting and distorting (Graff 1986, p. 72). Literacy is only one factor affecting socio-economic problems, and blaming the individual is not the solution. Later in this chapter, we shall see that being literate does not ensure employment. There are other political and economic forces at work, not the least of which is the move by multinationals to hire offshore, cheaper labour. So we need to be mindful of what literacy can reasonably be expected to do. In addition, we need to be aware of how statistics about literacy are used. Literacy 'myths' are often perpetuated (or manufactured) by social commentators who use a range of definitions and statistics to highlight (or invent) a 'literacy crisis'. As Cook-Gumperz argues:

> Literacy rates are seen as indicators of the health of the society and as a barometer of the social climate. As a result, illiteracy takes on a symbolic significance, reflecting any disappointment, not only with the workings of the education system, but with society as a whole (Cook-Gumperz 1987, p. 1).

Recently, OECD countries participated in an International Adult Literacy Survey (IALS) to identify literacy benchmarks. The survey used a five-point scale, level 3 of which is deemed to be the level which represents 'the ability to cope with a varied range of materials found in daily life and work [though not always] with a high level of proficiency' (McLennan 1997, p. x). Thus, as will be shown later in this chapter, the 'magical' level 3 has become the benchmark for entry-level training. The response to the large percentage of Australians at levels 1–3 has either been one of blaming the individual or, as Hodgens suggests, the relatively low skill levels are interpreted as 'an indicator of a deeper institutional malaise. The moral order of society itself is seen to be at stake' (Hodgens 1994, p. 17). This is highlighted in the following quotation from the OECD:

> In recent years, adult literacy has come to be seen as crucial to the economic performance of industrialised nations. Literacy is no longer defined merely in terms of a basic threshold of reading ability, mastered by almost all those growing up in developed countries. Rather, literacy is now being seen as how adults use written

information to function in society. Today, adults need a higher level of literacy to function well; society has become more complex and low-skill jobs are disappearing. *Therefore, inadequate levels of literacy among a broad section of the populations potentially threaten the strength of economies and the social cohesion of nations* (OECD 1995, p. 13) [emphasis added].

This rather alarming statement infers that a lack of literacy equates with some form of disease or deviance which could trigger a national crisis, hence the need for greater control and accountability—another 'back to basics' campaign—or targeting the socially disadvantaged—'learn to read or lose the dole'. As Gee asserts:

> Literacy is a socially contested term. We can choose to use this word in any of several different ways. Each such choice incorporates a tacit or overt ideological theory about the distribution of social goods and has important social and moral consequences (Gee 1990, p. 27).

In the next section, the focus turns to the second aim of the chapter: to review some of the theories and research relating to literacy. As 'read is a transitive verb, so literacy must have something to do with being able to read *something*' (Gee 1990, p. 42). So we need to ask which theories address literacy and learning: *how* do people read and write? And how do we *measure ability* in reading and writing? Which research and theories inform our understandings of literate practices: *what* do people read and write? For *what* or *whose purpose*? Finally, which theories and research present an alternative view to the dominant discourses and ask questions such as who *does not* have access to literacy? How can literacy be used *to transform* individuals or communities through social action? These questions underpin the various theories and pedagogies related to reading and writing.

LITERACY THEORIES, RESEARCH AND PRACTICE

Internationally, 'literacy studies' as an area of research came of age in 1990, given the prominence of literacy in 1990, UNESCO's International Literacy Year. Prior to this time, empirical research focused on the acquisition of skills such as reading or writing. Most often the research was child-centred and came from the disciplines of cognitive psychology and linguistics. Psycholinguistic researchers were interested in the processes of production and comprehension of texts, while some linguists focused on the style and grammar of the product. Research in relation to adults concentrated on studies in the armed forces and industry. Then, in the 1980s, while some researchers (e.g. Sticht, Mikulecky and others) continued their empirical studies, others who

Table 3.2 Reading, writing and literacy theory and practice

Research discipline/field	Associated theories	Associated teaching practices	Resources	Source of meaningfulness
Cognitive psychology & linguistics	Information processing (identifying, matching letter/sound)	Phonics programs. Decontextualised word/spelling lists	Basal readers	Decoding of meaning from letter/sound correspondence
	Psycholinguistics (prediction based on semantic, syntactic & grapho-phonic cues)	Reading for meaning; cloze exercises; language experience	Natural language readers; individual's spoken language written down	Reader brings innate knowledge of language to meaning-making
	Process writing	Pre-writing, drafting, responding, revising, editing, publishing	Use of templates. Conferencing protocols	Processes of constructing meaning made explicit
	Interactive model (reader's schema, contextual factors, metacognition & affect)	Range of reading strategies: top-level structure; graphic outlines; 3-level guides; retrieval charts	Range of texts reflecting different purposes for reading. Vocational texts	Meaning derived from matching strategy to text and purpose
Anthropology, sociology & linguistics	Roles of reader (code breaker, text participant, text user and text analyst)	Range of reading strategies, some relating to the reader's skills, others relating to practice in a particular context	Range of texts reflecting different purposes for reading; social, informational, vocational and workplace texts	Meaning derived from matching strategy to text and purpose in relation to the context; also includes a critical component

Research discipline/field	Associated theories	Associated teaching practices	Resources	Source of meaningfulness
	Social literacies. Concept of the literacy 'event'. Public v. vernacular literacies	Understanding the ways in which people use literacy	Social, public and workplace texts and tasks/events	Meaning constructed independently, with assistance or collaboratively; meaning depends on knowledge of codes
	Genre theory (genres are staged, purposeful, goal-oriented activities)	Spoken and written language is not arbitrary. Language in use conforms to certain generic structures which can be taught, e.g. report, procedure, exposition, persuasive	Explicit teaching of the genres or text types of vocational subjects, workplace or everyday texts	Language as social practice cannot be separated from the context; meanings vary according to the context, the topic, the power relationships among the people involved and the mode of communication
Critical literacy studies	Conscientisation	Transformation through social action: praxis	Grass-roots, community action	Meaning through dialogue and problematising
	Critical language studies. Discourse analysis	Examining how texts are socially and ideologically constructed, e.g. power within and behind the media	Addressing the social conditions around the production and interpretation of texts	Meaning is constituted by the relations of discourse, power and knowledge

were influenced by the work of social anthropologists in describing the actions of people within their own societal contexts adopted different research methodologies. This resulted in a series of seminal ethnographic studies in which, 'instead of conceiving literacy as involvement with written language that is the same everywhere and involves some fixed inventory of capacities, we began to think of literacy as a term applying to a varied and open set of activities with written language' (Scribner 1983, p. 5). So for Scribner (1983), Heath (1983), Street (1984, 1995) and others, literacy became a cultural and social construction of activity or practice in terms of recurrent, and interrelated, goal-directed actions. This is particularly important, as this model of literacy continues to inform much current adult literacy research and curricula.

The major research trends outlined above have been informed by, or resulted in, the development of related theories, which in turn have informed associated teaching practices. These linkages are summarised in Table 3.2. This is not a comprehensive analysis of the various schools of thought. Instead, the purpose here is to provide an overview of the theories, together with their associated pedagogies and resources, and to suggest how each contributes to meaning-making. Having scanned this information, it is possible to appreciate how the definitions of literacy, presented earlier in Table 3.1, have been derived. For example, psychologists have been interested in the individual, how the individual acquires reading or writing skills and how the individual makes meaning. On the other hand, socio-linguists are concerned about the individual as a member of society and how individuals use a range of literacies depending on particular social situations and cultural contexts. This does not mean that the skill of decoding is ignored, but social-linguists argue that to focus only on this decontextualised skill is extremely limiting and does not account for the range of literacies or language choices that individuals are faced with in making meaning in their daily lives.

In summary, this table provides an overview of the different schools of thought and their influence on teaching practices and meaning-making. However, as we saw in an earlier section, concepts of literacy are not value-free; they are inherently ideological. So the approach that one takes to planning and implementing literacy learning depends on one's ideological position. The next section explores some of the research which is associated with these ideologies in terms of four discourses of literacy: literacy as autonomy; literacy as technology; literacy as social practice; and multiliteracies.

Literacy as autonomy: basic skills

The 'autonomous' model of literacy as defined by Street (1984) is based on a narrow, culturally specific view of literacy practice. This view is premised on the assumption that the skills of reading and writing are context free, universal in time and space, and generate consequences for cognition, social progress and individual achievement. In short, reading and writing are considered to be generic skills. As a result, the teaching focus is on the individual and his or her ability to 'crack' the code or derive meaning from letter/sound correspondence: 'If in doubt, sound it out'. Failure to comprehend results in blaming the individual and deficit approaches to skills acquisition. However, resources associated with this approach such as decontextualised phonic word lists and spelling lists do little to assist adults with the highly situated texts and tasks which they have to perform daily.

As shown in the previous section, conservative governments have drawn on this 'basic skills' discourse to justify 'back to basics' campaigns (Bloom 1987; Hirsch 1987), to engage in public debates about falling 'literacy levels or standards' (Green et al. 1994; Hodgens 1994) and, more recently, to justify punitive measures against the long-term unemployed with low levels of literacy. Barton notes his concern at these developments in suggesting that this is conservatism 'in a very basic way of being resistant to change' (Barton 1994, p. 226). Even in the 1970s, Resnick and Resnick pointed out that 'the old tried and true approaches, which nostalgia prompts us to believe might solve current problems, were designed neither to achieve the literacy standard sought today nor assure successful literacy for everyone' (Resnick & Resnick 1977, p. 202). But, despite society becoming more complex with globalisation, the adoption of new technologies and risk management, some governments have retreated to standardised curricula and testing.

Other responses to autonomous views of literacy are found in the work of researchers such as Sticht (1975, 1977, 1982), who demonstrated that functional literacy is a cognitive skill which workers require in order to complete a task, and Mikulecky (1982, 1984), who argued that literacy is a variable construct. For example, Diehl and Mikulecky (1980) found that the level of reading ability required for successful work performance varied according to the job and, moreover, that reading practices also varied with context. Further, Mikulecky demonstrated that transference of literacy abilities from school (mainly 'reading-to-learn') to out-of-school and work contexts in which reading is used as an aid to performance (reading-to-do) 'is severely limited by differences in format, social support networks and required background information' (Mikulecky 1990, p. 25). These are all aspects of the 'demands hypothesis' outlined by Welch and Freebody (1993), who argue not only that work and school place different literacy demands on the individual but that, as jobs become more complex, there is a corresponding increase in functional demands on workers—a point which will be taken up later.

In summary, the adoption of skills-based approaches to literacy instruction and structured curricula reflects literacy education as being the acquisition of sets of decontextualised rules and patterns. This has important implications for pedagogical theory and practice. This reductionist view of education has been drawn on by governments to measure literacy and thus justify public expenditure through benchmarking literacy levels. As the earlier quotation from Cook-Gumperz asserted, by quantifying literacy in this way, governments measure the 'health' of nations. Further, as this 'autonomous' view of literacy becomes normalised, it is often used by governments, employers and others to adopt inappropriate entry tests, literacy screens and assessment practices.

Literacy as technology

Writing in response to the UNESCO campaigns, Oxenham (1980) sought to move away from the ideologies governing the campaigns by suggesting that state and commercial interests in literacy were concerned with the use of 'literacy as a technology', which could transform the user: 'Literacy, in short, is a technology, a "technical method of achieving a practical purpose"' (Oxenham 1980, p. 41). Historically, 'literacy as technology' has been used to control access to certain forms of knowledge. Only specific elites were permitted to compose and interpret information. In recent years, a new form of 'literacy as technology' has become part of the human capital discourse (Lankshear 1993). Today, a lack of—or inadequate—literacy means to be marginalised: that is, barred from access to new forms of knowledge and new modes of thinking. As we shall see later in relation to work, this means lack of access to training, and therefore the possibility of becoming a core or knowledge worker. Further, many individuals and disadvantaged groups in the community who have inadequate control of the 'institutional literacies' (Barton & Hamilton 1990; Castleton & McDonald 2002) essential for living healthy and independent lives, become increasingly dispossessed—particularly in times of decreasing social and welfare provision by the state (Lankshear 1993).

In a recasting of the 'literacy as autonomy' model, literacy is again being seen as a tool which is essential to gain access to this new knowledge. The 'literacy as technology' approach to literacy in the 'new work order' (Gee & Lankshear 1997) is being used to determine who needs what literacy, and how literacy skills or competencies should be measured. This technological discourse, Millar (1991) argues, constructs education as an assembly line producing human skills and capacities. It also allows for the codification of knowledge. Educational outcomes can be stated in advance and individual performance can be assessed in relation to the objectives, reported and audited. Hence governments, as well as commercial, military and business interests, see this discourse as particularly powerful. In recent times, many governments have adopted this discourse, based around the management of large systems or concepts, in order to manage the economy and skills development. It is argued here that this has resulted in a return to a recycled autonomous model of learning, which has reappeared in the form of competency-based training.

From this technicist perspective, literacy is perceived to be a tool or conduit for performance, a means of encoding and decoding information, a generic skill or key competency. This is the perspective of those who espouse a 'bolted-on' approach to vocational education and training. That is, the purpose of education is to ensure that students or trainees have generic literacy skills first, and then training can be undertaken. The assumptions are, firstly, that there are 'generic' literacy skills and, secondly, that these skills will transfer to different situations. However, this view was challenged in its early phase by cognitivists such as Kintsch (1977) and Rumelhart (1976), who reconceptualised the reading/comprehension process as one of interaction with the text and task, and later by socio-linguists who drew on the work of language philosophers (Wittgenstein 1958) and anthropologists such as Malinowski (1923) to analyse the social contexts in which literate practices took place. Constructing literacy as a social practice meant moving from a unitary notion of literacy as a single generic competence to a multiplicity or hierarchy of literacies (Levine 1986), with language and literacy being two of the many social semiotic systems through which people make meaning (Halliday 1975, 1985; Halliday & Hasan 1985).

Literacy as social practice

In contrast to the earlier representations of literacy, Street (1984) proposed an 'ideological' model. This view of literacy takes as its central premise the idea that 'the social and political significance of literacy ... derives largely from its role in creating and reproducing—or failing to reproduce—the social distribution of knowledge' (Levine 1986, p. 46). Reading, writing and enumerating are viewed as cultural practices, which are learnt in specific cultural contexts and which have epistemological significance—that is, uses of literacy and numeracy are meaningful, cannot be generalised across cultures, cannot be isolated or treated either as 'neutral' or as 'technical', and have implications for power relations. In other words, *how* literacy is used depends on the context and the relationships among participants. Gee (1990, 1996) discusses such social practices, or 'Discourses', as ways of talking, interacting, thinking, valuing and believing—all of which are socially and historically constructed, so that people have to be socialised into the practice of reading text A in way B. In this sense, Gee is building on Bourdieu's (1977) notion of 'expanded competence', or language as praxis, which introduces concepts of language being functional and strategic—it is not just knowing how to produce grammatically coherent sentences but knowing about 'appropriateness': 'when to speak, keep silent, speak in this or that style' (Bourdieu 1977, p. 646). In fact, given that the meaning of literacy depends upon the social context in which it is embedded, and that the particular reading and writing practices involved depend upon social structures and the institutions of education or training, there cannot be a single, autonomous 'literacy'. It would be more appropriate to refer to multiple 'literacies'.

It is argued here that the teaching of 'autonomous skills' should be replaced with developing a range of contextualised social literacy skills and practices. Rather than using highly structured reading schemes or phonic reading and spelling lists, students should be engaging with authentic, meaningful texts, taking on different roles depending on the tasks (Freebody & Luke 1990), ideally within a vocational or community context. However, some researchers and community activists would argue that this approach does not go far enough. They maintain that it only assists individuals to comply with dominant discourses—whether of governments or industry—rather than challenging the status quo and examining how texts are socially and ideologically constructed (Bradshaw 1998; Fairclough 2001; Gee 1990, 1996). Street (1995) refers to this approach as 'New Literacy Studies', grounded in new theories of language and literacy and new research methodologies. Others, such as Muspratt et al. (1997), refer to 'critical literacy' which has been informed by a range of discourses, including critical language studies, feminist theory and cultural studies. While recognising the social nature of language, these debates are also influenced by the sites of literacy activity, which cannot be 'neutral' as they are constituted by the relations of discourse, power and knowledge.

Multiliteracies

Recently, there has been a move to replace the above models of literacy with a model which addresses the complexities of multi-modal communication while recognising the pluralities of today's societies. If we take a critical-cultural view of society, we can see how globalisation and the increased dominance of technology have blurred the separation of public and private lives—for example, television programs such as *Survivor* and *Big Brother*. We have been introduced to a mass media culture (as evidenced by the media control of sporting events), a culture of technology (with text messaging, use of the Internet and telemarketing) and a global commodity culture (Microsoft, McDonald's and product marketing of children's films and television). In addition, we have an increase in 'infotainment' programs and the mediation or 'conversationalisation' of news and current affairs (Fairclough 2001).

As a response or challenge to what is seen as a 'cynical, manipulative, invasive and exploitative ... [appropriation] of private and community lifeworlds to serve commercial and institutional ends' (Cope & Kalantzis 2000), a group of ten US, UK and Australian researchers, known collectively as the New London Group, commenced the 'multi-literacies project'.

> Multiliteracies relate 'to the increasing multiplicity and integration of significant modes of meaning-making, where textual is also related to the visual, the audio, the spatial, the behavioural ... 'multimedia' and in electronic 'hypermedia' ... to focus on the realities of increasing local diversity and global connectedness. (Cope & Kalantzis 1995, p. 6)

The focus is on 'designs' of meaning. In other words the New London Group reconceptualises literacy in terms of available designs, the process of designing, and the outcome or 'redesigned'—all of which require multiple literacies. Its members recognise the different domains in which individuals operate (working lives, public lives and private lives), as well as the pluralistic nature of western societies. Members of the New London Group are concerned about the emergence of what Gee & Lankshear (1997) term 'fast capitalism', which has taken place at the same time as an invasion of private space and an associated decline in civic responsibility. The multiliteracies projects have focused on designing social futures which, in some respects, respond to the challenge of the OECD presented earlier in the chapter, in terms of 'productive diversity', developing civic pluralism and designing pedagogies which address the changing realities and 'multilayered lifeworlds' of the future.

Other researchers who are moving along similar paths are Barton and Hamilton (1990) in the United Kingdom who are exploring the nexus between what they refer to as public literacies (institutional literacies) and vernacular literacies (personal local literacies) and what this means for members of different communities. Similarly, Prinsloo and Breier (1996) have been researching social literacies in South Africa. The importance of such research is that it goes beyond the economic imperative to produce knowledge workers, to investigate the links with lifelong learning and possibilities of developing civic responsibility or social capital within communities.

In conclusion, it is advocated that a critical literacies model should be adopted. Such an approach would recognise the situatedness and pluralities of literacy. It would also reflect the ideological nature of language and uses of literacy for reasons of power and control. However, we also need to consider what the model of multiliteracies means for vocational educators. Firstly, we need to acknowledge different ways of knowing and meaning-making—collaborative learning in groups, assisted learning (with text, technology or mentor support) or independent learning. At the same time, we must recognise that learners may operate in a range of domains—work, public and private—and that increasingly there is slippage between them. In each of these domains, the learner may be using texts and undertaking tasks related to themselves (as a worker, citizen or family member) which focus on interacting in groups (at work, in the community, or family), as part of systems communication within an organisation, or communication with the broader community (ACTC 1993). Each of these forms of communication requires a different set of literacies: personal, cooperative, systems, procedural, public or technical—this is very different from the autonomous, often ethnocentric, view of literacy. So, in conceptualising a critical literacies model, there is a recognition of the dominant influence of socio-cultural contexts and multiple sites of literacy activity, which cannot be 'neutral' as they are constituted by social and power relations. It is to examples of these sites of contestation that we now turn.

LITERACY IN THE WORKPLACE

It has been demonstrated already that, throughout history, literacy as technology has been used successfully to control access to certain forms of knowledge. Most recently, the latest form of 'literacy as technology' has been appropriated by human capital discourses. The Australian economy, in line with many 'fast capitalist' (Gee 1994; Gee & Lankshear 1997) economies, has seen an increase in the tertiary or service sectors and also in information technologies (Luke 1992). Jobs that traditionally required minimal basic skills are becoming more complex, demanding higher levels of literacy and numeracy—hence the requirement for the long-term unemployed to acquire IALS level 3 literacy ability to be eligible for entry-level work. Further, new jobs are being created which require new levels and types of multi-modal communication skills. At the same time as the jobs themselves have been restructured, the nature of work has also been changing, with the introduction of new work practices and new technologies (Cope & Kalantzis 1995), all of which make new demands on the workforce (Adler 1992; Gee 2000). Following a brief overview of the changing nature of work, examples will be drawn from recent research in the hospitality and construction industries to explore literacy practices and discourses.

Changing nature of work

The move to globalisation and increased competitiveness among companies has resulted in greater demands being placed on enterprises to increase production with greater efficiency and reduced costs in terms of time, safety and potential litigation. As a result, the new 'high performance' workplaces are characterised by a commitment to continuous improvement and quality assurance principles, and the involvement of employees in decision-making processes relating to work (Adler 1992). Continuous improvement often uses a cycle of 'planning, executing, checking and refining operations to improve efficiencies'

(Jackson 2000 p. 265), all of which require extensive record-keeping and checklists as part of the daily tasks of employees. Quality assurance measures include documenting compliance with standard operating procedures, and with government and industry regulations, as well as monitoring performance and costs. All of these measures require an intensification of literacy practices which Darville (1999) refers to as 'textual orderings' and 'textualized accountings'. In addition, much of the work in this new work order is project based, giving rise to a new type of knowledge worker who becomes a skilled 'core' worker moving from project to project. At the same time, many enterprises are developing as learning organisations (Senge 1990). As a result, worker involvement is not only through participation in work teams and project meetings, designing and redesigning their own work practices, but also involves supervising, training and mentoring other members of the team while themselves gaining new skills and qualifications. Success is measured by the level of participation in decision-making, the auditing of work practices and the development of a culture of commitment and trust among employees. What this actually looks like in practice is the focus of the next sections.

Literacy in the hospitality and airline industries

Research into the literate practices of front office staff in motels (Searle 1996) and airline sales officers as they operate at the Customer Inquiry Counters at either domestic or international airports (Searle 1997) focused on the texts and tasks in a range of sites. The interest was in how the staff used the macroskills of reading, writing and viewing in order to make meaning, and whether meaning gained in one situation was transferable to another.

One of the most striking findings was the textualisation of all workplaces. However, when workplace documents were compared across sites, it was found that not all texts were used in all sites. Further, those apparently 'generic' texts which were common to several sites varied in terms of their language features—letterhead and layout in motels, or fare constructions and ticketing codes at airports. For workers, the reading and writing skills used were in relation to purposeful, goal-orientated, highly contextualised activities. For example, in routine tasks, 'reading-to-do' involved the matching of names and codes; scanning for names and codes; scrolling computer screens and flipping between screens in search of codes—as meaning was located in the codified data. Moreover, in motels, the computerised reservation systems also required staff to have navigational skills to follow detailed directions, to identify and understand the purpose of icons, codes, screen layout and sequence, menus or function keys. In this case, meaning was derived from a range of schemata deployed. The following extracts from transcriptions refer to the process of 'checking-out' a guest from a motel; however, it can be seen that the processes involved varied between the two motels.

Check-outs is menu 4, screen number 1—check-out, and that's all you use. You check off the manual list or you can check it in 'Check-out' going into no. 1. Now, she's going to say, is room 33 gone? If nothing comes up to 'Check-out' it means we've already checked it out of the system so you say 'Yep, 33's gone'. Same again 34—whatever number she asks you put it in and it's going to tell you that they're gone, simply because it won't bring up any information. (Site A)

I'm just going to double check them [departures] to make sure he's [the night auditor] departed them out of the computer . . . So . . . I type in the reservation number which is 005417 then hit [tab] which (looks like/matches) . . . the invoice number. And it's the same gentleman, and it is departed because that's missing. That's usually F3 for 'create today's tariff'; F4 is something else . . . If you press F2 it gives you your account. So he's departed. (Site C)

However, reading as practice—as meaning-making—is not just about knowledge of codes, tariffs and tariff structures, but about understanding the rules which govern those structures, which are known only to members of that specific workplace. Although the staff may bring some generic decoding skills to the job (from previous training or previous employment in a similar occupation), the actual use and interpretation of codes is learnt on the job so that such tasks become automatic and routine. As one employee stated: *You can learn computer inputs from training courses but really you learn everything on the job . . . we usually buddy up* (C:7). Further, as the databases used in most sites in the hospitality and airline industries are multi-user, the 'design' (Cope & Kalantzis 1995) of the program/database is given. It is authoritative, installed by management for efficiency and cost-effectiveness and cannot be 'redesigned' by staff. As Edelsky points out, 'if the print user is being controlled in her print use—if someone else decides what literacy event will occur, how it will begin, what it will be about, when it will end, and so on, then the print user is positioned as an Object' (cited in O'Connor 1994, p. 29).

In both the hospitality and airline industries, the focus is on accountability, so each has an audit trail of texts, either print (housemaids' instruction forms and guest registration cards) or computerised booking and accounting systems. Staff are aware that texts are constructed for particular purposes, usually by management, and as such represent one or more value systems—for example, efficiency, accuracy, accountability: *You have to have standard formats or you'd have people putting anything in these computers . . . it's not just us that read them either* (A:75). Staff are expected to comply with the work order and in these industries there is little room for 'redesigning' texts or critically analysing them. In addition, these service industry employees have to remain polite on all occasions when transacting with the public, despite having to deal with 'complainers' or unforeseen problems. They are aware of the value of 'keeping the guests happy' (Stevenson 1996). Staff are therefore put into a position of having to comply with a particular predetermined stance. There is some recognition within these industries of what the US Department of Labor Secretary's Commission on Achieving Necessary Skills (1992) refers to as 'basic' or 'enabling' skills as key competencies in reproducing codified knowledge. However, the individual literacies which underpin organisational communication, the staff attitudes and dispositions in relation to company or industry values are not as recognised and yet are crucial to successful communicative performance.

To sum up, the findings from this study indicate that workplaces are increasingly textualised but the texts themselves and the literacies required to use them are quite site-specific. As a result, much learning occurs on the job, and it is here that employees are 'socialised' into work routines, rules and company values. It was an interest in exploring these issues further which underpinned more recent research conducted in the construction industry (Searle & Kelly 2002). The examples in the next section are taken from interviews conducted within one particular construction company which was developing as a learning organisation.

Literacy in the construction industry

Initially, the research in the civil construction industry was concerned with identifying literacy-related issues in the implementation of the industry training package (Kelly & Searle 2000). Subsequent research focused on exploring the discourses of training and literacy through interviews with staff and workers at different levels within one company. While there has been a universal move to codify vocational and workplace knowledge and skills into sets or packages of competencies, in Australia these have been collated into industry-specific training packages which cover a range of occupational levels. It was found that there are fifteen units of competency within the first (entry) level of the Civil Construction training package, of which eleven are considered to be 'technical' in nature while the remaining four cover 'generic' skills. One of these generic units of competency is 'Carry out interactive workplace communication'. However, what this means in terms of workplace texts, tasks or the underpinning literacy skills is not made explicit. The assumption that workers will possess certain basic skills and, further, that these basic skills will transfer to training at Australian Qualifications Framework (AQF) Level II, infers an 'autonomous' view of literacy although, when interviewed (see extract below), the Training Coordinator appeared to indicate that higher-order skills or more specific literacies were required for AQF Level III.

> *Level II competency numeracy and literacy is still fairly low and people talk about Level II being a, say, a second-, third-year apprentice-type person who probably fills out basic things like a time sheet and some safety checklists and things like that. When they get into Level III, the trades level, they really have to start looking at quality documents and things like that and that's where we're really starting to find out where the problems are. [Training Coordinator]*

The training coordinator appears to espouse a 'literacy as technology' approach to the skills required at AQF Level II. That is, the focus is on reading-and-writing-to-do, to accomplish certain workplace requirements. These literacy technologies such as the ability to fill in forms and follow instructions are deemed to be 'desirable skills', as they maintain the social order of the workplace. However, it is also apparent that literacy relates to other core values such as cost effectiveness.

> *I mean we've spent x amount of dollars developing all these training manuals, it's no good if 90 per cent of the guys out there can't read and write, is it? You've wasted your time and money . . . The first round were paper based, book based, now we're starting to get them on CD ROM . . . all that sort of thing. [Training Coordinator]*

It can been seen from this excerpt that, in this case, literacy is again perceived to be an autonomous skill which a worker requires prior to training—the 'bolted-on' approach referred to earlier in the chapter—as it is more cost-effective to employ workers who would have a minimum of IALS Level 3 literacy ability. Further, the crucial role of literacy in relation to workplace health and safety, and assessment of risk, is indicated in the following extracts from interviews.

> *Pre-Start Checks for equipment. A bloke gets on a dozer in the morning, he does his pre-start bla bla bla and away he goes. Now again if he has literacy problems, is he actually understanding what is supposed to be in there or is he ticking the box so it keeps him out of trouble? [Training Coordinator]*

> *But I think when you delve deeper into it, more and more we ask people to fill out more forms because of safety and environmental legislation etc., etc. and probably insurance as well, I think we'll really open up a can of worms. [Training Coordinator]*

One of the characteristics of the 'high performance' workplace is that responsibility is passed down to the individual worker. As stated in the company policy documents, the bottom line is getting the job done right the first time, safely and within environmental guidelines, thus reducing costs. This has led to the increased 'textualisation' of the workplace as workers are required to complete pre-start checks, fill in forms for safety and environmental protection and so on. Therefore, as in the hospitality industry, the individual worker is positioned as being compliant and accountable not only for their own actions, but more broadly to protect the company from litigation. The final comment from the training coordinator cited above sums up what a number of the informants felt. Added to the metaphor of 'a can of worms' were statements such as a lack of literacy being 'an accepted evil' and 'it's frightening really'. Each represents a particular view of literacy as being related to deviance (which needs to be controlled), or ignorance (which may be resolved through training, although staff were uncertain about how this would be achieved), or a threat to the performance of the company, thus reflecting the OECD views stated earlier. What is apparent is that the industry is changing rapidly. Gone are the days when, as the safety officer commented, *all the industry wanted was a labourer from the neck down*. Now, with the increased use of technology and individuals having to take responsibility for their actions, workers are encouraged to problem solve, to question and, if unsure, to check. In addition, this company was developing as a learning organisation and to that end had instituted 'continuous improvement' initiatives as well as various systems of communication. These included the activities listed in Table 3.3.

Most of the activities listed in Table 3.3 were developed to increase efficiency and maintain the 'social organisation' of the workplace. Gee (1996) refers to such activities as being part of a 'socialisation' process—that is, enabling employees to work collaboratively . Although these practices are recognised by supervisors and management as important elements in quality assurance and in developing a learning organisation, the site-specific literacy skills involved, which range from decoding to critical analysis, are either assumed or neatly glossed under the generic competence 'Carry out interactive workplace communication'. An example of literacy as an enabling skill, useful in maintaining the social order of the workplace, is found in the following quotation.

Communication skills still remain a core basic requirement for a good outcome, and we've got things like Work Activity Briefings, Job Safety Analysis that we do and we record or document those, and more and more we're trying to thrust that responsibility back down to the workforce, to the people that do and carry out the work . . . So there's a need for someone in that part of the organisation to actually have literacy and numeracy skills to be able to carry out that function. [Systems Manager]

In this extract, the systems manager positions himself with management staff who are implementing a rather aggressive top-down approach of 'thrusting' responsibility on to the workforce. This binary opposition is also apparent in the comment on the need for good 'communication

Table 3.3 Workplace activities

Activity	Timing	Personnel	Purpose
Inductions	When hiring new employees	WH&S officer & new employee(s)	Induction to company, WH&S
Work Activity Briefing (WAB)	Commencement of new job	Whole crew	Site plans, training needs, equipment
Pre-start meetings	Every morning (sometimes evening)	Leading hand to whole crew	Objectives for the day Problem-solving Discussion of previous day
Pre-start checklists	Start of shift	Individual	Equipment checks Safety checks
Task specific briefings	Start of shift	Individual	Task objectives Problem-solving
Job Safety Analyses (JSA)	Commencement of new job or task	Whole crew	Analysis of safety procedures Environmental issues
Toolbox meetings on-the-job	Once a fortnight	Leading hand or foreman to crew	Job issues Safety issues

Source: Searle & Kelly (2002)

skills' in relation to management staff, but 'back down the workforce' this relates to 'someone in that part of the organisation' having literacy and numeracy skills. Thus it would appear that an autonomous view of literacy as 'basic' decoding skills applies to entry-level workers, whereas 'communication' at management levels may relate to certain higher-order, problem-solving literacy practices. Further, according to the systems manager, '*training will also enable you to have more skilled workers who can perform a variety of tasks and so reduce the level of workforce you might need*'. So the move is towards having a core of multiskilled, multiliterate workers who transfer from project to project. These 'compliant' workers will build up situated, but uncritical, expertise and literacies whilst at the same time be willing to engage in further training. The concept of the 'core worker' was defined by the engineer as being those workers '*that know our systems, understand our work ethic and culture, and help disseminate that to others that work in and around them*'—an example of the exercise of power through the manufacture of consent (Fairclough 2001). As a result of this system, hired labourers and most subcontracted labourers are excluded from training. In Gee and Lankshear's (1997) terms, these workers are likely to become the displaced, marginalised, 'disenchanted' workers.

Thus it is argued that this company subscribes to the discourse of 'literacy as technology', in which literacy is perceived as being an essential basic skill or tool for the safe and efficient performance and auditing of workplace tasks, as well as being a requirement for workplace training. However, while the necessity for good literacy skills in order for workers to participate successfully in workplace communication meetings is implied, it is not specifically addressed.

In summary, the effects of globalisation and industry competition following micro-economic reform and industry deregulation, together with the emergence of new technologies and new work practices, have changed our understandings of what literacy or multiliteracies are, who needs what literacies and how these should be measured. We have seen how the new post-Fordist workplace is designed around teams of project workers focusing on continuous improvement cycles and quality assurance. In such workplaces, facility with spoken and written language is crucial. While some commentators critique the new workplace as being a site of contested power relations and unequal access to training or distribution of work (Gee & Lankshear 1997; Reich 1992), others are more optimistic and view the move towards learning organisations as opening a space for social transformations (Senge 1990). What is certain is that today's workforce requires literacy skills which go way beyond the traditional 'basics' in order to gain meaning from texts which may be computer generated as tables, databases or graphics, and be menu or icon driven. To focus only on those 'autonomous' literacy skills which are required to perform certain tasks within the workplace is to lose sight of the social components of work such as membership of project teams and the social and organisational networks through which work practices are generated and sustained. What this means for vocational education and training is discussed in the next section.

IMPLICATIONS FOR TEACHING AND LEARNING

The following sections on curriculum design, instructional and assessment practices provide a guide to how some of the previously mentioned issues might be addressed.

Curriculum design

The adoption of competency-based training has significantly changed the way that education and training is conceptualised, planned, delivered and assessed. More than ever before, teachers and trainers are being called upon to interpret sets of competencies and related performance criteria in ways that are, firstly, responsive to industry and workplace environments and, secondly, legislatively, financially and morally accountable. Further, the endorsed competencies relate to specific work practices and it is the competent performance of those practices which is assessed, not abstract skills and knowledge. So the following general principles for literacy in the curriculum are proposed:

- *It is imperative that curriculum designers and instructors have an understanding of the discourses that operate within the specific sites in which teachers and trainers are operating.* As social practices, or Discourses—ways of interacting, valuing and being in the world—vary across domains (schooling, vocational institutions and individual workplaces), so instructors need to understand the site-specific organisational systems, work practices and underpinning values. This is partly for pragmatic reasons (training is organised to suit project needs or climatic/economic conditions) and partly in order to contextualise learning and build a rapport or positive learning environment.
- *As workplace literacies are highly contextualised, the teacher or trainer requires an in-depth knowledge of the site-specific texts and tasks.* As we have seen in the previous section, although training occurred in relation to industry competencies, the literacies required to participate in workplace activities and auditing processes were not addressed. Further, with the move towards developing a learning culture within the workplace, there is a necessity for all workers to engage in a range of communicative activities and learn new literacy practices.
- *The literacies which underpin competencies should be perceived by curriculum designers and instructors as embedded within those competencies and not as additions or prerequisites to the competencies.* There is a view that workers should possess generic literacy skills which are transferable or, if they have inadequate skills, that they should be 'fixed up' prior to, or 'bolted-on' to, training. However, evidence presented earlier suggests that literacies are highly situated and cannot be generalised in this way. Therefore, in developing a curriculum, attention should be given to those technical literacies which are required to achieve the stated competence, and these should be taught alongside the technical competence using the relevant workplace texts.
- *There is a need for curriculum designers and instructors to include critical literacy within the curriculum.* We have seen how the move towards increased employee accountability has led to increased textualisation in the workplace. As a result,

> there is a need for appropriate training so that *all* workers have the skills and understandings to undertake different literacy roles. For example, a worker could be a text decoder and text user when completing a form or checklist correctly, but could also become a text analyst in understanding the significance of compliance or non-compliance with continuous improvement systems or in becoming a critical participant in decision-making processes.

In summary, educators and trainers should strive to provide integrated training programs in which the technical and social literacies of the workplace are embedded with the training. The next section suggests some approaches which could be taken.

Instructional practices

The starting point for this section is to unpack the concept of an 'integrated training program'. Vocational education and training programs which integrate language, literacy and numeracy within them have four key characteristics:

> - They identify the language, literacy and numeracy competencies (or learning outcomes) essential for work performance (or those which underpin the stated industry competencies), and address these competencies as part of the curriculum. They should also identify the social literacies of the workplace, which are often not made explicit.
> - They take into account the language, literacy and numeracy competence and needs of the learner and develop these as part of, not separate from, vocational competence.
> - They ensure that the instructional and assessment language and processes used in the vocational program are consistent with those required on the job or in the vocational area, and are appropriate for the learner.
> - They assess language, literacy and numeracy outcomes in terms of successful performance of relevant and authentic tasks.

Integrated programs should address the relevant literacies in all three phases of learning: orientating, enhancing and synthesising.

> - *Orientation* introduces the competence or learning outcome, the tasks involved and criteria for assessment. This is the time when the learner's prior knowledge of the literacies involved may be assessed or learners could self-assess their own facility with the relevant texts. Use questions to access the learner's prior knowledge of the topic so the reading process is likely to

be successful. Demonstrate how to use workshop manuals or how to look up specific standards. Introduce new language such as technical terms, everyday words used in a technical way and colloquialisms. The language of instruction and assessment should also be introduced.

- *Enhancing* is about mastering new technical knowledge and the associated literacies. This may take place on site or in a training room using authentic texts and tasks, simulations and role-play. It may require moving from the traditional classroom to a training room set up as a workplace with the requisite furniture and equipment. As far as possible, the environment should simulate actual work conditions in order that learners experience the need to develop skills in prioritising work, coping with interruptions and developing the social literacies so essential for high-performance workplaces. At the same time, learners should be made aware of the competing discourses apparent in workplaces. In addition, opportunities should be given for learners to work independently, with assistance (which could be computer-aided assistance) or in collaborative groups. If this training takes place on the job, new employees could observe and work with experienced workers in a mentoring situation, to learn the communication patterns of the workplace, including use of insider terminology and use of site-specific documents, while at the same time becoming socialised into the workplace culture.

  Using a 'teaching–learning' cycle (Hammond et al. 1992), the following site-specific literacies should be taught:
  - understanding the context and purposes for reading and writing;
  - understanding and being able to adopt the following roles of the reader (Freebody & Luke 1990) to suit the purpose for reading: code breaker (how do I crack this?); text participant (what does this mean?); text user (what do I do with this, here and now?) and text analyst (what does all this do to me?);
  - understanding the generic structure of workplace/ vocational texts and the associated language features in order to make meaning; and
  - other more specific strategies, which were presented earlier in Table 3.2.

- *Synthesising* is the phase in which learners bring together the new knowledges and literacies to form part of their conceptual framework, as a basis for further thought and action. Activities associated with this phase include reflection on what has been learnt and/or summative assessment.

Assessment

The previous discussion mentioned two forms of assessment: initial assessment and summative assessment. Initial assessment, as part of the orienting phase of learning, is concerned with making a judgement about the current literacy skills of learners in relation to training and/or on-the-job texts and tasks. Summative assessment comes at the end of a program of training and indicates whether the learner is competent or has achieved the required standard of performance. The following principles apply in either situation:

- *Assessment should be holistic.* Rather than concentrating on the performance of discrete, often decontextualised skills (word recognition or spelling lists), it should be possible to address a range of competencies or learning outcomes through a more holistic approach (an authentic task).
- *Assessment should be appropriate to the context.* The validity of performance-based assessment depends on the extent to which the assessment measures what it is intended to measure. Therefore, standardised tests are usually inappropriate and should be discarded in favour of using relevant workplace texts and tasks for assessment purposes.
- *Assessment should be reliable and fair.* The instructions for assessment tasks should be clear, explicit and ordered. The learner should know what is expected, including the time allowed and the criteria on which their performance will be measured. The language of assessment should reflect the language of instruction. If the learner does not have a good understanding of the English language or has inadequate literacy for the task, decisions need to be made about alternative assessment processes. These may include assessment in the first language and use of oral assessment.

In summary, assessment tasks should be contextualised and reflect what learners/workers are required to do. For example, if reading is required as part of a training program or workplace task, then the assessment should reflect the reading process in which the reader draws on prior knowledge of the subject, knowledge of how to read for a particular purpose, and the four components of reading performance: text decoder, text user, text participant and text analyst (Freebody & Luke 1990).

CONCLUSION

It has been argued that an increase in global competition and international benchmarks for performance on a range of social and economic measures has resulted in pressure from governments for the development of a more knowledgeable workforce. At the same time, the need for industry to be efficient and competitive has led to an increased commitment to training on the part of enterprises. However, the concerns raised in this chapter have been, firstly, that this training relates only to those knowledges and skills which have been codified as competencies, and secondly, that only some workers have access to training. Further, it is apparent that the way in which literacy is being constructed as a technology has allowed governments to link social welfare and civic well-being in a punitive way to individuals' literacy acquisition, while some employers utilise inappropriate literacy screens to select potential employees. So literacy continues to be used as a means of control by powerful groups with vested interests.

The position which has been advocated in this chapter is to move away from the construction of literacy as a technology towards adopting a critical literacies framework for curriculum development. Using this approach, attention is focused on meeting the literacy needs of the individual learner rather than instruction being based on a reductionist set of pre-determined competencies. A critical literacies framework acknowledges that individuals are required to operate across a range of domains (civic, work, private), while allowing for the pluralistic nature of society. Instruction should be contextualised, using authentic texts and tasks and allowing for multiple modes of meaning-making. Further, and more importantly, how literacy is used within any activity or social situation marks the social and power relations within that context. Therefore it is essential that learners be made aware of the ideological nature of language and literacy. Finally, we should be concerned that vocational education and training systems are inclusive, opening up new pathways for young people, encouraging older workers to access training and providing for those who are perceived as lacking certain privileged forms of language and literacy.

REFERENCES

Adler, P. 1992, *Technology and the Future of Work*, Oxford University Press, New York

Australian Committee of TAFE Curriculum (ACTC) 1993, *National Framework of Adult English Language Literacy and Numeracy Competence*, ACTRAC Products Ltd, Frankston

Barton, D. 1994, *Literacy: An Introduction to the Ecology of Written Language*, Basil Blackwell, Oxford

Barton, D. & Hamilton, M. 1990, *Researching Literacy in Industrialised Countries: Trends and Prospects*, UIE UNESCO, Hamburg

Bloom, A. 1987, *The Closing of the American Mind*, Simon & Schuster, New York
Bourdieu, P. 1977, 'The economies of linguistic exchange', *Social Science Information*, vol. 6, pp. 645–68
Bradshaw, D. 1998, *Knowledge of Texts: Theory and Practice in Critical Literacy*, Language Australia, Melbourne
Castleton, G. & McDonald, M. 2002, *Multiple Literacies and Social Transformation*, Language Australia, Melbourne
Cook-Gumperz, J. 1987, *The Social Construction of Literacy*, Cambridge University Press, London
Cope, B. & Kalantzis, M. 1995, 'Designing social futures', *Education Australia*, issue 30, p. 6
—— eds 2000, *Multiliteracies. Literacy Learning and the Design of Social Futures*, Macmillan, Melbourne
Darville, R. 1999, 'Knowledges of adult literacy: surveying for competitiveness', *International Journal of Educational Development*, vol. 19, nos 4–5, pp. 273–85
Diehl, W. & Mikulecky, L. 1980, 'The nature of reading at work', *Journal of Reading*, vol. 24, no. 3, pp. 221–7
Fairclough, N. 2001, *Language and Power*, 2nd edn, Pearson Education, London
Freebody, P. & Luke, A. 1990, ' "Literacies" ' programs: debates and demands in cultural context', *Prospect*, vol. 5, no. 3, pp. 7-16
Freire, P. & Macedo, D. 1987, *Literacy: Reading the Word and the World*, Bergin & Garvey, South Hadley, MA
Gee, J.P. 1990, *Social Linguistics and Literacies: Ideologies in Discourses*, Falmer, London
——1994, 'New alignments and old literacies: critical literacy, postmodernism and fast capitalism', in *Thinking Work Vol. 1: Theoretical Perspectives on Workers' Literacies*, ed. P. O'Connor, ALBSAC, Sydney, pp. 82–104.
——1996, *Social Linguistics and Literacies: Ideologies in Discourses*, 2nd edn, Taylor & Francis, London
——2000, 'The new capitalism: what's new?' *Proceedings from the Working Knowledge Conference*, University of Technology Sydney, Sydney, pp. 189–94
Gee, J.P. & Lankshear, C. 1997, 'Language, literacy and the new work order', in *Changing Literacies*, eds C. Lankshear with J. Gee, M. Nobel & C. Searle, Open University Press, Buckingham, pp. 83–102
Graff, H. 1986, 'The legacies of literacy: continuities and contradictions in western society and culture', in *Literacy, Society and Schooling: A Reader*, eds S. de Castell, A. Luke & K. Egans, Cambridge University Press, New York, pp. 82–91
Green, B., Hodgens, J. & Luke, A. 1994, 'Debating literacy in Australia: a documentary history 1945–1994', in *Towards a History of Adult Literacy in Australia. A Record of the History of Adult*

Literacy Weekend November 1994, eds P. Ward & R. Wickert, National Languages and Literacy Institute of Australia, New South Wales Adult Literacy Research Network & University of Technology Sydney, Sydney, pp. 37–44

Halliday, M. 1975, *Learning How to Mean: Explorations in the Development of Language*, Edward Arnold, London

—— 1985, *Spoken and Written Language*, Deakin University Press, Geelong

Halliday, M. & Hasan, R. 1985, *Language Context and Text: A Social Semiotic Perspective*, Deakin University Press, Geelong

Hammond, J., Burns, A., Joyce, H., Brosnan, D. & Gerot, L. 1992, *English for Social Purposes*, NCELTR, Sydney

Heath, S.B. 1983, *Ways with Words*, Cambridge University Press, Cambridge

Hirsch, E. 1987, *Cultural Literacy: What Every American Needs to Know*, Houghton Milin, Boston

Hodgens, J. 1994, 'How adult literacy became a public issue in Australia', *Open Letter*, vol. 4, no. 2, pp. 13–24

Jackson, N. 2000, 'Writing-up people at work: investigations of workplace literacy', *Proceedings from the Working Knowledge Conference*, University of Technology Sydney, Sydney, pp. 263–72

Kelly, A. & Searle, J. 2000, *Literacy on the Motorway: An Examination of the Effects of the Inclusion of Literacy and Numeracy in Industry Standards in Training Packages on the Quality of Learning and Work Outcomes*, Language Australia, Melbourne

Kintsch, W. 1977, 'On comprehending stories', in *Cognitive Processes in Comprehension*, eds M. Just & P. Carpenter, Lawrence Erlbaum, Hillsdale, pp. 33–62

Kirsch, I. & Jungeblut, A. 1986, *Literacy: Profiles of America's Young Adults*, final report, Education Testing Service, National Assessment of Educational Progress, Princeton

Lankshear, C. 1993, 'Curriculum as literacy: reading and writing in "New Times"', in *The Insistence of the Letter: Literacy Studies and Curriculum Theorizing*, ed. B. Green, Falmer, London, pp. 154–74

Levine, K. 1986, *The Social Context of Literacy*, Routledge & Kegan Paul, London

Luke, A. 1992, 'Literacy and work in "New Times"', *Open Letter*, vol. 3, no. 1, pp. 3–15

McLennan, W. 1997, *Aspects of Literacy: Assessed Skill Levels, Australia 1996*, Australian Bureau of Statistics, Canberra

Malinowski, B. 1923, 'The problem of meaning in primitive languages', supplement to *The Meaning of Meaning*, eds C. Ogden & I. Richards, Routledge & Kegan Paul, London

Mikulecky, L. 1982, 'Job literacy—the relationship between school preparation and workplace actuality', *Reading Research Quarterly*, vol. 17, no. 3, pp. 400–19

—— 1984, 'Preparing students for workplace literacy demands', *Journal of Reading*, vol. 28, no. 3, pp. 253–7
—— 1990, 'Basic skills impediments to communication between management and hourly employees', *Management Communication Quarterly*, vol. 3, no. 4, pp. 452–73
Millar, C. 1991, 'Critical reflection for educators of adults: getting a grip on the scripts for professional action', *Studies in Continuing Education*, vol. 13, no. 1, pp. 15–23
Muspratt, S., Luke, A. & Freebody, P. eds 1997, *Constructing Critical Literacies*, Allen & Unwin, Sydney
O'Connor, P. ed. 1994, *Thinking Work Vol. 1: Theoretical Perspectives on Workers' Literacies*, ALBSAC, Sydney
OECD (Organisation for Economic Co-operation and Development) 1995, *Literacy, Economy and Society*, OECD & the Canadian Ministry of Industry, Paris
Oxenham, J. 1980, *Literacy: Writing, Reading and Social Organisation*, Routledge & Kegan Paul, London
Prinsloo, M. & Breier, M. eds 1996, *The Social Uses of Literacy: Theory and Practice in Contemporary South Africa*, Sached Books, Cape Town
Reich, R. 1992, *The Work of Nations*, Vintage Books, New York
Resnick, D. & Resnick, L. 1977, 'The nature of literacy: an historical exploration', *Harvard Educational Review*, vol. 47, pp. 263–91
Rummelhart, D.E. 1976, *Toward an Interactive Model of Reading*, University of San Diego, CA
Scribner, S. 1983, 'Mind in action: a functional approach to thinking', invited lecture, biennial meeting, Society for Research in Child Development, The Graduate School & University Centre, CUNY, New York
Searle, J. 1996, 'Language and literacy competencies', in *Learning in the Workplace: Tourism and Hospitality*, ed. J. Stevenson, Centre for Learning and Work Research, Griffith University, Brisbane, pp. 22–50
—— 1997, 'Workplace language and literacy competencies', in *Skill Formation in the Airline Sector of the Transport Industry*, ed. F. Beven, Centre for Learning and Work Research, Griffith University, Brisbane, pp. 19–57
Searle, J. & Kelly, A. 2002, *Acting Smart: An Investigation of Assumptions and Principles which Underpin Training and Assessment within One Civil Construction Company*, Language Australia, Melbourne
Senge, P.M. 1990, *The Fifth Discipline: The Art and Practice of the Learning Organisation*, Doubleday, New York
Stevenson, J. 1996, 'Values underlying attitudes, dispositions and actions', in *Learning in the Workplace: Tourism and Hospitality*, ed. J. Stevenson, Centre for Learning and Work Research, Griffith University, Brisbane, pp. 145–78

Sticht, T. 1975, *Reading for Working: A Functional Literacy Anthology*, Human Resources Research Organisation, Alexandria
—— 1977, 'Comprehending reading at work', in *Cognition Processes in Comprehension*, eds M. Just & P. Carpenter, Lawrence Erlbaum Associates, Hillsdale, NJ, pp. 221–46
—— 1982, *Basic Skills in Defence*, Human Resources Research Organisation, Alexandria
Street, B.V. 1984, *Literacy in Theory and Practice*, Cambridge University Press, Cambridge
—— 1992, 'The new literacy studies', in *Cross-Cultural Approaches to Literacy*, ed. B. Street, Cambridge University Press, Cambridge
—— 1995, *Social Literacies: Critical Approach to Literacy in Development, Ethnography and Education*, Longman, London
US Department of Labor Secretary's Commission on Achieving Necessary Skills 1992, 'Learning a living: a blue print for high performance', *A SCANS Report for America 2000*, US Department of Labor, Washington DC
Welch, A.R. & Freebody, P. 1993, 'Introduction: explanations of the current international "literacy crises" ', in *Knowledge Culture and Power: International Perspectives on Literacy as Policy and Practice*, eds P. Freebody & A.R. Welch, Falmer, London, pp. 6–22
Wickert, R. 1989, *No Single Measure: A Survey of Australian Adult Literacy*, Institute of Technical and Adult Teacher Education, Sydney
Wittgenstein, L. 1958, *Philosophical Investigations*, Basil Blackwell, Oxford

4

Developing numeracy

Clive Kanes

INTRODUCTION

In this chapter I advance a theory about how people engage with numeracy. That is, I explore themes relating to how people describe and think about numeracy; how numeracy is used; and how it is produced. My approach to these topics is cultural-historical. By this I mean I am more concerned with how the social environment shapes and determines our behaviours and thoughts about numeracy, and less concerned with what (if anything) determines numeracy *independently* of human interactions. In this, my approach follows the neo-pragmatist views of, say, Richard Rorty (1998), rather than the realist concerns of John Searle (1999). This means my concerns are about numeracy as a form of human activity rather than as an aspect of any independent reality. In terms of the treatment of material, the chapter is divided into a number of sections. The first deals with the concept of numerical practice, and each of the following three sections deals with a different theme commonly found among such practices. This leads to a statement of learning and teaching principles useful to practitioners. Next, a number of dilemmas and tensions among the themes of numeracy are considered, and these are theorised in the context of a cultural-historical activity theoretic model of curriculum development for numeracy. The chapter concludes with a statement relating to implications for practice arising from this work.

NUMERICAL PRACTICES

Common views about numeracy include the following: it is a kind of elementary or watered down mathematics; it is mainly to do with numbers—counting, calculating and measuring; it is a kind of knowledge which, at least in terms of the school curriculum, is virtually unique in being little changed from one generation to the next, a kind of educational constant; it is a kind of literacy, a compilation of albeit specialised texts, legitimate readings and so forth. Whatever the merits of these views (and later in the chapter I will return to them), it is safe to say that numeracy is certainly thought about, managed and used in a wide variety of situations and contexts. For instance, numeracy is found in school classrooms as well as shopping centres and real-life situations; in university mathematics departments, schools and training colleges; in diverse workplace situations such as factories, workrooms and offices; among policy-makers, textbook writers, curriculum experts and parent groups as well as everyday people. It is also evident in the things people in all cultures and traditions do and think about. Numeracy is also present in different ways under the pressure of new technologies and new ways of producing wealth. In short, we find numeracy working in a multitude of what, following Walkerdine (1988), I want to call *numerical practices*.

Various attempts have been made to come to terms with the variety of numerical practices found in real life. For instance, drawing on Bishop (1988), we can say a numerical practice is one in which numeracy helps to analyse, count, position, play with and design the things people manipulate and do. Similarly, the authors of the *Literacy and Numeracy Strategy* argue that numerical practices involve:

> abilities which include interpreting, applying and communicating mathematical information in commonly encountered situations to enable full, critical and effective participation in a wide range of life roles (Department of Education, Queensland, Australia, 1994, p. 9).

Broader definitions of numerical practice have also been sought. For example, the Australian Association of Mathematics Teachers suggests that numeracy 'involves using some mathematics to achieve some purpose in a particular context' (AAMT 1997, p. 13). On this view, because numeracy involves the interrelation of both mathematical knowledge and the context of its use, it certainly cannot be reduced to mathematics alone.

However, attempts such as these at characterising numerical practice run into problems. First, they each beg further questions—for example, what is it to analyse something using numerical knowledge? What is it to count? What is mathematics? And so on. Responses to these new inquiries soon run either into circularities or the need for more definitions and inevitably more questions. So attempts to build up more knowledge about numeracy by directly answering 'what?' questions concerning numeracy come to very little. A second problem with common attempts to understand more about numeracy is that what information is obtained about numeracy tends not to help to advance practical questions about teaching and learning numeracy or curriculum, or help us understand how numeracy is actually used in real-life settings. Simply put, the information we obtain is not practical enough to help us better shape our curriculum concerns with numeracy.

A thematic approach to considering numerical practice

Therefore, instead of addressing the question 'what is a numerical practice?' head on, I intend to explore themes often associated with numerical practices in thinking, writing and talking about numeracy; in teaching and learning and curriculum contexts (in school, workplace, tertiary and vocational settings); in workplace and everyday contexts; and in research contexts. These include the key themes of *visibility* (in which what is counted as a numerical practice by practitioners is made explicit), of *useability* (focusing on uses of numeracy) and of *constructibility* (concerning how numerical knowledge is generated and developed) (Noss 1998). Although this alternative enquiry cannot yield a philosophical answer to the question of the nature of numerical knowledge, it can help us with practical questions to do with numeracy. My thesis is that studying the key themes of numeracy and the tensions between them helps us to better understand the complex body of knowledge that is numeracy, and this ultimately helps us to understand how better to provide opportunities for more effective curriculum development and more effective teaching and learning in numeracy.

For instance, arithmetic as we understand it in western culture makes use of abstract symbols (the ten digits) and the concepts of place, value and numeration. By this means, we discuss and specify numerical relationships, making these distinctive and therefore open to both demonstration and manipulation. Because these relationships have been made visible, they become tools by which we are able to discuss and solve problems. Moreover, teachers and curriculum managers, for instance, find making numeracy visible an important first step in creating and managing a numeracy curriculum. Thus the theme of visibility, for example, helps us focus on the kinds of ways we discuss numeracy in our communications with each other about numerical knowledge, its management and its control.

Richard Noss, however, makes the important observation that not all numeracy is visible in that some 'lies beneath the surface of practices and cultures' (Noss 1998, p. 3). Typically this occurs when numeracy is in use in real-life situations such as work and home life. This underscores the theme of useability that directs our attention to the way numerical knowledge is used in practice.

The third theme that helps us to understand numeracy is constructibility. This theme describes how numerical knowledge as a cultural phenomenon has come to be, and how it comes to be learned. It helps us understand the origins of numeracy as an historically evolved body of knowledge and to understand the origins of numeracy in the lives of individual people and communities. In other words, the theme of constructibility is about the history of numeracy and about teaching and learning numeracy or, more simply, about how numeracy is created in the lives of people and of a community.

In summary, the theme of visibility is about how we formalise and control numerical knowledge; the theme of useability is about its use; and the theme of constructibility is about its origins both as a cultural-historical phenomenon and as an individual attainment.

In the following sections, I explore and illustrate these themes as they apply to numeracy in greater detail.

THE THEME OF VISIBILITY

The theme of visibility among numerical practices is demonstrated by the application of a specialised vocabulary (mathematical terms and expressions), symbolic systems (mathematical signs and symbols and their conventions) and the organisation of numeracy content into topic headings (e.g. arithmetic, ratio and proportion, measurement, percentage, etc.) and content domains (e.g. algebra, geometry, calculus, etc.). Mathematics itself affords an obvious example of this.

Other examples of this theme at work are found in numerical practices relating to curriculum work in numeracy. For instance, mathematics syllabi and curriculum documents informing these are typically organised by mathematics content areas and topics. Consider, for example, the Australian Education Council's 1994 report entitled *Mathematics—A Curriculum Profile for Australian Schools*, the purpose of which is to underscore the development of compatible mathematics curricula among Australian states and territories. In this work, mathematics content areas ('strands' and 'strand organisers') are set out. These are listed in Table 4.1. In this table, the specialised vocabulary of mathematics is evident. Associated with each of the strand organisers is detailed reference to mathematics content knowledge and its symbolic systems.

The concerns of visibility are also clearly represented in mathematics teaching and learning. For instance, textbooks and other teaching aids including teaching methods and their literature illustrate numerical practices in which this theme plays a vital role. Moreover, various pedagogic traditions in numeracy have been shaped by issues relating to visibility of

Table 4.1 Strands and strand organisers for *Mathematics —A Curriculum Profile for Australian Schools* (Australian Education Council 1994)

Strand	*Strand organiser*
Number	Count and order Number patterns Equations Applying numbers Mental computation Written computation Calculators
Measurement	Choosing units Measuring Estimating Time Using relationships
Space	Using spatial ideas, tools and techniques to interpret, draw and make Visualising, analysing and representing arrangements and locations Visualising, analysing and representing shapes
Chance and data	Understanding, estimating and measuring chance variation Collecting data Organising data Displaying and summarising data Interpreting data
Algebra	Expressing generality Function Equations and inequalities
Working mathematically	Investigating Conjecturing Using problem-solving strategies Applying and verifying Using mathematical language Working in context

numerical knowledge. For instance, Edward Thorndike's 1922 classic of mathematics pedagogy, *The Psychology of Arithmetic,* lays down a blueprint for teaching number concepts and numeration by breaking down mathematical concepts and processes into arithmetical 'bonds'. Thorndike's idea was that, in order to learn arithmetic, the student needs to have these bonds 'stamped in' by a system of suitable rewards and reinforcement. Another example is provided by the New Maths movement of the 1960s. In this approach to teaching mathematics, a congruence was sought between the structure and content of mathematics and mathematics pedagogy. Teaching methods and organisation were developed around the principles and formalisms of mathematics. Visibility was thus a key theme in the development of teaching from this perspective.

As these examples suggest, the theme of visibility assists the management of the numeracy curriculum. Further, writing about the effects of integrating literacy and numeracy into training packages, the Adult Literacy and Numeracy Australian Research Consortium notes that:

> [It] may be necessary to . . . find ways of making literacy and numeracy competencies more explicit . . . in order to make [these] more visible [sic] and to make trainers more accountable for literacy/numeracy outcomes (ALNARC 2000, p. 34).

and

> [the] 'invisible' nature of language, literacy and *numeracy* skills created a difficult job for teachers and trainers and [does] nothing to reinforce the significance of literacy and numeracy provision (ALNARC 2000, p. 33) [emphasis added].

In other words, visibility tends to promote the interests of numeracy in the curriculum—the less visible it is, the less likely it is that these interests will be addressed. This suggests that visibility is a powerful theme in political debates surrounding the nature and needs of the numeracy curriculum.

THE THEME OF USEABILITY

The theme of useability is apparent where the concerns are with the application of numeracy. This may be in the everyday or workplace tasks numeracy helps to perform, the problems it helps to solve or situations it helps to analyse and better understand. An early (1958) study by Brownell and Chazal (cited in Resnick & Ford 1981) illustrated that, when people actually use numerical knowledge in everyday situations, they tend to utilise techniques and strategies they have developed from experience, rather than learned in school or other formal settings. In other words, in order to understand numeracy, we have to understand how numeracy is used.

More recently, in her now classic study, Sylvia Scribner (1997) showed that when we use numerical concepts we not only adapt them to a specific context, but transform them depending on that context. As she followed dairy workers around their daily routines, she observed that workers with experience developed numerical routines and methods that facilitated more efficient work practices. In so doing, workers were observed to amend and adapt numerical concepts and formal routines and generate new routines as needed to meet workplace tasks. More recently, Jean Lave has investigated the useable numeracy of 'just plain folks' in supermarket contexts (1988). Nunes et al. (1993) and Saxe (1988, 1991) have studied numerical proficiencies of candy sellers on the streets of South American cities. Each of these studies has illustrated that using numerical knowledge is not merely a matter of transferring it from the learning context to the everyday/workplace context; rather, using numeracy is about the transformation and modification of numeracy.

In the following material, I illustrate these ideas further by giving examples of how numeracy is used in practice. I do this by examining the transcripts of real-life work situations observed in over-the-counter transactions within the hospitality industry. These show what numeracy looks like in actual workplace situations and illustrate the theme of useability. Examples involve interactions among the client services officer (CSO), clients (C) and the researcher (R). To aid presentation, I have grouped the episodes discussed according to workplace tasks, such as constructing accounts in order to facilitate the sale of services and striking room rates.

Constructing accounts

Managing the flow of money is fundamental to the operations of commercial enterprises. Such flows certainly afford examples of visible numeracy in operation. For example, in Episode A the CSO demonstrates knowledge of multiplication and how it applies in order to construct a client's telephone account.

Episode A
R: *Can I just ask you—when you check the phone charges, can you bring the number up on the switch?*
CSO: We bring up the extension number of the room and that reads as 28 meter pulses and we multiply that by 0.60—it's 60 cents a meter pulse.

Nevertheless, constructing accounts is found to routinely engage more complex processes and forms of reasoning. For instance, in Episode B and Episode C, even though room charges are automatically tabulated, the CSO must appropriately identify the kind of service being offered.

Episode B
R: *And up there you've got—oh, your room charges.*
CSO: Yes, this is all the room charges and room number. Because [in

the computer] you've got the charge table [depending on] what rate you [can] check in. And the ultimate charge [inaudible] and we charge according to the number of people in the room. You can go in and change it—for example [charge for a double] which is for two people and we have the single charge which is for one person in a double room.

R: *So do you refer to this much?*

CSO: No, it's sort of habit to you, once you know it. It's really—yeah I guess it's up there for newcomers really. Yeah, and just in case people aren't sure, then they can go through and check it. Once reception staff . . . once they use it, they get [to remember] what charge is what.

Episode C

R: *Do you then enter that into the computer?*

CSO: Well first we have to go directly behind me which is to our 'bible'. Now, this bible has to be correct at all times. 'Cause we go by the whole motel with this. So hopefully this is always correct. I do have a room available for them [inaudible] so I'll have to put them in, otherwise someone else will let that room go. [inaudible]

OK. I've got them booked into a suite. So therefore I have to enter into the 'suite/double/or single'. It'll come up a charge type. So there's two occupants [inaudible] staying in room 102. That's getting into the normal rates and charge tables. [inaudible] If he was going to get 5 per cent discount because he's a corporate cardholder or something we would then go to '1', press [enter] and it changes the rate straight away.

I have shown that these episodes make use of charge variables including: room configuration (single, double, or suite); number of people in a room; and whether a discount applies. My analysis continues as follows:

> In constructing an account, the CSO must choose values for these variables. Furthermore, some codes for these variables formalise naturalistic meanings—for example, if three people share a suite, then the key reflecting this number is '3'—whereas other codes adopt arbitrarily imposed signifiers—for example, if a corporate discount applies, the CSO must signify this with the numerical code '1'. This means the CSO must manage a range of variables and codes crossing numerous domains—some visibly numerical, others not. Throughout these operations, the CSO must manipulate numerical variables, but know when and where to visit characteristically numerical meaning upon them. In other words, the worker must know which aspects of a presented situation require outright quantification, which require codification though not quantification, and

which can be (or need to be) ignored. These examples illustrate that, even for apparently straightforward workplace tasks, useable numeracy proficiency requires more than the visible manipulation of arithmetic values (Kane 2002, p. 344).

Striking rates

Striking rates for services illustrates the kinds of complexity involved in useable numeracy manipulations. For example, in Episode D, C requests a rate for a sixteen-day stay in a motel.

Episode D: People checking out room return to reception.
CSO: How was that?
C: Very nice.
CSO: Now you want to know how much?—I've been trying to think—sixteen days is a long stay, so we will do our best for you. They're normally $85 a night, we normally would let them go say on a weekly basis for say $70 which is $525. But if you're staying the sixteen days I'll let you have it for $500.
C: $500 a week—that's thousand and a bit.
CSO: Leave it at a thousand—that's two nights that we give you. How does that sound?
C: [inaudible] thanks for your time [inaudible]
CSO: Good. Yeah. No problem—you're welcome. Ta ta [to the kids], see you later.
CSO: (to R) It makes it very hard when it's so competitive—as soon as the different times drop off—it's sort of—how much do we actually charge them to keep it? you know—you know it's really hard to know what to do, but I offered them the room for $1000 for the sixteen days, so basically $500 a week.

Guests enter.

In response, the CSO engages in a chain of complex reasoning as follows. The normal rate is $85 per night, which amounts to $595 for one week. However, a discount of $70 applies in such cases, bringing the total to $525. Using this as the basis, the CSO now strikes a rate for sixteen nights by further reducing the discount by $25 and thus arrives at a new rate of $500 per week. In a final step, the CSO further discounts the rate in order to bring the final amount to a round $1000.

Whilst the CSO shows knowledge of relevant arithmetic relationships ($85 per night for seven night equals $595, minus $70 discount equals $525), these only form part of the knowledge required in order to strike a suitable rate. As the CSO concedes, striking a rate is 'very hard'. The market is 'so competitive' and this means the 'actual' rate cannot be merely the application of a set protocol. It is notable, however, that the CSO's techniques involved successively rounding down quoted amounts: first from $525 per week to $500 per week, and then from $1000 per fortnight (fourteen days) to $1000 per sixteen days. This procedure required the close coordination of two kinds of knowledge: numerical criteria for selecting rounding target (nearest hundred, nearest whole week) as well as business criteria relating to the maintenance of a competitive pricing. Further, it would seem, maintenance of a competitive edge required not only that the routine pricing protocol be manipulated, but that the reasoning on which this manipulation depended be made explicit. Merely quoting a discounted rate would not do for competitive purposes. The episode shows that the CSO 'sells' the discount to the client by firstly articulating the process of reasoning by which the discount was computed, and secondly translating discounted values into equivalent service items ('leave it at a thousand— that's two nights we give you').

This example illustrates that there is no clear demarcation between numerical procedures and other kinds of specifically work-related knowledge used to strike competitive rates. In other words, when used, numeracy is intimately shaped by the workplace environment itself.

Likewise, Episode E illustrates that no clear demarcations can be made between setting the terms of the service and figuring the related cost structure of the service. That is, numeracy viewed from the perspectives of use extends in the direction of specific workplace knowledge.

Episode E
R: *Have they taken any action against anyone?*
CSO: Not yet, but there have been threats of action. You get a kid call in [inaudible] last year when all this came out what we decided was the only way around it was have schoolies [school leavers] and schoolies only here and then we're not discriminating because then everybody's under the same umbrella right? We had young girls calling 'do you have rooms available?'—what do you mean you charge a bond—that's discriminating. And I just said 'Look sweetheart [sic]. You've been reading too many newspapers. If you want to stay, fine, you pay a bond. If you don't want to pay a bond you just don't stay here I'm sorry.' So they can go and take us to court or whatever, but I just don't know where it's all going to end [inaudible]. But also see when we've got schoolies here, when I close up at six o'clock at night security starts. When I open at 8 o'clock in the morning, security finishes. Otherwise we'd have parties and 50 people in a room and all kinds of things. Security has to try and vet some of those people coming through. If we can't charge a bond—who's going to pay for security? That's $15 an hour. Add that up over twelve to fourteen hours that's a lot of money. That's more than what they're paying for the room basically, so what do you do? It's very difficult. It'll be very interesting to see what comes out of it.

In this example, a complex interaction is observed between the perceptions of risk associated with providing service (damage to rooms and property) and the cost of hedging against these kinds of risk (security at '$15 per hour for twelve to fourteen hours') and litigation on the grounds of 'discrimination'. Rather than detailed specification of cost, a sketch of the cost structure is provided and this serves as a rationale for hedging measures built around the rhetorical question 'who's going to pay for security?'. Numerical knowledge is engaged by foreshadowing possible cost calculations (useability) rather than specifying calculated amounts for operational purposes (visibility).

Similarly, in Episode F the CSO sketches an outline of the cost structure relating to the servicing of motel rooms in order to explain why overnight stays are profitable in one establishment, though sometimes not in others.

Episode F

R: Do you have many overnight bookings?

CSO: We do. A lot of places don't take overnighters. But the reason is simply because those people that were just here—they contract the cleaning of the rooms, and it's quite expensive. But my housemaids are on $11 an hour—it would take them say half an hour to clean a small room so we're looking at about $6. But of course, we've got the linen costs, the electricity and the supplies and everything else to take into consideration, but it wouldn't come to $20. But they would—we charge $50 for a room and they're going to charge $20 to clean it. Right? So—it's not for us—because we do have overnighters. Other hotels that have three, four and five nighter only, no less than three—it's OK for them. But I wanted to contract the cleaning out at those costs. It's too expensive. But what were we originally talking about?

R: *Oh, the question was whether you get many overnighters or whether it's . . .*

CSO: We do take overnighters because we charge them $50 for a room and its going to cost me—I costed it out once and I can't remember exactly, so on weekday it costs say $14 taking linen and everything else into consideration out of $50 right? And that's also taking into consideration the housemaid's wages, superannuation, all that sort of thing as well. On a weekend, on a Saturday it's a little bit more expensive and of course it's more expensive than that so that's why we try and hold the rooms over—we pay $13.30 or something like that per hour on Sundays, so it gets a lot more expensive. But I think we'll stick to our casual housemaids, it's going to be a lot cheaper. So overnighters—no problems.

At the core of this argument is the logic that engaging housemaids to clean rooms at a casual rate is cheaper than committing the motel to a cleaning contract. Of interest is the way in which this is expressed. On the one hand, the all-up cost of servicing a room at casual rates 'wouldn't come to $20', whereas at contract rates 'they're going to charge $20 to clean it'. Note that, in this example, the CSO makes no attempt to be precise with the numerical values quoted. Instead, approximations and estimated values are utilised in order to maximise the rhetorical impact of the argument. In this case, numeracy is shaped by reasoning which is only loosely coordinated with actual numerical values. What the CSO offers is not a mathematical 'proof', but a roughly worked argument.

These examples not only show that the way numeracy is used is embedded in the context, but that numeracy itself is shaped by its context.

THE THEME OF CONSTRUCTIBILITY

As indicated previously, the theme of constructibility concerns the origins of numeracy both as culturally available knowledge and as learned knowledge residing in individuals. The first of these relates to the history and philosophy of mathematics. Here we see the theme of constructibility playing a key role in the evolution of mathematics and of the ways in which mathematical knowledge is validated. For instance, in early Greek geometry, knowledge was generated and verified by the technique of geometric constructions. Later, in Euclid's geometry, the art of geometrical construction developed into what we know as the axiomatic method. In modern times, the method of Descartes illustrated how algebraic and geometrical knowledge could be synthesised, thereby showing that the notion of construction applied broadly to a wide variety of mathematical objects. Similarly, Leibnitz (1646–1716) argued that mathematical problems were essentially problems of computability, and therefore could be solved in principle by methods of construction.

The work of these authors has served as the basis for a range of more recent attempts at showing that mathematical knowledge is constructed knowledge and that constructibility is a key criterion when evaluating the validity of mathematical knowledge—for instance, the constructionism of Brouwer (1881–1966) and the formalism of Hilbert (1862–1943). These efforts in viewing mathematical knowledge as constructed knowledge stand in contrast to another equally ancient tradition: the view that mathematical knowledge is governed by the metaphor of vision. To know a piece of mathematics is to 'see' the logic of it, rather than prepare a construction for it. This view is linked to Plato's theory that the purest form of knowledge, *noesis*, is the direct intuitive perception of it, and that mathematical knowledge, at least in its 'higher' forms, is of this kind. Now a tension exists between these views of mathematical knowledge—one, constructibility, built around the metaphor of 'doing', and the other, visibility, built around the metaphor of 'seeing'. For instance, in teaching contexts, these are very often expressed in the supposed differences between so-called rote learning (which focuses on the development of specific numerical skills) and learning for understanding (which purports to focus on the development of numerical concepts). In the former, emphasis is on the development of appropriate procedures; in the latter, it is on the development of insight into mathematical relationships. Often, these alternatives are presented in value-laden terms—such as, for instance, the belief that rote learning is more suitable for vocational-oriented learning contexts and conceptual learning for those destined for professional occupations.

Principles of learning and teaching numeracy

As indicated above, important examples of the theme of constructibility relate to numerical practices operating around the learning and teaching of numeracy. Here, as I have argued previously, two lines of development have been significant:

> In the first [line of development], made problematic by more recent mathematics education research, numeracy is typically associated with developing the habits of numerical thinking (i.e. the building of hierarchically organised bonds or associations), as in the work of Thorndike (1922). This approach sees learning numeracy as a behaviouristic phenomenon in which the most important feature is the inculcation of salient responses to given stimuli. Rote learning of numerical relationships, so much a feature of traditional school experience, is consistent with this view. More recent theorisations of this approach to learning have been provided by information processes psychology (Gagné 1970). In this view, context plays an extrinsic role in the learning process.
> In the second line of development, learning is identified with the learner's ability to use prior learning and the learning context to formulate meanings for the manipulations which make up learned numeracy experience (Brownell 1947). This focus on building adequate meanings for learning mathematical concepts and processes has been variously theorised by Gestalt psychologists (Wertheimer 1945), cognitive psychologists such as Piaget, Bruner (1960) and Dienes (1960), and social constructivists such as Steffe, von Glasersfeld (1995), Cobb et al. (1992) and Cobb (1994a). Because many cognitively based theories share the view that the learner actively constructs new knowledge by modifying, extending, replacing and transforming existing knowledge, they have come to be known by the umbrella term 'constructivism'. According to the constructivist view, learning numeracy corresponds with the purposeful construction of powerful meanings (i.e. those that deliver a problem-solving outcome) in a given learning context. Whilst much has been left out

in this story, the central point is that learning numeracy and constructing numerical knowledge adequate to a problem-giving situation are seen as one and the same process.

Now the switch to the constructible—the so called 'constructivist turn' in mathematics education—involves a valuing of context and the conditions of learning mathematics as intrinsic to the learning process. This, in turn, has given rise to views of learning mathematics in which social, historical, cultural and economic contexts are integral rather than peripheral to learning processes. It follows from this analysis that examples of the theme of constructibility are seen in those views of numeracy which emanate from studies which assume and support understanding of the socially constructed nature of numerical knowledge. Examples of these views include the anthropological studies of Bishop (1988), Saxe (1991) and Nunes et al. (1993); the sociological and linguistic studies of Bloor (1983), Lave (1988) and Solomon (1989); the micro-sociological analyses of Bauersfeld (1991), Voigt (1993) and Cobb (1994b); and the discourse theory approaches of Walkerdine (1988, 1994) (Kanes 2002, pp. 344–5).

Arising from the above, a set of learning principles for numeracy can be distilled, as follows.

- *Numeracy learning is always shaped by the setting within which it is embedded.* Whether the setting is a workplace or is created by a learning institution or learning materials, learning is referenced to a setting. As Lave and Wenger (1991) argue, this means that features of a setting, together with tools (both physical and psychological) and economic, social and cultural relations of the setting create opportunities for learning and characterise the kinds of learning which takes place.
- *Learning numeracy is about generating meaningful and powerful skills and concepts.* Learning is about making meaning—without meanings, there is no learning. Brownell (1947) offers a useful characterisation of meaning as being of two kinds: meanings *of* numerical knowledge (concept of process); and meanings *for* numerical knowledge. However, meanings must also have power in the particular setting in which they arise (Cobb et al. 1992). This means that meanings must be consistent with workable or legitimate solutions to problems within the problem setting.
- *Learning numeracy is about actively solving the problems of adaptation to new settings or new aspects of received settings.* 'Problem' means a dilemma or conceptual challenge to the learner arising from the presentation of a new or novel circumstance. Problems require conscious, decisive action.

'Adaptation' means the process of generating workable procedures or valid meanings within the context of the problem's setting. Adaptation requires that the learner generates new skills and meanings by extending, modifying, developing and transforming existing skills and meanings.

- *Learning numeracy involves reflective thinking.* Generating meaning requires the learner to consciously reflect on the knowledge already acquired (whether concepts or skills). The purpose of reflection is to transform meaning associated with a setting in a particular instance to other instances and settings. In so doing, the learner constructs new meanings, and generates new concepts and skills.
- *Learning numeracy is a socially interactive process.* Not only do all learning settings have a social dimension, but learning itself is a social process. This is because learning is about making meaning, and making meaning is a pre-eminent feature of social life. In addition, meaning-making in numeracy requires that the learner engage with multiple sets of perspectives and resources. These must frame numerical knowledge in a range of different ways including linguistically, concretely and symbolically.
- *Learning numeracy requires a pedagogically sequenced curriculum.* Because numerical knowledge is in part hierarchically organised, sequencing of knowledge in learning is important. A pedagogical sequence must respect both the logical hierarchy of numerical knowledge and the sequence imposed by an ordered development of numerical meanings.

Effective teaching requires that curriculum workers make choices that best facilitate learning. Thus principles of teaching and associated methods should be closely related to the learning principles from which they are derived. Table 4.2 sets out teaching principles and methods against each of the learning principles indicated above. As this table shows, flexible learning is affected by a wide variety of teaching methods.

Having now sketched an outline of three leading themes related to the question of numeracy and its scope, the next section considers how they are related to each other. For instance, when considering questions related to the numeracy curriculum, do these different themes complement each other? To what extent do they conflict?

DILEMMAS AND CONFLICTS

Over the last twenty years, there has been a rich literature which I believe demonstrates tensions between the themes of visibility and useability in numeracy. Starting, for instance, with the publication in

Table 4.2 Principles for the learning and teaching of numeracy and indicative teaching methods

Numeracy learning principle*	*Derived teaching principle*	*Indicative teaching methods*
Numeracy learning is shaped by the setting within which it is embedded	Teaching must utilise characteristics of settings in which numeracy is to be utilised	Draw examples from professional and vocational contexts, use authentic settings in the presentation of content
		Generate a rich environment of numerical tools, numerical procedures and problems, e.g. concrete manipulables, spread sheets, numerical and graphical calculators, statistics software and other relevant software.
Learning numeracy is about generating meaningful and powerful skills and concepts	Teaching must create opportunities for students to manipulate, extend, modify and develop their existing knowledge of numerical skills and concepts	Utilise authentic tools and scenarios relating to numerical knowledge
Learning numeracy is about actively solving the problems of adaptation to new settings or new aspects of received settings	Teaching must not only afford learners a cognitively challenging environment, but also one in which challenges are appropriately supported	Utilise drill and practice where skills are to be formed
		Enrich problem-solving exercises with video cueing techniques
		Flag cues and clues for active participation
		Use problem-solving heuristic tools
Learning numeracy involves reflective thinking	Teaching must prompt learners to consciously think about their learning and mastery of skills and concepts	Prompt students with open-style questions
		Utilise student questions as tools to prompt reflective thinking

Numeracy learning principle	Derived teaching principle	Indicative teaching methods
		Respond to student questions with questions designed to elicit student knowledge
		Create opportunities for students to critically appraise their own knowledge base, e.g. by use of journals
Learning numeracy is a socially interactive process	Teaching must involve methods that encourage learners to articulate and share their knowledge with others; teaching must deploy a variety of tools and strategies and thus engage multiple ways of giving meaning to knowledge targeted for growth	Prompt students to act as peer tutors—in this way, students must monitor and transform their own knowledge
		Use video recordings of students engaged in collective problem-solving activities in order to prompt dialogue and discussion of numerical ideas
		Utilise authentic tasks and tools
Learning numeracy requires the development of numerical skills and concepts to be organised in a pedagogic sequence, i.e. one which is both mathematically and pedagogically significant	Teaching must be organised around the pedagogic sequencing of numerical content knowledge	

*(adapted from Donnan's 1999, p. 104 interpretation of Basiel (1999)

1982 in Britain of the Cockroft report, which had the task of considering 'the mathematics required in further and higher education, employment and adult life generally'(DES 1982, p. ix, cited in Noss 1998, p. 2), a clear tension between the demands of useability and visibility in numeracy emerges as an issue to be contended with. As noted in Noss (1998, p. 3), the report observes that workplace practices seldom demand standard arithmetic operations 'such as $\frac{2}{5} + \frac{3}{7}$' and that the need for algebra, 'let alone such mathematical ideas as proof, modelling and mathematical rigour'(Noss 1998, p. 3), was almost nil. From this it concludes that 'it is possible to summarise a very large part of the mathematical needs of employment as a feeling for measurement' (DES 1982, p. 24, cited in Noss 1998, p. 3). In other words, the thrust of the report throws into question the utility value of a broad-ranging numeracy curriculum. As a consequence, those maintaining the value of such a curriculum need to advance arguments other than the direct significance of mathematical terms and expressions when explaining the use of the numeracy curriculum for employment and general life purposes. In short, as Noss (1998) argues, a focus on useability in numeracy diminishes the focus on visibility, and vice versa. This point is further illustrated by Strässer (1999) in his study of weighing machines in delicatessens; and Wolf (1984, cited in Noss 1998) provides evidence that workers make use of mathematics without needing or wishing to make this fact visible.

In Australia, Kanes (1999) has shown in an investigation of over-the-counter operations in the motel and airline industry that, of the six mathematics content strands of the profiles (see Table 4.1), three strands—Number, Chance and data and Working mathematically—were ranked highly in terms of the visibility of these content areas in the workplace settings (see Table 4.3). Consistent with Cockroft, algebra was found to be least visible. These results support the view that useability and visibility tend to crowd each other out of curriculum questions in numeracy.

Further, Noss (1998) has argued that the problematic relationship between what is identified here as visibility and useability gives rise to a number of curriculum paradoxes along the following lines. For, as I have argued:

> If we merely restrict our view to the 'surface of arithmetical activities' (1998, p. 3) in adult working lives, then we are bound to find only 'traces and shadows' (1998, p. 3) of mathematics in actual use. The paradox arises when such a finding is used to conclude that the mathematical needs of adult life are not strong, for such a conclusion

Table 4.3 Cluster analysis of overall strand site ranks

Cluster	Strand
Low strand ascription	Algebra
Medium strand ascription	Space
	Measurement
High strand ascription	Working mathematically
	Chance and data
	Number

Source: Kanes (1999)

is bound to activate a utilitarian principle relating to the usefulness of school mathematics and see school mathematics become more and more narrowly defined and thus, paradoxically, less and less useful. In terms set up in this paper, concentration on the interests of creating visibility oversimplifies issues relating to useability in numeracy, and this leads to numeracy becoming less 'useable' than would otherwise be the case (Kanes 2002, p. 346).

Second, given that there exists a 'lack of mathematical confidence and alienation on the part of the many' (Noss 1998, p. 3), the numeracy curriculum in response has tended to be oversimplified, and this in turn has tended to compromise numeracy's 'broader roots in science and technology' (ibid.). Thus, 'in trying to connect mathematics with what is learnable, we have disconnected school mathematics from what is genuinely useful' (ibid.). Now, as I argued above, under the rubric of constructivism learnability is an aspect of the theme of constructibility. Thus one way to interpret Noss's second paradox is that the themes of useability and constructibility crowd each other out in discussions around the issue, for instance, of the alignment of numerical curriculum with workplace needs. Noss is suggesting that a focus on constructibiliity (learnability) generates a tension with useability and that this tension permeates curriculum concerns in numeracy.

As I have pointed out, 'these paradoxes illustrate that the development of numeracy is governed by highly problematic situations' (Kanes 2002, p. 346). Discussions of numeracy require engagement with the themes of visibility, useability and constructibility, yet a focus on any one of these themes tends to exclude the interests of the others. Nevertheless, it is only this broader set of interests that addresses the needs of students, industry and mathematics.

I now return briefly to comments made earlier in this chapter, in which I outlined certain views about numeracy. I am now in a position of explain these views further and show in what sense they are erroneous.

Firstly, numeracy is not a watered down mathematics—instead, 'mathematics' (by which I am referring to the academic discipline) is a particular kind of numeracy. To be more exact, mathematics is numeracy seen under the rubric of the theme of visibility. Typically, its concerns are with proof and demonstrability, logical argumentation and rigour, abstract symbolism and so on, by which operations are made explicit and clear themselves. Unlike numeracy viewed from the perspective of useability, mathematics privileges the formalisms in which it is codified. Unlike numeracy viewed from the perspective of constructibility, mathematics is not so much concerned with the meanings of its definitions and theorems for people as it is concerned with the logical and conceptual demonstrability of its findings.

Secondly, numeracy is not limited by number concepts and numeration processes; instead, numerical practice typically involves the concrete (i.e. in situ) management of a repertoire of concepts including number, space, data, chance and abstractions of these. This follows, once again, from the recognition that useable-numeracy and constructible-numeracy extend the domain of the numerical.

Thirdly, numeracy is not ahistorical. Instead, like any other social and cultural phenomenon, it has a history, a past, a present and a future. In this history, not only does the body of knowledge within numeracy develop as a direct result of new technologies and methods of production, but also as a result of their interactions and the needs of useability and constructibility which arise as a consequence of these.

Fourthly, numeracy is not a kind of literacy—though numerical practices are often associated with discursive acts, they are not themselves typically discursive. If literacy is taken broadly to be associated with acts of communication, then it becomes clear why numeracy cannot be reduced to a form of literacy. Quite simply, numeracy is only partly concerned with communication (imparting information, say)—more typically, it is about applying methods to solve problems. Whether these are problems of rigour and certainty, or problems of quantities and configuration, communication is not the salient task.

My analysis now moves towards a cultural-historical framework for understanding the development of numeracy. My central claim is that the dilemmas and conflicts depicted above be seen as intrinsic to the nature of numeracy, rather than as anomalies extrinsic to an otherwise ordered and coherent system of knowledge. I argue that tensions of the kind described are responsible for the development of numeracy and that a fuller understanding of these offers a way to develop and explore curriculum issues for numeracy using an activity theory approach.

NUMERACY CURRICULUM DEVELOPMENT

When thinking about the development of numeracy for specific educational purposes, a full range of value positions and stakeholder interests needs to be considered (Pinar 1995; Slattery 1995). Effective numeracy curriculum development must speak to the needs of students, teachers and trainers, mathematicians, employers, policy-makers, administrators and everyday citizens (those who Lave (1988) describes as 'just plain folks'). Moreover, as the preceding analysis suggests, numeracy is a dynamic activity depending on the relationship among different kinds of people—and this activity is depicted by the themes of visibility, useability and constructibility.

Therefore, in order to extend our understanding of the curriculum development of numeracy, we must grasp the process of change leading to its cultural and historical development. What theoretical framework can assist us in bringing together the insights we have so far generated and help us to embark on the needed cultural and historical analysis indicated above? This question is addressed in this section.

Numeracy as a cultural-historical activity system

It is difficult to summarise in a short space the tenets of cultural-historical activity theory, however I have presented these as follows:

Cultural-historical activity theory follows in the tradition of Vygotskian psychology (1978) and offers a way of conceptualising the transformation of human systems of production (Engeström 1987, 1991, 1999a, 1999b; Leont'ev 1981; Scribner 1997; Suchman 1996; Wertsch 1981, 1985). Social interactions and the role of cultural artefacts in the mediation of activity are at the heart of this theory. An activity system is a social entity that uses cultural artefacts to mediate its common primary motive or driving force. In the activity theory jargon, this motive is known as the 'object' (it is used in the sense of the word 'objective' or purpose). For Engeström (1987, 1991, 1999a, 1999b), cultural artefacts include the tools and instruments (physical and psychological), rules and protocols, community context and social roles, and the division of labour associated with practice. As an activity system progresses, human subjects take up operations and goal-directed actions, and outcomes are generated.

These relations are depicted in Engeström's diagram [see Figure 2.1, Chapter 2].

Three key features of the theory relate to the development ('expansion' or 'remediation' are jargon terms also used) of the object. These are as follows. Firstly, contradictions within practice are construed to generate the creative impetus for the historico-cultural development of the system. Activity theory is a theory of crisis. The primary impetus for historical development is derived from the need to resolve crises induced by conflicting tendencies, double-bind situations and paradoxes in the nature of the activity system.

Secondly, an activity system faced with the need to resolve crises struggles to develop into a 'culturally more advanced form' by the process of 'remediation'. For Engeström, this is a process whereby the system makes use of newly deployed artefacts in order to facilitate desired outcomes. And thirdly, the object or motive is double-sided in the sense that it both orientates the subject in a direction for action and, in turn, is shaped by the multiple domains of mediation constituting the activity. Simultaneously, actions lead to the continual revision and reconstruction of the object in the

DEVELOPING VOCATIONAL EXPERTISE

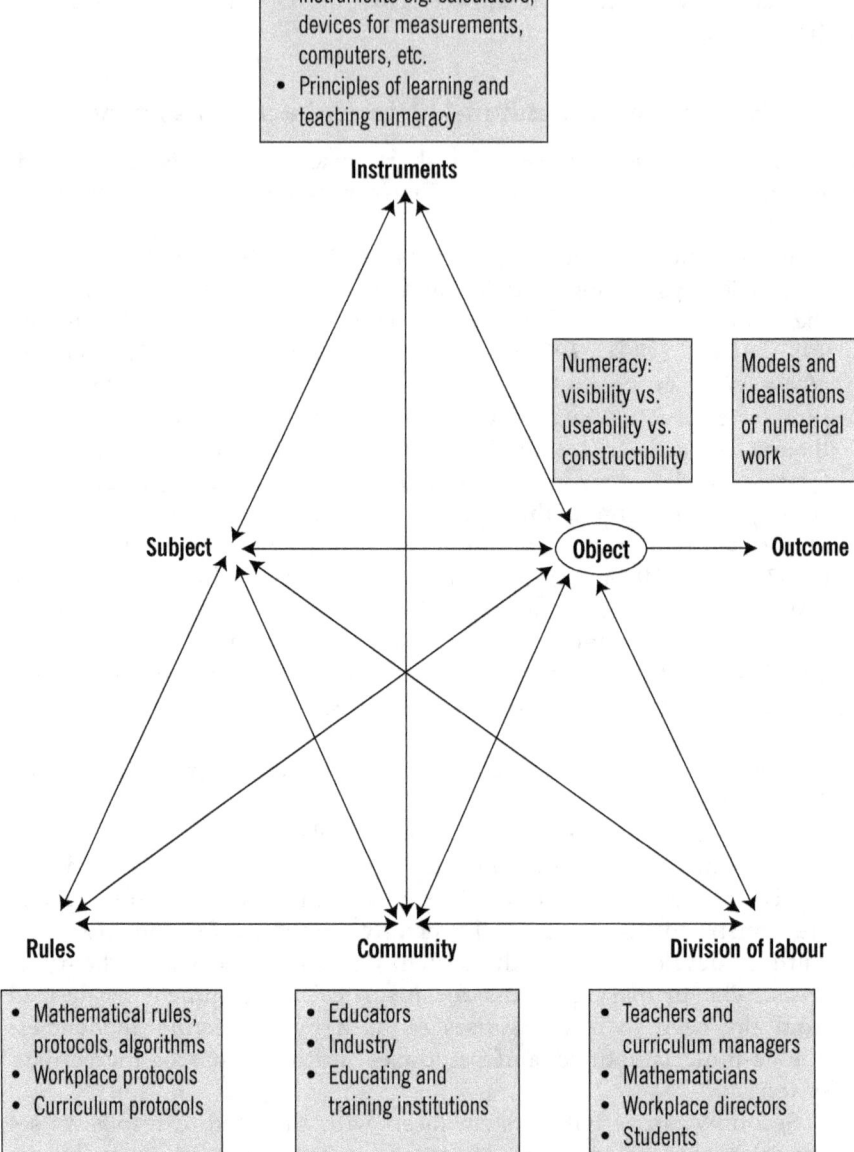

Figure 4.1 Model of numeracy as a cultural-historical activity system as in Kanes (2001, p. 49; 2002, p. 348)

light of intermediate goals being reached and the recognition of obstacles to progress (Kanes 2002, pp. 346-7).

As I have shown (Kanes 2001, 2002), activity theory enables us to now give a more comprehensive view of numeracy and its interacting components, as depicted in Figure 4.1 (derived from Engeström 1999b—see Figure 2.1).

Numeracy is seen as the object or motive of a numerical practice, and we observe this motive expressed in the themes of visibility, useability and constructibility. Tools used by students and teachers, workers and mathematicians, curriculum developers and managers to implement actions relating to these themes respectively include:

- mathematical tools, such as calculators, computers and their software, instruments, and so on;
- tools and instruments associated with the operation of numerical knowledge in order to achieve a context-defined goal; and
- curriculum documents, principles for learning and teaching numeracy.

As activity proceeds, all components of the activity system are in actual or potential interaction. Conflicts are produced (as among visibility, useability and constructibility, for instance) and the resolution of these leads to the development of the activity system.

Thus far I have used the activity theory model of numeracy to analyse and illustrate different themes and tensions relevant to numeracy. The many ways that numeracy is engineered in an actual instance are thereby made explicit and amenable to critical exploration. However, the model is not limited to studies such as these: it can also be used to advance changes in numerical practices. Engeström (1999a) shows the way forward here with his concept of 'expansive visibilisation'. This multistage developmental process involves the depiction of the numeracy activity system in its contemporary form and theorises the projection of new forms with a view to identifying prospects and actual pathways for change and development. Stages in expansive visibilisation include:

- mirroring and analysing tensions within approaches to numeracy;
- modelling numeracy curriculum development activity systems;
- designing and implementing new numeracy curricula; and
- reviewing and revising these plans.

Moreover, because expansive visibilisation exists both as a description of a developmental process and as an artefact mediating change, it can itself be conceptualised as a tool within the numeracy activity system.

This chapter contributes an outline of the first two of the stages of the expansive visibilisation of numeracy. In my elaboration of key themes and analyses of tensions and dilemmas within numerical practice, an outline of the first stage is provided; the second stage is advanced in Figure 4.1. Future collaborative efforts of workers participating within the activity system of numeracy will move the process of expansion to the third and fourth stages. Central to this work as a whole is the task of weaving together plans for using new learning technologies with new roles for those involved with the numeracy curriculum; new kinds of social interactions; and new rules for supporting the achievement of goals and purposes. As Engeström argues, this weaving together is not driven by a 'list of discrete rationally predetermined goals but by a dialectical movement between activity-level visions and action-level concretisations' (Engeström 1999a, pp. 91–2). That is, curriculum workers must use reflection on their *plans* for the numeracy curriculum as tools for developing and transforming their concrete practice; and, vice versa, reflection on *concrete practice* must be used as a tool to transform plans for the numeracy curriculum.

IMPLICATIONS FOR PRACTICE

In this chapter I have provided various tools for implementation when engaging with numerical practices. For instance, numeracy teachers make use of schedules of numerical knowledge (for example, Table 4.1), together with learning principles and teaching principals and methods, in order to specify learning goals and design learning experiences for students that will achieve them (Table 4.2). In working towards these achievements, teachers use a variety of mathematical tools and instruments (mathematical concepts, processes, symbols, calculating devices, computing devices, etc.) and pedagogic tools and instruments (for instance, concrete manipulables, software, etc.) In addition, the teacher's numeracy curriculum goals are shaped by assessment tools and standards, often imposed on the teacher by the environment external to the teaching and learning interaction with students.

But in implementing these tools, the teacher's work is not without conflict. Being concerned with student learning, the teacher's concerns are with the potential and actual quality of the knowledge students construct as a result of learning experiences they have undertaken. In addition—particularly in the vocational curriculum—there is a concern with the useability of the knowledge developed. However, curriculum documentation and procedures (including assessment requirements leading to vocational accreditation) which draw more on the theme of visibility and less on the themes of constructibility and useability are also principal concerns of educators. That is, educators often are 'and perhaps must be' more concerned with the achievement of formal learning outcomes (as in, for instance, outcomes-based criteria), and less concerned with how this knowledge stands in relation to actual use or understanding. This situation gives rise to conflicting interests and opportunities for curriculum development via the application of the 'expansive visibilisation' tool introduced in the previous section. Expansive visibilisation provides opportunities for teachers to identify and understand the conflicting tensions of their work; model the activity system which has numeracy as its purpose; and propose and implement curriculum development in numeracy, leading to further monitoring and transformation practice.

Policy managers and syllabus writers also find tensions relating to the themes of useability and visibility of numeracy in their work. For these workers, for instance, a concern for the use of numerical knowledge in work-related contexts makes it difficult to align curriculum documents against formal statements of specifically numerical knowledge, and this compromises curriculum accountability. Expansive visibilisation provides for a planned response to this problem. In the first stage, an explication of the problematic nature of accountability in a use-oriented curriculum is undertaken. This leads to the collaborative identification of tools, protocols, roles of curriculum workers, the values and goals of the teaching and training institutions and joint analysis of the multiple ways in which such a curriculum is facilitated and implemented. A model of the activity system that has numeracy as its purpose is then developed and shared among numeracy curriculum workers. Next, workers design and implement new tools and strategies in order to resolve tensions made explicitly. Implementation is monitored and plans are revised accordingly. Thus the process of visibilising curriculum work leads to an expanded and collectively shared development of teaching practice.

Expansive visibilisation provides a way to make explicit and co-ordinate the evolving interests of the various themes of numerical practice. This encourages the development of new tools and ways of operating in workplaces and learning institutions which have as their purpose more effective implementation of operations, actions and activities related to numeracy.

CONCLUSION

This chapter has firstly explored what kind of knowledge numeracy is. In accomplishing this task, it has introduced a new framework for numeracy that draws on cultural-historical activity theory. Next, the themes of visibility, useability and constructibility were identified and used to explore the way numerical knowledge is identified, utilised and generated. I have argued that tensions exist among these themes, and that these are the source of creative developments in numeracy. This has led to my suggestion that curriculum developments in numeracy are able to benefit from a close understanding of numeracy as an activity system. The chapter included a brief overview of learning and teaching principles for numeracy. These were conceptualised as tools with the numeracy activity system.

Note: This chapter is a revised and expanded version of Kanes (2002).

REFERENCES

Adult Literacy and Numeracy Australian Research Consortium (ALNARC) 2000, *Building Literacy and Numeracy into Training: A Synthesis of Recent Research into the Effects of Integrating Literacy and Numeracy into Training Packages*, ALNARC, Melbourne

Australian Association of Mathematics Teachers (AAMT) 1997, *Numeracy—Everyone's Business*, Australian Association of Mathematics Teachers, Melbourne

Australian Education Council 1994, *Mathematics—A Curriculum Profile for Australian Schools*, Curriculum Corporation, Melbourne

Basiel, A. 1966, 'Web-constructivism using Javascript', in *Proceedings of ED-MEDIA 99, World Conference Educational Multimedia, Hypermedia and Telecommunications*, eds B. Collis & R. Oliver, AACE, Seattle, Washington, pp. 178–83

Bauersfeld, H. 1991, 'The structuring of the structures', in *Constructivism and Education*, ed. L. Steffe, Lawrence Erlbaum Associates, Hillsdale, N.J.

Bishop, A. 1988, *Mathematical Enculturation*, Kluver, Dordrecht

Bloor, D. 1983, *Wittgenstein: A Social Theory of Knowledge*, Columbia University Press, New York

Brownell, W. 1947, 'The place of meaning in the teaching of arithmetic', *Elementary School Journal*, January, pp. 256–65

Brownell, W. & Chazal, C. 1958, 'Premature drill', in *Research in the Three R's*, eds C. Hunnicutt & W. Iverson, Harper, New York

Bruner, J. 1960, 'On learning mathematics', *The Mathematics Teacher*, December, pp. 610–9

Cobb, P. 1994a, *Learning Mathematics: Constructivist and Interactionist Theories of Mathematical Development*, Kluwer, Dordrecht

—— 1994b, 'Where is the mind? Constructivist and sociocultural perspectives on mathematical development', *Educational Researcher*, vol. 23, no. 7, pp. 13–20

Cobb, P., Yackel, E. & Wood, T. 1992, 'A constructivist alternative to the representation view of mind in mathematics education', *Journal for Research in Mathematics Education*, vol. 23, no. 1

Department of Education, Queensland 1994, *Literacy and Numeracy Strategy: 1994-98*, Department of Education, Queensland, Brisbane

DES 1982, *Mathematics Counts*, HMSO, London

Dienes, Z. 1960, *Building Up Mathematics*, Hutchinson, New York

Donnan, P. 1999, 'Web course development tolls: boom or bust for instructional designers?', in *Open, Flexible and Distance Learning: Challenges of the New Millennium, Collected Papers from the 14th Biennial Forum of the Open and Distance Learning Association of Australia*, pp. 103-10

Engeström, Y. 1987, *Learning by Expanding: An Activity-theoretical Approach to Developmental Research*, Orienta-Konsultit Oy, Helsinki

—— 1991, 'Non scolae sed vitae discimus: toward overcoming the encapsulation of school learning', *Learning and Instruction*, vol. 1, pp. 243-59

—— 1999a, 'Expansive visibilization of work: an activity-theoretical perspective', *Computer Supported Cooperative Work*, vol. 8, pp. 63-93

—— 1999b, 'Expansive learning at work: toward an activity-theoretical reconceptualization', keynote address, *Changing Practice through Research: Changing Research through Practice*, 7th Annual International Conference of the Centre for Learning and Work Research, Griffith University, Brisbane

Gagné, R. 1970, *The Conditions of Learning*, Holt, Rinehart & Winston, New York

Kanes, C. 1999, 'What kind of knowledge is "Vocational Mathematics"?', *Australian Vocational Education Review*, vol. 6, no. 2, pp. 1-14

—— 2001, 'Numeracy as a cultural-historical object', *Australian Vocational Education Review*, vol. 8, no. 1, pp. 43-51

—— 2002, 'Towards numeracy as a cultural-historical activity system', in *Proceedings of the Third International Mathematics Education and Society Conference*, eds P. Valero & O. Skovsmose, Helsingør, Denmark, pp. 341-50

Lave, J. 1988, *Cognition in Practice: Mind, Mathematics and Culture in Everyday Life*, Cambridge University Press, Cambridge

Lave, J. & Wenger, E. 1991, *Situated Learning: Legitimate Peripheral Participation*, Cambridge University Press, Cambridge

Leont'ev, A.N. 1981, *Problems of the Development of the Mind*, Progress, Moscow

Noss, R. 1998, 'New numeracies for a technological culture', *For the Learning of Mathematics*, vol. 18, no. 2, pp. 2-12

Nunes, T., Schlieman, A.D. & Carraher, D.W. 1993, *Street Mathematics and School Mathematics*, Cambridge University Press, New York

Pinar, W. ed. 1995, *Contemporary Curriculum Discourses: Twenty Years of JCT*, Peter Lang, New York

Rorty, R. 1998, *Truth and Progress: Philosophical Papers*, Cambridge University Press, Cambridge

Resnick, L. & Ford, W. 1981, *The Psychology of Mathematics for Instruction*, Lawrence Erlbaum, London

Saxe, G. 1988, 'Candy selling and math learning', *Educational Researcher*, vol. 17, no. 6, pp. 14–21

—— 1991, *Culture and Cognitive Development: Studies in Mathematical Understanding*, Lawrence Erlbaum Associates, Hillsdale, NJ

Scribner, S. 1997, *Mind and Social Practice: Selected Writings of Sylvia Scribner*, eds E. Tobach, R. Joffe Falmagne, M. Parlee, L. Marting & A. Scribner Kapelman, Cambridge University Press, New York

Searle, J. 1999, *Mind, Language and Society*, Weidenfeld & Nicholson, London

Slattery, P. 1995, *Curriculum Development in the Postmodern Era*, Garland Publishing, New York

Solomon, Y. 1989, *The Practice of Mathematics*, Routledge, London

Strässer, R. 1999, 'On the disappearance of mathematics from societal perception', in *Changing Practice Through Research: Changing Research Through Practice, Proceedings of the 7th Annual International Conference on Post-Compulsory Education and Training, Vol. 1*, Surfers Paradise, 6–8 December, Centre for Learning and Work Research, Brisbane, pp. 55–65

Suchman, L. 1996, 'Constituting shared workspaces', in *Cognition and Communication at Work*, eds Y. Engeström & D. Middleton, Cambridge University Press, Cambridge

Thorndike, E. 1922, *The Psychology of Arithmetic*, Norwood Press, Norwood

von Glasersfeld, E. 1995, *Radical Constructivism: A Way of Knowing and Learning*, Falmer, Washington, DC

Voigt, J. 1993, 'Ascribing mathematical meaning to empirical phenomena', paper presented at the Conference *The Culture of the Mathematics Classroom: Analyzing and Reflecting Upon the Conditions of Change*, 11–15 October, Osnabrück

Vygotsky, L.S. 1978, *Mind in Society: The Development of Higher Psychological Processes*, Harvard University Press, Cambridge, MA

Walkerdine, V. 1988, *The Mastery of Reason*, Cambridge University Press, Cambridge

—— 1994, 'Reasoning in a post-modern age', in *Mathematics, Education and Philosophy: An International Perspective*, ed. P. Ernest, Falmer, London

Wertheimer, M. 1945, *Productive Thinking*, Associated Book Publishers, Tavistock Publications, London

Wertsch, J. ed. 1981, *The Concept of Activity in Soviet Psychology*, M.E. Sharpe, Armonk, New York

—— 1985, *Vygotsky and the Social Formation of Mind*, Harvard University Press, Cambridge, MA

Wolf, A. 1984, *Practical Mathematics at Work: Learning Through YTS*, Manpower Services Commission, Sheffield

5

Developing information literacy

Fred Beven

BACKGROUND

This chapter explains the concept of information literacy by drawing upon recent examinations of its use in the workplace and more generally. This includes ideas about information literacy as a fundamental competency, ideas of how information literacy should be developed for work, an examination of information literacy in workplace practice, as well as ideas from the literature on the efficient use of software and hypermedia. Finally, the chapter discusses how approaches to curriculum development and teaching and learning might be fashioned as a consequence.

There has recently been a major shift in the way in which we live, learn and work as part of a global change—the coming of the information age. The National Office for the Information Economy in Australia (1998) reported these changes as follows. In many places around the world, learners now use computers at home and at school as part of everyday practice. Governments are increasingly providing services and information online. People undertake banking, borrowing and investing of monies electronically. Businesses offer goods and services on Websites and, correspondingly, consumers make purchases by browsing virtual shops. The Internet makes it possible to make payments, and to stay in touch with friends and family members across great distances. Businesses and governments can exchange documents, students can do university degrees, corporations can do training and like-minded people from around the world can use chatrooms to share common interests. Intending travellers can visit other parts of their country or the rest of the world and make reservations. You can visit the most influential art galleries and libraries, as well as the most famous national parks. At the heart of the information revolution is that the way people do the central things in life—leisure and work—is changing.

What we now have is a world of electronic commerce where distance is of little consequence and where commerce and human activities are seamlessly global. This new kind of economy has been termed the 'knowledge economy' and is seen to be that which is replacing the industrial economy of the past.

Information is becoming a critical resource and every day we are seeing its volume grow exponentially. As a consequence, critical new skills are necessary to enable one to deal effectively with this resource. For example, it is no longer enough to know how to get information relevant to a task; it is also necessary to know how to extract meaning from it as well. Such new skills are seen to be linked to one's potential income-earning capacity. For example, Lepani (1998) argues that, within a knowledge economy, one creates value by going up the hierarchy of knowledge and this demands a progression from simple cognition to meta-cognition to epistemic cognition, and finally to wisdom cognition. Thus developing skills to manage and manipulate information (information literacy) is seen as a core skill necessary to function effectively in the world today.

WORK IN THE KNOWLEDGE ECONOMY

The information age is clearly reshaping life generally and work in particular (Zuboff 1988). This reshaping in relation to new work practices in manufacturing and business services is discussed below. These two disparate contexts of work were examined by Hirschhorn and Mokray (1992) and serve to highlight the similarities to the changes to work practice that are the consequence of the impact of information technology and a knowledge economy. Hirschhorn and Mokray note that whereas hands once made a quality product, now a machine makes it while we watch through an interface. The workers they studied noted that they more often used their heads than their hands. That is, they had to cope with greater variety and complexity and consequently had to remember more. Skills, therefore, have become more head-based and linked to the activities of controlling, planning and consciously remembering.

Workers have shifted their focus to a broader perspective and, rather than focus on the instantaneous interaction between tools and materials, now observe a broader pattern of events. Hirschhorn and Mokray (1992) summarise these shifts in the nature of tools as from 'a single tool' to a 'system of tools'; from 'a discontinuity between material and tool' to 'a seamless interaction of material and tool'; from 'a sensory feedback at the juncture of the tool and materials' to 'cognitive feedback at the interface between the system and the person'; and from 'tools that narrow the worker's focus' to 'tools that broaden the worker's focus' (Hirschhorn & Mockray 1990, p. 21).

As a consequence, workers are now required to master a greater range of problem situations, and this quantitative shift also restructures the problem domain. As workers are increasingly using automated tools systems, problem-solving is becoming more both more abstract and complex in nature. Hirschhorn and Mokray (1992) suggest that this in turn requires workers to focus on 'flow and pattern rather than on a single piece and the particular puzzle it presents'. They articulate this changing nature of problems from 'a few parameters' to 'many parameters'; from 'correcting' to 'preventing variance'; from 'sustaining levels of output' to 'variances sustaining quality'; from 'puzzles: a single piece' to 'patterns: the flow, the linkages'; and from 'within a single operation' to 'across several operations' (Hirschhorn & Mockray 1990, p. 23).

Problem-solving has always been linked to the act of undertaking work in both routine and non-routine ways. However, the nature of this problem-solving has been reshaped by the changing nature of work itself. Much of this problem-solving relies on the capacity to extract meaning from the information relevant to the task and to be able to engage with this information as it provides the interface between systems and individuals.

Two examples of this reshaping, identified earlier, are discussed next as a way of understanding the impact of the knowledge economy on work. The manufacturing and business services sectors are the examples used. By business services I mean the administrative functions that support business operations and therefore can be found across all industries, including manufacturing.

Manufacturing

Hirschhorn and Mokray (1992) examined the competencies necessary for organisations and workers in manufacturing industries as they took up computer technology. They found that competencies were shaped by skills and roles and argue that skills are shaped by a plant's technical infrastructure, and roles by the plant's social system. This suggests that the skills workers need are shaped by the tools they use and the problems they face. Workers facing difficult problems using simple tools need significant skills. Those working with powerful tools may still need significant skills, especially when they must solve continually changing problems. Hirschhorn and Mokray (1992) argue that the concept of skill alone is insufficient to understand a person's efficacy at work. Skills must always be potentiated by the context in which they are exercised.

With new computer-controlled plant, the ways in which workers interact between raw materials and tools change significantly. Firstly, tools systems have become more integrated and there is less disjunction between the raw materials and the tools for transforming them. For example, a manufacturing worker undertaking a manual task would physically control the interactions between the tools (e.g. saw or drill) and the materials with which they are working. The new worker does not experience these interactions in the same way. Within computer-controlled systems, there is a continuous interaction between tools and material and the worker observes the consequences of this interaction. Thus the tools and the materials are integrated and the worker no longer gets direct sensory data from this interplay, but instead gets data from an interface (e.g. computer screen or printed report). Thus the role of the worker has shifted from a capacity to manage the interactions between tools and materials to managing data as the information passing between the system and the individual.

Business services

An important phenomenon of the early twenty-first century is the ubiquity of the computer in the workplace. The western world, in particular, has been moving towards a knowledge- and information-based economy as manufacturing industries have contracted. This has given rise to a workforce that uses computers as a tool for everyday work tasks, collectively referred to as 'information workers'. There are two commonly accepted types of information workers: *knowledge workers* (those who primarily create new information and knowledge); and *data workers* (who primarily use, manipulate or disseminate information) (Laudon & Laudon 1991). Knowledge workers are spread across all industries, whereas data workers are concentrated in service industries, finance and government (Laudon & Laudon 1991).

Like workers in the manufacturing industries, the tool systems used by knowledge and data workers are becoming more integrated (e.g. Microsoft Office, high-level programming languages and phone and data systems). For data workers, the nature of their work is increasingly hidden from them by the tools they employ to undertake that work. That is, the transformation of the data they input is facilitated, in a largely opaque or invisible way, by the computer-controlled systems they operate. Thus the information they produce is a result of the automation of the tools they use rather than the physical manipulation of tools (cash book, filing cabinet) and the materials (raw data and source documents), as was the case before the pervasive use of computers.

INFORMATION LITERACY FOR WORK

The previous sections argue that having information literacy for work requires one to possess a capacity to employ a system of (information) tools that allows for the interaction of materials with these tools in order to solve problems of increasing complexity. Hirschhorn and Mokray (1992) contend that such a competence is a function of both skills and roles, arguing that skills must always be potentiated by the context in which they are exercised.

Clearly, then, information literacy is something that most of us accept as necessary for living and working in the knowledge society in which we currently find ourselves. Most of us would believe that we understand what 'information literacy' means, yet these understandings will be shown to vary considerably according to our individual functions, purposes and experiences in using them. What is meant by the term 'information literacy' will largely depend upon whom you ask and in what circumstances.

The *Oxford Dictionary* offers a starting point for developing an understanding of this term. It describes information as 'telling; what is told; knowledge; news'. This is not particularly useful, however, as most of us would consider information to be more than just telling or being told. Further, we would consider information as something capable of allowing us to build the knowledge necessary to make sense of our world. At any given moment, we are receiving all kinds of information via our senses. As a result, we are constantly 'awash' with information of various kinds. Thus information takes on many and complex forms. Seeing, touching and smelling would seem as important as hearing and saying.

The information with which we work is also stored in a number of ways. The dictionary definition tends to suggest that the storage takes place in our memories (telling, and being told); however, for many thousands of years information has been stored by humans in other ways. Far back in time we know that humans stored information by way of recording it outside of their brain (e.g. cave paintings). In fact, anthropologists argue that this human capacity, along with language, has led to the development of our mental superiority over other species. Thus information has many manifestations in the modern world.

Literacy, on the other hand, is described by the *Oxford Dictionary* as 'the ability to read and write'. In Chapter 3, Jean Searle convincingly argues that this is a somewhat narrow view of literacy. Joining these two dictionary definitions seems to be inadequate in describing what 'information literacy' is.

The work of Gee (1990) is helpful in this regard, as he broadens the concept of literacy and contends 'that most traditional approaches to literacy talk about literacy as an individual possession, a set of capacities that resides somewhere in the individual brain' (Gee 1990, p. 42), much like the dictionary. He suggests that this approach is problematic and that: 'Literacy surely means nothing unless it has something to do with the ability to read. "Read" is a transitive verb. So literacy must have something to do with being able to read *something*' (Gee 1990, p. 42). To read something meaningfully requires the reader to have different types of background knowledge in order to derive meaning from the something. Further, Scribner (1983) puts forward the view that literacy is a social practice and suggests that we see it as a term applying to a varied and open set of activities with written language.

From this we are able to suggest that 'information literacy' is having a capacity to be able to do something meaningfully with information in its multiple manifestations. What it is exactly you might meaningfully do with information will largely depend on the way in which you might engage with it, and for what purpose. For example, it might be that you do nothing further with it, or that you trade information (e.g. casual conversation or educating a sibling), or that you use information in your social or working life. Clearly, then, the term 'information literacy' will have multiple meanings depending on the circumstances and the context of its use.

In the print society, literacy has been the ability to read and write, and through this to be able to be a fully participating member of society (Lepani 1998). In the global knowledge society, with its technological infrastructure of computers and multimedia, literacy is being extended beyond reading print and writing with a pen. The resulting information literacy is electronically based and includes complex visual and aural language. Lepani (1998) suggests that, in the knowledge society with its informational mode of production, we will need to become knowledge navigators as both learners and workers.

In this chapter, 'information literacy' will be confined to its meaning as a capacity to collect, store and transform the information required for workplace application. Thus it will be examined from the context of it being a work-based skill. This has not been done to diminish the significance of other ways of defining it, but rather to focus this chapter on one important aspect: that of its workplace significance. Workplaces are being transformed as a consequence of the move towards a knowledge economy, and some aspects of this are discussed next.

It is therefore not surprising that the importance of 'information literacy' skills has been associated with the employment and education policy of national governments throughout the world during the last decade. Many of these policies conceive of 'information literacy' as being a functional competence necessary for the modern workplace and capable of being defined and learnt. In this context, 'information literacy' as a functional competence is afforded description in a number of ways. These include descriptions by national governments, educations systems, academics, teachers and industry, each of which attempts to give information literacy application. Each of these descriptions is explored below.

Government

Descriptions by western governments have generally been cast in terms of seeing information literacy as a workplace competence. Increased usage of competency models to drive workplace learning has taken place in the United States (Boyatzis & Kolb 1995), the United Kingdom (Newton & Wilkenson 1995), Australia (Beven 1997; Stevenson 1996) and the Scandinavian countries (Mabon 1995). This can be attributed to the stances taken by the national governments in these countries on the benefits that can accrue through the creation and adoption of recognisable competency standards. As a result, 'information literacy' has received attention in these standards as there is broad agreement that knowledge processes and products are central to success in the competitive environment of the new economy.

A key platform in this movement has been a concern to identify sets of essential generic workplace skills that employers need. During the late 1980s and early 1990s, similar development efforts took place in the United States, Australia and the United Kingdom (see Table 5.1).

Kearns (2001) reports that these countries have adopted two alternative approaches to key workplace competencies. He argues that the US model involves a broader, more flexible and more holistic set of generic skills which include basic skills, personal attributes, values and ethics, learning to learn as well as workplace competencies. The Anglo/Australian model, on the other hand, was influenced by the approach to competency-based training adopted in both countries, which has resulted in a more narrowly focused and instrumental set of key skills/key competencies that are broadly similar, but with one significant difference. In both countries, personal attributes and values have largely been excluded.

In a recent review of research on generic skills for the Australian government, Kearns (2001) has mapped a comparison of the Australian Key Competencies against the key skills from the United States, the United

Table 5.1 Generic (key) workplace skills frameworks

Country	Initiative	Year
United States	American Society of Training and Development and Department of Labor (ASTD/DOL); Workplace Basics: The Skills Employers Want	1988
	SCANS Commission Framework of Workplace Know-how	1992
United Kingdom	Key Skills (Core Skills)	1990
Australia	Mayer Key Competencies	1992

Table 5.2 Comparison of key skills in Australia, the United States and New Zealand

Key Competencies (Australia)	UK (NCVQ) Core Skills	US (SCANS) Workplace Know-how	NZ Essential Skills
Collecting, analysing and organising information	Communication	Information; Foundations skills: basic skills	Information skills
Communicating ideas and information	Communication; personal skills: improving own learning and performance	Communication skills	
Planning and organising activities	Personal skills: improving own learning and performance	Resources: foundation skills; personal qualities	Self-management skills; work study skills
Working with others and in teams	Personal skills: working with others	Interpersonal skills	Social skills; work study skills
Using mathematical ideas and techniques	Numeracy: application of number	Foundation skills: basic skills	Numeracy skills
Solving problems	Problem-solving	Foundation skills: thinking skills	Problem-solving and decision-making skills
Using technology	Information technology; modern foreign language	Technology systems	Information skills; communication skills

Note: Where the UK Core Skills, US Workplace Know-how and NZ Essential Skills are comparable with more than one key competency, they have been repeated.
Source: Mayer (1992, p. 11) as reproduced in Kearns (2001, p. 15)

Kingdom and New Zealand. The similarities between these frameworks are evident, as is the inclusion of information literacy skills in each.

This comparison clearly shows the importance placed on information literacy by various governments when developing their various sets of 'key' workplace competencies. In the Australian framework, information literacy is accounted for primarily in the 'Collecting, analysing and organising ideas and information' key competency, although aspects of 'Using technology' are also involved. 'Collecting, analysing and organising ideas and information' is seen as the processes of gathering and managing information that are constantly changing and evolving under the impact of technological development. The summary statement that the development committee issued (see Table 5.3) best illustrates this.

In contrast, 'Using technology' is seen as the capacity to use technological processes, systems, equipment and materials. The notion of 'using' is seen as extending from the skills of operating equipment to the use of technology to explore ideas, in order to pursue understanding (see Table 5.4). Thus competencies in gathering, managing and the analysis of information, as well as using technology, were seen as both emergent and critical in 1992.

Therefore, using the technology of computing for informational purposes could, for example, relate to the:

- skills necessary for data workers to manipulate technology for routine work related purposes;
- skills necessary for knowledge workers who use computers as a more transformative tool; and
- capacity of manufacturing workers to use technology to produce products.

Clearly, during the last decade, governments throughout the world have found it important to focus attention on the identification of a set

Table 5.3 Extract from the summary of the key competency 'Collecting, analysing and organising ideas and information'

Key Competency strand	Performance Level 1	Performance Level 2	Performance Level 3
Collecting, analysing and organising ideas and information	Access and record pieces of information from a single source	Access, select and organise information from more than one source	Access, evaluate and organise information from a range of sources

Source: Mayer (1992)

Table 5.4 Extract from the summary of the key competency 'Using technology'

Key Competency strand	Performance Level 1	Performance Level 2	Performance Level 3
Using technology	Reproduce or present a basic product or service	Construct, organise or operate products or services	Design or tailor products or services

Source: Mayer (1992)

of key functional employment-related competencies as an aspect of economic policy. This is particularly true of those countries that have adopted a competency approach to vocational education (Garavan & McGuire 2001). The inclusion of information literacy as part of this suite of skills does seem congruent with and reflective of the requirements of a knowledge-based economy. Consequently, these key workplace skills are seen as an essential component of any curriculum associated with preparing individuals for work. Thus information literacy in its various guises is viewed as an essential component of all work-related curricula.

With information literacy becoming more pervasive within vocational curriculum, it has received the attention of both researchers and teachers. Researchers have tried to give it meaning by examining it within workplace practice in an effort both to define it better and to gain an understanding of its relationship with other aspects of work. Teachers, on the other hand, have been trying to give it application in learning—that is, to situate it within its various contexts of practice. These two aspects are discussed next.

RESEARCH

The notion of information literacy is multi-faceted and, as a consequence, research is occurring across many disciplines and contexts. In this section of the chapter, three areas of research are discussed: information literacy at work; efficient use of software; and hypermedia. I am not suggesting that this is representative of all the research taking place, but rather that these three areas might represent the richness of this research.

Examining information literacy in the workplace

As key skills are described in a generic way, they necessarily have multiple meanings related to their specific use in practice. Examination of workplace practice is starting to provide a better understanding of information literacy as it applies to specific tasks undertaken as part of various kinds of employment. Information literacy practices amongst front office staff of motels (Beven 1996) and airline service officers operating customer service counters (Beven 1997) provide some insights into the kinds of skills and capacities that staff employ when using computer (database) software to engage in their work practice. These studies attempted to ascertain the nature of the knowledge (information literacy) that was being deployed by workers and the extent to which competence gained in one setting might be transferable to other settings.

'Domain-specific' knowledge and skills were taken as providing a worker with the ability to undertake tasks proficiently (Gott 1989). In contrast, 'generic' knowledge and skills were taken as being more domain-independent, and as being transferable across and between tasks (Stasz et al. 1990). Using such a framework in the workplace, then, competent practice would require a practitioner to draw upon both 'domain-specific' and 'generic' knowledge and skills. The purpose of these studies was to examine such a hypothesised separation of specific and generic knowledge in the workplace.

Database software required users to undertake tasks within structured menus and predetermined screen layouts designed by the software author. To manipulate data within the software effectively, users were required to use icons, codes, keys assigned specific functions and a variety of key sequences both to navigate through the system and to enter data. By its very nature, computer software is often very deterministic and unforgiving, and requires the user to be very precise. It also requires the user to develop a well-defined conceptual map of the systems and sub-systems. Thus proficient use of the software requires not only system knowledge including skills, but also the development of system-specific literacy and numeracy skills. Moreover, the effective use of the software requires an appropriate interaction between the above-mentioned skills.

A taxonomy of database knowledge was used as a framework against which to map the knowledge used in the workplace. The map provided a structure from which to examine the nature of the knowledge and skills used in operating computerised motel and airline reservation systems. Whether or not the knowledge required to work effectively was shared across sites enabled the researchers to determine the extent to which it was context-specific or 'generic'.

Motel front office practice

The first study was of the use of database software by front office staff who manage motel reservations processes and associated management systems. Two analyses undertaken in this study indicate that considerations about the 'generic' nature of knowledge and skills can be made at different levels of generality and abstraction. For example, the use of software menus can be regarded as having similarities (being conceptually generic) at an abstract level, across sites. For instance, similar tasks could be accessed via a menu (see Figures 5.1, 5.2 and 5.3) at each of the investigation sites.

However, at a more specific level from an operator's standpoint, little similarity existed between the menu structures at each site. That is, the abstract similarities were not meaningful at the concrete level of operation because an operator was required to deploy different keystrokes for each menu. Similarly, while the analysis of data entry strategies could be conceptualised as similar across sites (i.e. use of function keys, look-up tables, on-screen instruction), at a more concrete level of operations, little commonality was found to exist in the strategies used across sites in undertaking the same activity. For example, to check in a new reservation at each of the sites required the informant at Site A to Enter numeric key 1, at Site C to press the ENTER key; and at Site D to press the Function key 2 (F2).

It is clear that the levels of abstraction and generality have a significant effect on the validity of assigning a 'generic' label to the knowledge identified in this study. The more concrete the level of examination, the less likely it is that the knowledge or skill can be labelled 'generic'.

RESERVATIONS
Thursday November 8 1995

	Functions		**Inquiries**
1.	Check in	20.	Guest inquiry
2.	Group check in	21.	Today waitlist inquiry
3.	Reservation for today	22.	Guest history inquiry
		23.	VCP inquiry
		24.	Group master inquiry
4.	Change guest information	25.	Availability inquiry
		26.	Blocked rooms inquiry
6.	Same day cancellations	27.	Room back inquiry
7.	Maintain links	28.	House count inquiry
		29.	Floor plan inquiry
9.	Flagged comments maintenance		

	Inquiries		**Alternative Functions**
30.	Expected arrivals inquiry	61.	Check in
31.	Room reserve calendar	62.	Check out
32.	Guest information inquiry	63.	Guest transaction posting
33.	Room availability	64.	Room availability inquiry
		65.	Reservation inquiry
Enter Selection:		66.	Guest inquiry

Figure 5.1 Main menu at Site A

```
DMS Version 2.35              RESERVATIONS              8:41 am 12/08/95

                              New Reservation

                     Press ENTER to begin a New Reservation

                           Find Existing Reservation

                       By:              Current           All
                Guest Name =              F1              F7
               Phone Number =             F2              F8
               Room Number =              F3              F9
                Group Name =              F4              F10
                Registration =            F5              F11
                Other Fields =            F6              F12

              Registration Number =      [TAB]


Reservation Required:
```

Figure 5.2 Main menu at Site C

```
Front Menu              XXXXX Lodge XXXXX         11/11/95  12:40:33 pm

                              Front Menu

         F1     For System Help                        Manual Ref

         F2     Reservations                               3
         F3     Registration                               4
         F4     Check Out and Cashier                      5
         F5     Operator Assistance                       6–1
         F6     Availability Summary                     2.2.3
         F7     Availability Report                      2.2.2
         F8     Housekeeping Menu                          6
         F9     In-House Financial Summary              9.3.16
```

Figure 5.3 Main menu at Site D

It would seem that the labelling of skills and knowledge as 'generic' can be validated at an abstract 'conceptual' level; however, the genericity falls down at a more concrete or 'operational' level. That is, the generic label is not useful for practical activity. Moreover, the knowledge needed for the activity would not be known in terms of the 'generic' label. Further, if it were known in terms of the generic label, it would not necessarily be accessible as such for the tasks.

Thus the 'generic' knowledge identified in this investigation may not be sufficient to complete tasks successfully at a more concrete (operational) level. At this operational level, success seems to depend much more on 'domain-specific' knowledge. This is not to suggest that 'generic' skills are therefore worthless, but rather supports the view that 'generic' skills may be impossible to apply if the user lacks 'domain-specific' knowledge (Resnick 1987). Knowing that a function of a reservation system is available through a menu structure is important; however, the lack of knowledge of the correct synonym to enable the process will inhibit its successful completion. Therefore, attempting to teach knowledge only as 'generic' might in fact be non-productive. Evidence to this effect has been provided by Lester, who reported 'that teaching students about problem-solving strategies and heuristic methods and phases of problem-solving does little to improve students' ability to solve mathematical problems' (Lester 1994, p. 666).

Airline customer service

The use of a computer database by airline customer service staff was the focus of a second investigation. The respondents worked on customer service counters where they engaged with the flying public and dealt with a diverse range of customer inquiries ranging from simple flight changes through to very complex reticketing and fare recalculations often associated with multiple carriers. From the first study, it was concluded that the more concrete the level of examination, the less likely it is that the knowledge or skills can be labelled 'generic'. That study revealed that the level of abstraction of knowledge necessary to make it 'generic' may reduce its meaningfulness for successful completion of a task, without accompanying 'domain-specific' knowledge. This study sought to establish whether the previous findings would hold in a different, but allied, workplace context.

Airline customer service officers interact with database software to inform their dealings with customers. To do so, they need to be able to communicate effectively with the database. These communications have two important aspects: firstly, a capacity to construct a request; and secondly, a capacity to interpret a response. In the workplaces examined in this study, the informants made database requests by constructing mnemonic forms, and received responses as screen displays. Different kinds of knowledge were needed to undertake both aspects effectively.

Making requests to the database required knowledge of the language, abbreviations and codes that made up a mnemonic, as well as knowledge of the general principles of mnemonic construction. During the period under investigation, one informant constructed 427 mnemonics within 60 transactions. These mnemonics ranged from a simple '\l' to a complex 'BAV5445643991093113,02-98, K W WHITTONs', as well as coded remarks such as 'RMK TKT WAS LEFT BY COLLEAGUES FOR PAX WAS TO BE REBKD AND PAY UPG BUT THEY DID NOT RBK SO NOSHOWED'. Correct construction of the mnemonic was vital to succeeding with any action. It was apparent that the lead characters (usually 2–5) of the mnemonic were significant in informing the software of the type of request.

Some of the knowledge needed to construct mnemonics was 'context-specific' and centred around unique software commands. Additionally, knowledge of 'generic' principles of mnemonic construction, as well as 'generic' knowledge about where to obtain critical data, was also necessary. The 'generic' knowledge identified here seemed vital to the ability of the informant to construct so many codes in the course of the day. Yet this 'generic' knowledge was incapable of being useful alone. It was the 'context-specific' knowledge of the software codes (the initial part of the mnemonic) that the computer also acted upon. What was apparent was the synergy of both kinds of knowledge to the process of database manipulation. It would be impossible for the informant to memorise all the possible computations of data as codes, and therefore they must be capable of drawing upon the 'generic' principles of mnemonic construction to produce them effectively.

The informant often had to make use of the only available data. Data such as names, flight numbers and dates of travel were critical to the construction of many of the mnemonics, yet often the data could not be supplied by the customer at the commencement of a transaction. As a consequence, 'similar' transactions were constructed differently, and those with limited data were often more complex than those in which the necessary data were available. This point was highlighted where, across six transactions of a similar task (see Table 5.5), the number of sub-actions in which the informant used a mnemonic ranged from three to 39. Such variations suggest that it would be difficult to learn this task as a series of structured steps.

In dealing with highly codified screens, the informant had developed ways to reduce the cognitive load by training himself to see only those aspects of the screen that he regularly dealt with. Further, he had developed a capacity to access similar types of data in appropriate informational contexts. This capacity often enabled him to reduce the number of transactions (*actions*) necessary to complete a task (*event*). Another skill observed was selecting shortcut or 'linking' mnemonics to move between screens. These had the effect of reducing the complexity of mnemonics, as well as narrowing the search to a smaller data set.

Table 5.5 Comparison of mnemonics used in generic context 5 of Event 'Issuing Ticket'

Event 1	Event 2
BADC136473866895856,03-96,G N PETERS	RTBOOTH549.BNESYD
DT	RFB964984
SYS00	RTBOOTH506-SYDBNE
RTHLGFW	RTWILLIAMS
SG586ESYD	506-SYDBNE
BNEKK1	RT3
XE	SG586Y.SYD
\	BNE1
	XE2
	SG549.BNE
	SD1
	Adds 'Y' to above data - SG549Y.BNE
	SYD1
	BADC13647548877153383.05-98, C D WILLIAMS
	T
	CTSYD/132628
	DT
	RTBOOTH586-SYD
	SG506Y.SYD
	BNE1
	E2
	SGS549Y.BNE
	SYD1
	ADC136474587690696,11-97 C BOOTH
	DT
	TSYD/
	TELSTRA
	DT
	SY586

Event 3	Event 4
RTHT42E	RTHT42E
DAVC544948259971,05-97, J C LEWIS/P1	DAVC544848259971,05-97, J C LEWIS/P1
DTP1	DTP1

Event 5	Event 6
RTHALL482.SYDGOL	PD508,1MIL
PM	RT2
RTHALL486.SYDGOL	PN
FP	PF
RT	PN
CHQ80627923219658,WESP AC	DTC/P2
DT	
PD417.1GRIF	
PD: QF417/30MA YBSYD,GRI1	

continued

Event 5	Event 6
PR2	
RT 2	
PW	
P	
T	

The random accessibility provided no logical linking between screens, nor did it provide the informant with any sense of structure. None of the screens provided screen-based links to, or associations with, any other screen. Consequently, navigating between screens relied on the informant having an holistic understanding of the complete screen set. This random accessibility, whilst providing maximum flexibility in terms of access (i.e. no screen was more than a mnemonic away), gave little assistance to the informant. As a consequence, mnemonic constructions appeared to be situationally determined and context-specific in nature.

There were also 'generic' features in display across all screens that can be identified in command driven software. For example, the end of a display was always signalled by the return of the cursor; mnemonics, once entered, were overwritten by the displayed data; data were not automatically removed from the screen—rather, the screen scrolled, having the effect of leaving a history of actions; data that could be subject to a linking mnemonic was identified with a line number; and the data contained in 'Passenger Information' screens always commenced with line numbers. Knowledge of these 'generic' features permitted the informant to recognise structure in the displays, identify possible linking points and make changes as required. Unlike many database programs with more graphical displays, delineation between label and data is much less obvious on these text-based screens.

As in the case of making requests to the database, understanding displays required the informant to draw upon both 'generic' and 'context-dependent' knowledge. Whilst the 'generic' knowledge identified here was critical for the informant to both locate and order data for interpretation, 'context-specific' knowledge associated with the idiosyncratic nature of the data display and of the codification of that display was also necessary.

Examination of the data showed that, to use database software effectively, a user has to call upon aspects of both 'generic' and 'context-specific' knowledge. Both sorts of knowledge played a crucial but different role in the process examined. This analysis indicates that 'generic' knowledge and skills can be conceptualised only at a more abstract level of the task. In contrast, 'context-specific' knowledge seems to be involved in operating at a more concrete transactional level of the task. At the more abstract level, similarities that allow tasks to be grouped 'generically' can be identified. However, examination of tasks at the operational or concrete level shows little evidence of generality. What is clear from this study is that 'generic' knowledge may not be sufficient to complete tasks successfully at a more concrete (operational) level. At a concrete level, success seems to depend much more on 'context-specific' knowledge. What was apparent in this study was the synergy of the role between both kinds of knowledge in the process of database manipulation.

In the work practices examined in both studies, there appeared to be a boundary between different types of workplace knowledge—in particular, between the more abstract conceptualisation of knowledge and the more concrete use of that knowledge. These studies add further support to the view that 'generic' skills may be impossible to apply if the user lacks 'context-specific' knowledge. Further, conceiving of knowledge as being either 'generic' or 'specific' might not be useful educationally. The studies have shown that, in the workplaces examined, the knowledge required for effective practice was both rich in nature and adapted to its particular situation. Although knowledge could be abstracted to a level of genericity, its loss of meaningfulness seemed to render such an abstraction pointless.

Efficient use of software

Research by Bhavnani (2000) and Bhavnani et al. (2001) found that, despite experience, many users do not make efficient use of complex computer applications. They argue that this is due to a lack of strategic knowledge, which they assert is difficult to acquire just by knowing how to use commands. In a controlled study, they compared experimental groups in which they taught both strategic knowledge as well as commands with control groups who were taught the traditional method of just commands. These experiments showed that strategic knowledge can be explicitly and successfully taught in combination with commands, and that more that half of the students in an experimental group employed these strategies in a post-test. What was harder for them to qualify was the extent to which the strategy knowledge had taken on a general form and was then applied in other situations. However, if the strategy is not learned at a general level, it is less likely to be used in other situations involving different commands.

Whilst these experiments showed that some strategies might be acquired automatically just by learning commands, they also showed that other important strategies are not acquired easily but can be learned as a result of explicit instruction. Further, the authors claim that learning both strategic knowledge and command knowledge does not require extra time or harm the acquisition of command knowledge. They also assert that the addition of strategic knowledge to teaching has the potential to enable transfer of strategic knowledge across different applications.

These findings complement the findings from the workplace study detailed previously. That is, a focus only on command knowledge (specific knowledge) is counter-productive when developing information literacy skills in software usage. The efficient use of computer software seems to be dependent upon the acquisition of both strategic (generic) and command (specific) knowledge.

Hypermedia

Hypermedia is a new form of information access which is highly attractive to users because, on the surface at least, it leaves them in full control of that access while at the same time making it extremely easy. Hypermedia provides an environment that promotes the active, personal exploration of information for both comprehension and facts (Welsh 1995). Some characteristics of hypertext are that it is hierarchically organised information (text, pictures, graphics, sound, video) 'with associative or referential links able to be manipulated using a graphical user interface (GUI)' (Lai & Waugh 1995, p. 26). It is a network of ideas/concepts connected on the bases of their associative or referential links in addition to organisational links and suitable for information searching and retrieval. Duchastel (1990) sees the important features of hypermedia as being:

- non-linear access to information;
- varied information access;
- integrated information access;
- ease of access to information; and
- free access to information.

This implies that information-seeking is the fundamental underlying hypermedia activity, one which Jonassen and Grabinger (1990) describe as 'a fundamental learning activity, precursive to many others' (1990, p. 13), and which Marchionini sees as a 'special case of problem-solving' (1989, p. 57). Research shows that information searchers prefer facilities such as keyword search or index mechanisms (Joseph et al. 1989); however, where search questions are vague, people tend to resort to browsing or exploring strategies (Marchionini & Shneiderman 1988). Marchionini (1992) proposes a framework for information-seeking tasks that reflects the iterative, non-linear and opportunistic characteristics he sees as typical of end-user information-seeking patterns. In contrast, Wright (1990, pp. 176–8) attempts to impose some structure on the search process by proposing that six different types of search tasks can be identified. He describes these as:

- search target simple and fully known;
- search target simple but only partially known;
- search target complex and fully known;
- search target computed from online tradeoffs and feedback from the computer;
- search target simple but unspecifiable to a computer; and
- search target unrecognisable for the purposes of terminating the search.

Identifying search processes in this way seems to be useful for two reasons. Firstly, these processes can be thought of as a range of strategies available to users to reach different information search outcomes. Secondly, this diversity of search processes would also require users to develop and make use of a range of cognitive activities and structures.

The cognitive processes involved in hypermedia usage are similar to those involved in two other domains: information retrieval and reading (Duchastel 1990). Duchastel states that the information retrieval aspects of hypermedia lie in its navigational capabilities, which involve searching and browsing. In terms of the reading aspects of hypermedia, it is not concerned with the processing of language, but rather with aspects involved with comprehension, and includes knowledge processing from both graphical and textual information. Duchastel identifies four cognitive processes that seem central to hypermedia interaction: browsing; searching; integrating; and angling:

> *Browsing* is what hypermedia is principally for. Browsing is encouraged by the presence of buttons (links) which signal to the user that related information is available. *Searching* is another cognitive process continually activated by hypermedia. Searching occurs in response to a question that might be quite specific through to quite broad. The more specific the question the more straightforward the search is. *Integrating* is the global process of learning that cognitive psychology recognises most clearly. It involves the structural character of knowledge as knowledge is constructed by the learner. It is the active process involved in understanding, and consists in interrelating conceptual elements of knowledge in a coherent semantic net. *Angling* is the term used to denote the active process involved in establishing different perspectives on a topic of knowledge (viewing it from different angles). Being capable of examining multiple perspectives not only adds to the learner's knowledge of the topic, but also can potentially enhance higher skills such as critical thinking (Duchastel 1990, p. 227).

These four cognitive processes can be grouped into two broader processes. Browsing and searching together form the user's capacity to reach out into an information space. The user goes out to access new information. Integrating and angling, on the other hand, form an internal review of information in order to consolidate the information retrieved. The user looks inwards to ensure coherence in the understanding of the information to hand. Thus, in a hypermedia interaction, there is a constant and dynamic flow outwards and inwards in the processing of information. These cognitive processes would seem to have important implications for both work and education for work. That is, the development of these capacities is critical to workers who manipulate information.

Summary

This section has attempted to show how research is able to provide important and often different insights regarding information literacy and how it might best be developed. In summary, it informs us that conceiving of information literacy as a 'generic' skill that can be separately identified and taught has a tendency to both trivialise its complexity and devalue its importance in the development of workplace skills. The examination of workplace practice suggests that it is important for learners to develop their information literacies holistically within the context of their workplace application. This does not render obsolete the need to make explicit those aspects that are 'generic' and transferable to other tasks and contexts. The hypermedia literature provides an understanding about how information can be accessed as well as the kinds of cognitive skills needed to do this successfully. It also provides clues to educators about how they might construct learning to help learners to both reach into information spaces and to consolidate and make sense of the information they retrieve. The research by Bhavnani (2000) demonstrates that generic (or strategic) knowledge, as well as the context-specific (command) knowledge, can be taught and learned synergistically, using no more time and with greater success as measured by test results. These aspects have consequences for both curriculum development and teaching practice, which are discussed next.

IMPLICATIONS FOR CURRICULUM DEVELOPMENT

Literacy commentators have recently foreshadowed the need for change in our thinking about literacy curricula. For example, Lepani (1998) wrote about the end of the print society in which literacy has been the ability to read and write in order to become a fully participating member of a democratic society. This was usually accomplished through a Kindergarten to Year 12 compulsory education system, followed sometimes by some form of higher or vocational education. She believes that, in the emerging global knowledge society and its technological infrastructure of computers and multimedia, education is becoming lifelong and literacy has to be extended beyond reading print and writing with a pen. Spender (1995) supports this view with her assertion that literacy is more than the mechanics of comprehension; it is about the making and communicating of meaning. She argues that, in future education systems, it may also no longer be a matter of knowing information, but a matter of doing it. The previous section of this chapter provides a preliminary insight into what 'doing it' might mean.

Yet current practices of curriculum development in the western world (discussed earlier) seem overly simplistic and largely ignore what this research is saying. For example, the development of 'generic' competencies like the Australian example of 'Using technology' seems to ignore the context-specificity highlighted as critical in the research literature. Current curriculum documents continue to identify 'generic' competencies as important but separate entities. As a consequence, this causes a press on vocational educators to teach 'generic' skills which might in fact be non-productive, as research indicates that 'generically identified knowledge' alone is insufficient to secure success at a task. What needs more attention in both curriculum documents and training practice is a recognition of the importance of both kinds of knowledge and the synergistic relationship they have in securing successful workplace practice. Therefore, seeing information literacy as the highly complex, integrated and interconnected notion that it is becomes the first step in ensuring that the teaching and learning strategies adopted to develop it are appropriate. Some recommendations for teaching, drawn from research, follow.

RECOMMENDATIONS FOR TEACHING

The following is a set of specific recommendations for curriculum developers and teachers developing classroom practice. These are a distillation of the argument and recommendations drawn from the many works that have been used in constructing this chapter. Whilst they specifically address the acquisition of information literacy, they ought also to be viewed as having wider application.

1. Recalling prior knowledge from identical or similar actions is central to competent workplace learning. Teachers need to ensure they make such connections explicit to learners.
2. Contextual aspects of the workplace, as well as a focus on functional tasks, are important to learning for work. Learning from only paper-based examples (as is often the case in classrooms) denies the learner access to the nuances and conditional aspects

of, for example, interacting with a customer. When assessing competencies associated with non-routine skills such as issuing tickets, a problem-based action learning approach may prove more effective.
3. The current tendency is to teach computing skills by taking the learner through highly structured exercises, often using self-paced modules. This may serve to develop routine procedural skills. However, this method is unlikely to produce skills for non-routine tasks that would better be served by scenario-based approaches.
4. When teaching non-routine skills in which the computer is used in problem-solving, a focus on the construction of software search algorithms will assist the learner to generalise the problem-solving skills.
5. To ensure that learners know that efficient strategies exist to perform various kinds of tasks, the instruction must provide explicit strategies and indicate their effect on performance. That is, some strategies—whilst enabling task completion—are not as efficient as others.
6. To help learners know when to use a strategy, they should be given opportunities to explore alternative methods, and to decide how to select efficient methods. Furthermore, learners should be given opportunities to examine why they chose one method over the others, and to understand the tradeoffs involved.
7. To help learners learn how to deploy strategies, they must firstly have adequate practice in executing commands in the context of simple tasks, prior to executing commands on more complex tasks with the aid of suitable strategies.
8. To enable learners to transfer strategies across applications, teachers must ensure that learners use these strategies in the context of other applications, and recognise that they are the same strategies.
9. The open sharing of knowledge and information drives effective workplaces. The focus on individual development and assessment in formal learning settings (classrooms) has a tendency to discourage the same levels of sharing. A focus on more collaboration in learning could assist in minimising this effect.

REFERENCES

Beven, F. 1996, 'Using technology' in *Learning in the Workplace: Tourism and Hospitality*, ed. J. Stevenson, Centre for Learning and Work Research, Griffith University, Brisbane

—— 1997, in *Learning in the Workplace: Airline Customer Service*, ed. F. Beven, Centre for Learning and Work Research, Griffith University, Brisbane

Bhavnani, S.K. 2000, 'Designs conducive to the use of efficient strategies', *Proceedings from the DIS2000 Online Conference*, New York City, pp. 338-45

Bhavnani, S.K., Reif, F. & John, B.E. 2001, 'Beyond command knowledge: identifying and teaching strategic knowledge for using complex computer applications' , *Proceedings from the CHI 2001 Conference on Human Factors in Computing Systems*, Seattle, Washington, pp. 229-36

Boyatzis, R.E. & Kolb, D.N. 1995, 'From learning styles to learning skills: the executive skills profile', *Journal of Managerial Psychology*, vol. 10, no. 5, pp. 24-7

Duchastel, P. 1990, 'Examining cognitive processing in hypermedia usage', *Hypermedia*, vol. 2, no 3, pp. 221-33

Garavan, T.N. & McGuire, D. 2001, 'Competencies and workplace learning: some reflections on the rhetoric and the reality', *Journal of Workplace Learning*, vol. 13, no. 4, pp. 144-63

Gee J.P. 1990, *Social Linguistics and Literacies: Ideologies in Discourses*, Falmer, London

Gott, S.P. 1989, 'Apprenticeship instruction for real-world tasks: the co-ordination of procedures, mental modes, and strategies', *Review of Research in Education*, vol. 15, no 3, pp. 97-169

Hirschhorn, L. & Mokray, J. 1992, 'Automation and competency requirements in manufacturing: a case study', in *Technology and the Future of Work*, ed. P.S. Adler, Oxford University Press, New York

Jonassen, D.H. & Grabinger, R.S. 1990, 'Problems and issues in designing hypertext/hypermedia for learning', in *Designing Hypermedia for Learning*, eds D.H. Jonassen & H. Mandl, Springer-Verlag, New York

Joseph, B., Steinberg, E.R. & Jones, A.R. 1989, 'User perceptions and expectations of an information retrieval system', *Behaviour and Information Technology*, vol. 8, no. 2, pp. 77-88

Kearns, P. 2001, *Review of Research: Generic Skills for the New Economy*, National Centre for Vocational Education Research, Adelaide

Lai, Y. & Waugh, M.L. 1995, 'Effects of three different hypertextual menu designs on various information searching activities', *Journal of Educational Multimedia and Hypermedia*, vol. 4, no. 1, pp. 25-52

Laudon, K.C. & Laudon, J.P. 1991, *Managing Information Systems: A Contemporary Perspective*, 2nd edn, Maxwell McMillan International Editions, New York

Lepani, B. 1998, 'Information literacy—the challenges of the digital age', invited keynote address, *Proceedings from the 3rd National*

Information Literacy Conference, Australian Council of Adult Literacy, Canberra

Lester, F.J. 1994, 'Musing about mathematical problem solving research: 1970-1994', *Journal for Research in Mathematics Education*, vol. 25, no. 6, pp. 660-75

Mabon, H. 1995, 'Human resource management in Sweden', *Employee Relations*, vol. 17, no. 7, pp. 57-83

Marchionini, G. 1989, 'Information-seeking strategies for novices using a full-text electronic encyclopedia', *Journal of the American Society for Information Science*, vol. 40, no. 1, pp. 54-66

—— 1992, 'Interfaces for end user information seeking', *Journal of the American Society for Information Science*, vol. 43, no. 2, pp. 156-63

Marchionini, G. & Shneiderman, B. 1988, 'Finding facts vs. browsing knowledge in hypertext systems', *IEEE Computer*, vol. 21, no. 1, pp. 70-80

Mayer, E. 1992, *Employment-related Key Competencies for Post-compulsory Education and Training: A Discussion Paper*, The Mayer Committee, Australian College of Education, Melbourne

National Office for the Information Economy 1998, *Towards an Australian Strategy for the Information Economy*, Ministerial Council for the Information Economy, AGPS, Canberra

Newton, R. & Wilkenson, M.J. 1995, 'A portfolio approach to management development: the Ashworth model', *Health Manpower Management*, vol. 21, no. 3, pp. 16-31

Resnick, L. 1987, *Education and Learning to Think*, National Research Council, National Academy Press, Washington DC

Scribner, S. 1983, 'Mind in action: a functional approach to thinking', invited lecture, *Biennial meeting Society for Research in Child Development*, The Graduate School and University Center, CUNY, New York

Spender, D. 1995, *Nattering on the Net*, Spinifex, Melbourne

Stasz, C., McArthur, D., Lewis, M. & Ramsey, K. 1990, *Teaching and Learning Generic Skills in the Workplace*, National Center for Research in Vocational Education, Berkeley, CA

Stevenson, J. 1996, *Learning in the Workplace: Tourism and Hospitality*, Centre for Learning and Work Research, Griffith University, Brisbane

Welsh, T.M. 1995, 'Simplifying hypermedia usage for learners: the effect of visual and manual filtering capabilities on efficiency, perceptions and usability, and performance', *Journal of Educational Multimedia and Hypermedia*, vol. 4, no. 4, pp. 275-304

Wright, P. 1990, 'Hypertexts as an interface for learners: some human factors issues', in *Designing Hypermedia for Learning*, eds D.H. Jonassen & H. Mandl, Springer-Verlag, New York

Zuboff, S. 1988, *In the Age of the Smart Machine: The Future of Work and Power*, Basic Books Inc., New York

6

Developing problem-solving skills

Howard Middleton

INTRODUCTION

This chapter outlines the importance of various kinds of problem-solving in contemporary vocations. It draws on cognitive theory to outline and examine models of problem-solving for well-defined and ill-defined problems. On the basis of these models, approaches are outlined for the teaching and learning of the knowledge needed for solving the kinds of problems that will constitute contemporary and future work.

The ability to solve problems is an important attribute in most contemporary workplaces. The kinds of problems that are encountered can vary from routine tasks like packing supermarket shelves to more complex problems like predicting demand for particular products. In recent years there has been a shift in the kinds of problem-solving required, with the ability to solve complex, ill-defined problems being regarded as important to the success of certain enterprises. The need to be able to deal with complex problems has occurred because of social, economic and workplace changes. These problems occur, for example, in new small businesses in the tourism and hospitality industry (Middleton 1996). The ability to provide creative solutions to complex problems is also seen to be increasingly important in many occupations (Yashin-Shaw, this volume). In some occupations, high levels of problem-solving ability are equated with expertise (Stevenson, this volume). However, there are many conceptions of what constitutes problem-solving—and indeed, of what constitutes problems. At the outset I will define *problems* as tasks that workers encounter, and are required to solve, where there is some impediment to completing the task successfully.

Problem-solving has been addressed in the literature. It has been defined variously as a specific activity and as a more general process. For example, Polya (1965) regards problem-solving as 'attaining an aim that was not immediately attainable' (1965, p. 9), while Mayer (1991) regards the terms *thinking*, *problem-solving* and *cognition* as interchangeable. The various approaches have attempted to address questions that include:

- What are problems?
- What makes some problems difficult?
- How do people represent problems?
- How do people solve problems?
- How do people become expert problem-solvers?

PROBLEMS

People encounter problems on a regular basis during work, at home and as part of social activities. Problems can be classified both in terms of the ways in which it is thought that people represent the problem (Greeno 1978; Greeno & Simon 1988; Newell & Simon 1972) and in terms of the cognitive action they take to solve them (Anderson 1982). One model that has been useful in characterising problems is the *problem space model* (Newell 1980; Newell & Simon 1972). In this model, problems are defined as having three components that occur within the problem space. The first component is called the *problem state*. This represents all the information the problem-solver has about the problem. The second component is the *goal state*, which describes the attributes of a successful solution. The final component is the *search space*, which is the range of information the problem-solver has in memory, or can access, that might be used to move from the problem state to the goal state. In this conceptualisation, problem-solving is sometimes described as 'navigating' the search space to move from problem state to goal state.

To illustrate the problem space model, one can use a problem most people face at some stage. The problem is changing houses. The problem state is the absence of suitable housing, possibly due to getting married or having children. The goal state is a house with a suitable number of rooms with appropriate facilities and configuration for the changed circumstances. The search space might include contacting a builder, locating a suitable block of land, establishing a budget, and so on.

The problem space model was developed alongside information processing theory. This theory posits thinking and problem-solving as the processing of information in ways analogous to a computer. The explanatory orientation is cognitive, and validation is sought using computer simulation. That is, if a computer can be programmed to solve a problem in observable ways that appear human-like, this is regarded as evidence that the underlying computer programming which allowed the computer to solve the problem resembles the way a mind might process the information to solve the problem.

A general method to explain the way people move from the problem state, through the search space to reach the goal state has been developed. The method is called a *production system* (Anderson 1982). Production systems consist of a set of productions, which are rules and actions for solving a problem. A simple production consists of a goal, some application tests and an action. An example of a simple production in driving and its expression is as follows:

IF   the goal is to drive a standard transmission car and the car is in first gear
and the car is going more than 10 miles an hour
THEN shift the car to second gear
(Anderson 1990, p. 243).

The information processing explanation of problems and of problem-solving has been challenged on a number of grounds. Schön (1990) argues that, for a production systems approach to work, it is necessary to be able to specify all aspects of the problem prior to attempting to solve it. The problem space model was developed from puzzles and games and by examining how people solve mathematical problems under specific, controlled situations. Schön argues that many everyday and work problems cannot be specified in this way. This can certainly be the case in industries developing new products or systems.

A more recent formulation of the problem space has been developed to account for complex and ill-defined problems, and problems that require a creative solution (Middleton 1996) (see Figure 6.1). In this formulation, the problem state has been replaced with a *problem zone*, the goal state with a *satisficing zone* and the search space with a *search and construction space*.

In ill-defined problems, the problem zone is defined as that portion of the problem space from which a representation of the problem is derived. The problem zone comprises the information that exists prior to the problem-solving process commencing. However, there are different ways in which a problem-solver might represent the problem. For example, one architect might represent the information provided by a client differently from another architect.

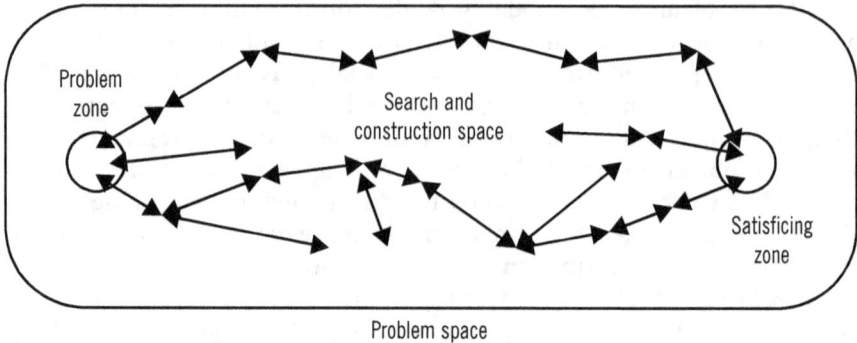

Figure 6.1 Revised concept of a problem space
Source: Middleton (1996, p. 113)

The problem zone captures the way that the starting point for some problems is ill-defined and can be interpreted and represented in various ways. It also captures the notion of problem finding (Getzels & Csikszentmihalya 1976) as an important aspect of problem-solving. Constructing a representation of the problem zone from information presented by customers was identified as an issue in a study of airline customer service officers:

> Most problems have pretty much got the same sort of approach to them in that you sort of say 'you tell me what it is that you want' and then we have to think about and think 'OK, is this what the person really wants?' ... Sometimes it doesn't make any sense right up, so you sort of sift through in your own head, you verify individual parts with them and ask them questions related to those parts and sometimes you can find out, the story, as they are perceiving it, is quite different to what it really is and you can start to see what the real story is' (Middleton 1997, p. 104).

The search and construction space of ill-defined problems is regarded as the portion of the problem space the problem-solver navigates to reach the solution. Ill-defined problems can have a complex search and construction space for a number of reasons. There may be many different ways to solve the problem—for example, in the building industry a house may be constructed from a variety of materials and, depending on the choice of materials, a variety of construction methods will be possible. Some steps in solving the problem may be opaque—that is, it may not be obvious to the problem-solver which procedures to take to solve the problem. For example, in diagnosing a malfunction in the electronics of a car engine, the steps to rectify the problem may be neither audible nor visible, and thus not obvious to the mechanic. In some problems there can be complex relations between procedures. For example, in designing an item such as a chair, the material selected for its construction will determine the range of construction methods that can be used. Both material and construction methods are linked to and determine the cost of production. Altering one will affect the others.

The term 'satisficing' was coined by Simon (1981) to describe design solutions. The term 'satisficing zone' refers to the stage of a problem when it is possible to make the judgement that a solution has been achieved. In complex problems, this satisficing zone contains aspects that are ill-defined and often opaque (Simon 1981), with goal criteria that may be linked and contradictory (Schön 1990) and which may emerge during problem-solving (Schön 1990). Ill-defined problems in areas such as design also have the requirement that the solutions be creative (Perkins 1990).

Simon (1981) argued that one cannot describe design solutions as correct, but only say that a particular solution satisfies known goal criteria at a particularly time. For these reasons, design solutions are described here as being located in a satisficing zone. Thus, in Figure 6.1, the satisficing zone is represented as an area bounded by a line, indicating an area in which various solutions may reside, rather than as a point indicating a single, correct solution (Simon 1981). The example used to illustrate complex, ill-defined problems is a design problem; however, many everyday and workplace problems have these features. For example, in medicine it is generally not possible to establish the level of recovery that might be possible for a given patient with a given ailment being treated with a particular treatment. Medical treatment thus has features of the satisficing zone similar to design problems.

Engeström (1999) has challenged cognitive theories in general because he argues that they are based on the assumption that people solve problems as individuals and that these problems are stable over time. Engeström suggests that in many workplaces new kinds of problems are emerging, often as a consequence of the introduction of new and novel technologies. Engeström defined these problems in terms of two related categories. The first he calls disturbances or breakdowns, while the second he describes as rapid overall transformations (Engeström 1999).

Often when a new technology is introduced into a workplace, new organisational patterns are required. These new patterns increase the possibilities of disturbances and breakdowns and these problems are often addressed through new technological or organisational solutions, hence leading to rapid overall transformations. This becomes recurring and cyclical, and thus workers are continually being required to solve new problems in novel situations, where expertise cannot be gained through practice in a stable situation (Engeström 1999).

Engeström (1999) argues that people do manage to solve problems in these new working environments, but the way they solve them cannot be explained in terms of existing theories. The evidence for this, according to Engeström, is that the solutions appear to go beyond the application of individuals' knowledge and problem-solving abilities. Engeström has proposed a theory of expansive learning based on cultural-historical activity theory (Engeström 1987; Vygotsky 1978).

PROBLEMS AS CHALLENGES

Perkins (1990) has developed a framework for describing problems based on the criteria that appear to determine whether a problem is complex or simple. Perkins uses the criteria of stability, transparency, simplicity/complexity and deliberation.

Perkins identifies six problem types which he calls challenges. The categories (and the corresponding challenge) include: *performance problems*, which are involved in many sports, where the challenge is to execute operations successfully; *strategic problems*, such as chess, where the challenge is to plan far ahead; *probabilistic problems*, such as card games, where the challenge is to reason well in terms of probabilities; *formal problems*, such as producing a theorem proof in geometry, where the challenge is to find a path; *routine problems*, such as making a cake from a recipe, where the challenge is to complete the task with precision; and *creative problems*, such as designing, where the challenge is to find the goal as well as the solution. One result of Perkins' classification is that there is a widening of the kinds of activities that are regarded as problematic to include both performance and routine problems.

To illustrate Perkins' framework, we can look at the example of creative problems. In Perkins' framework, creative problems are defined as *unstable*, in that the problem may change over time, and *non-transparent*, in that all of the strategies that may be applied to solve the problem are not obvious or observable at the outset of problem-solving. Perkins also suggests that creative problems contain a *non-simple* goal test, in that the determination that a solution is satisfactory requires subtle judgement.

Getzels and Csikszentmihalya (1976) examined the factors that might predict success in solving problems requiring a creative response for successful resolution. They conducted a twelve-year longitudinal study of a group of art students. The study commenced when the students entered university and finished eight years after they graduated. The subjects examined at the twelve-year point were those students who had been with the study from the beginning and had entered occupations where creative abilities were regarded as important to the success of the enterprise.

The single consistent finding was that people who were successful in occupations requiring creativity engaged in what Getzels and Csikszentmihalya called *problem-finding*. *Problem-finding* was defined as exploring alternative ways to represent a problem, exploring different directions extensively before settling on a course and remaining ready to change direction when alternative possibilities presented themselves. Thus the Getzels and Csikszentmihalya (1976) study can be conceptualised as examining the predictors of success for students engaged in solving problems that Perkins (1990) has defined as unstable, non-transparent, and with a non-simple goal test—in other words, problems that can be defined as complex and ill-defined. Moreover, the study emphasised the importance of the way problem-solving knowledge is represented.

WHAT MAKES PROBLEMS DIFFICULT?

Problem-solving involves undertaking a task where there is some impediment to completing the task; however, the difficulty of the task will not be the same for all people. People who have solved the problem (or one very similar to it) previously will not experience the same difficulty as those who are attempting the problem for the first time. Thus the nature of problems cannot be examined fully without reference to the experience of the person solving them.

Many elements

Some problems are complex because there are many parts to them. The task of preparing a materials order for the construction of a house can be said to be complex because of the numerous items required and the possibility that some items will be left out. However, these problems are what Schön (1990) calls additively complex in that there are seen to be relatively simple relations between each of the components. For example, if one vertical support member is omitted, it only has consequences for the vertical members next to it.

For other problems, complexity is a function of the nature of the relations between aspects of the problem or of proposed solutions. For example, while it is a relatively simple task to learn individual words in a language, to learn to communicate within that language is a much more complex task because it requires that the learner understand the syntactic and semantic relations among words.

Contradictory

In some problems encountered in occupations, the relations between aspects of problems represent contradictions, and these constitute another kind of complexity. For example, an industrial designer can be faced with the task of designing a chair that is lightweight, but strong. The lighter the chair is, the harder it becomes to also make it strong.

Opaque

Some problems are complex because it is not possible to see all the elements of the problem. In electronic troubleshooting, for example, diagnosing the problem can be complex because modern electronic systems provide many functions, there are complex relations between the parts of the systems that provide these functions and most of the system is not directly visible to the problem-solver.

Ill-defined

Complex problems are sometimes complex because the dimensions of the problem are not apparent to the problem solver. This lack of precise detail can include each of the three elements of the problem space model. For example, the information a client provides to an architect will generally provide details such as the number of rooms, but will leave other details for the architect to work out. This means the architect has to solve the problem without a clear idea of the problem zone, the details of the most appropriate path to take to navigate the search and construction space, or the precise details of a solution within the satisficing zone.

Emergent criteria

Problems in new industries can be complex because of the lack of established knowledge of the industry. This can mean that criteria for establishing suitable solutions emerge during problem-solving. For example, establishing specialist tourist facilities in remote locations such as some national parks and wilderness areas requires staff with particular skills. However, living conditions in these remote locations may determine that hiring staff meeting the ideal criteria for the enterprise may not be possible and that different criteria may need to be established. The establishment of these emergent criteria adds another dimension of complexity to the problem.

Need to be creative

Enterprises engaged in the design of commercial products encounter problems that are complex because of the legal requirement to be original. That is, to satisfy patent laws in most countries, products must be 25 per cent different from existing products. This requirement to be original provides a high level of complexity to the problem for two reasons. Firstly, engaging in creative activity is generally regarded as complex. Secondly, there is no precise way of defining the nature of the 25 per cent difference. For example, the car manufacturer Rolls-Royce sued another company that produced after-market radiator grilles for Volkswagens which resembled Rolls-Royce radiator grilles.

The complexity of problems is sometimes a function of the way in which the problem is represented. This has two aspects. On the one hand, there is the way in which a problem is presented to a problem-solver. For example, the problem may be presented as a textual description either verbally or in writing, or as a sketch or some type of visual representation, with or without text. On the other hand, there is the way in which the problem-solver represents the problem in memory. For example, they might create a visual image from a verbal description or verbal labels for a sketch or diagram. The issue of representation and the influence it has on the degree of difficulty people experience when solving problems has been examined and is explored in the following section.

REPRESENTING PROBLEMS

The ways in which problems are presented to people and the way in which they represent the problem in memory affects the ease with which the problem can be solved (Kotovsky et al., 1985; Kotovsky & Fallside 1989; Larkin 1989). In some taxonomies, there is the implication that the knowledge used in solving a problem is represented as abstract symbols, such as mathematical formulae or in language or language-like codes. This symbolic representation of knowledge appears to be the case with some kinds of mathematical problem-solving. Indeed, there have been periods where psychologists have argued that all thinking was represented by these abstract symbols and that such representations as mental imagery and tacit knowledge do not exist (Pylyshyn 1973, 1981).

More recent research in neurophysiology (Kosslyn 1994) has been able to provide evidence that different parts of the brain are activated by different modality stimuli. Different regions are activated by visual and verbal stimuli. Kosslyn interprets the neurophysiological findings as providing strong evidence of the existence of imaginal representations in memory. Kosslyn used positron-emission tomography to demonstrate the presence of images. Knowledge represented as images in memory appears to have different characteristics to knowledge represented in more abstract ways.

People can experience difficulty solving problems if the problem is presented as diagrams and notes where the notes related to the diagrams are not integrated with the diagrams. People have to search the text, locate relevant sections and mentally integrate them with the parts of the diagrams they are associated with. According to Sweller and

Chandler (1994), this integration of the spatially separated information creates a high cognitive load and thus makes the problem more difficult to solve than if the text were integrated with the diagrams. Sweller and Chandler call the phenomenon the *split-attention effect*.

The use of different combinations of images and text (either as text or as audio) has become of increasing importance in both education and industry, with the World Wide Web (WWW) and multimedia being used for communication and as a problem-solving tool. Mayer (2001) found the split attention effect present when researching the use of various combinations of words and images in multimedia formats. Mayer argues that cognitive load during problem-solving can be reduced by observing what he describes as the *spatial contiguity principle*—that is, ensuring that diagrams are spatially near, or integrated with, the text that relates to them.

The use of multimedia tools in workplace settings has introduced another dimension of complexity to problem-solving concerned with modality. Mayer (2001) argues that there are at least two perceptual channels by which humans receive information or interact with multimedia systems. One is visual and the other auditory. Mayer found that problem-solving was more efficient if problem information was presented in a combination of modalities that had the effect of sharing the processing load. For example, information about a problem presented as diagrams and audio was more effective than information presented as diagrams and text. Mayer's explanation is that when information is presented as diagram and text, the problem-solver overloads their visual processing capacity while not utilising their auditory processing capacity.

Problem-solving difficulty is increased if additional material that is not necessary to solving the problem is included with the description of the problem. This appears to be the case whether the additional material is interesting or not. Sweller and Chandler (1994) describe the phenomena as the *redundancy effect* and argue that the additional, unnecessary material serves to distract the problem-solver from attending only to the material that is relevant for solving the problem. Mayer (2001) found that the redundancy also applied when using multimedia. This is an interesting finding given the current tendency with Web-based material to include non-relevant material.

In some explanations of thinking and problem-solving, all knowledge is thought to be represented in an abstract code (Pylyshyn 1981). Challenges to the abstract code theories have led to the identification of further categories of problems that are of interest to workplace settings. The two are performance problems and routine problems (Perkins 1990). Both of these involve non-abstract representations of knowledge, and both are problems that are often encountered in the workplace.

In performance problems such as in driving a racing car, the driver is able to describe the actions involved in driving the car on a race circuit. However, expert drivers are not able to describe what it is they do that allows them to win over another driver who is not quite so expert. What discriminates between an expert racing car driver and a competent driver is knowledge that is almost certainly tacit, action knowledge and knowledge represented in working memory as dynamic mental images rather than a set of abstract propositions.

In the case of routine problems, Perkins defines the challenge as being contained in the requirement to complete the task with precision. If we take the example of planing a piece of timber flat, it is possible to see this as a non-problematic task that can be described in terms of a series of steps prescribing ways of holding the timber and the plane, and of the action of planing. However, planing a piece of timber flat with accuracy requires a high degree of skill, and this skill is developed in action that cannot be described in any meaningful way.

The way problems are presented to a problem-solver and represented in the problem-solver's memory seems to be important in terms of a problem-solver's ability to overcome the phenomenon generally described as mental blocks. Two blocks to problem-solving are *functional fixedness* (Duncker 1945) and *mechanisation bias* (Antonietti 1991). *Functional fixedness* is the inability to see objects used in other than their familiar role, while *mechanisation bias* is the tendency to employ familiar reasoning strategies in situations where they are not appropriate. Antonietti found that if a problem-solver represented those kinds of problems that tended to induce functional fixedness or mechanisation bias as visual mental images, prior to attempting to solve them, they were more likely to achieve success.

Antonietti (1991) conducted experiments to study the effects of mental visualisation on functional fixedness. Antonietti used the 'cord' problem developed by Maier (1930) with two groups of sixteen–twenty-year-old secondary school students. The control, or verbal, group was given the verbal formulation of the problem. The visualisation group was instructed to visualise the problem situation and was invited to imagine any changes to the situation, if they wished. After visualisation, the visualisation group was given the problem and allowed ten minutes to find a solution. The wording of the cord problem is as follows:

> Suppose you are in a room where two cords are hung from the ceiling. The two cords are of such a length that, when you hold one cord in either hand, you cannot reach the other. Your task is to tie the ends of these cords together. The room is empty. You have only a bunch of keys (Antonietti 1991, p. 217).

One solution to the cord problem is to tie the keys to one cord and to swing them like a pendulum. The other cord can be brought to the centre, so that the swinging cord can be caught as it approaches the centre, and then the two cords can be tied together. The solution to the cord problem requires the problem-solver to overcome functional fixedness, because the critical element (the bunch of keys) has to be used in an unusual way (as a pendulum).

Subjects were classified as productive solvers if they employed the critical elements in unusual ways and unproductive solvers if they gave responses that involved common applications of the critical objects. In the cord problems, the visualisation groups produced the highest percentage of solutions that were judged to be productive (84 per cent for the cord problem).

The results of the experiments using the cord problem support the theory that visualisation of the elements of a problem situation, prior to solving the problem, reduces the tendency to employ elements in familiar ways, and thus increases the probability that problem-solvers will employ elements in unusual ways. Thus using representations of problems that resemble rather than represent problems appears to reduce the complexity of certain problems. Or, put another way, the more concretely a problem is represented, the more likely it is that the problem will be solved.

Antonietti (1991) conducted an experiment to see whether visual mental imagery helps people to overcome the tendency to resort to apparently useful, but inappropriate, procedures, suggesting that they were influenced by mechanisation bias. Antonietti used the 'alarm clock' problem developed by Rausdepp (1980):

> John went to sleep at 8.00 p.m., having previously wound up his old alarm clock and set the hands to wake him up at 9.00 a.m. He slept soundly until the alarm rang. How many hours did John sleep? (Antonietti 1991, p. 213).

A common response to this question is 13 hours, because people calculate the number of hours between 8.00 p.m. and 9.00 a.m., not realising that nine is after eight on the alarm clock, and therefore the clock will ring after one hour. Antonietti (1991) used three groups of thirteen–fourteen-year-old secondary students for the experiment. One group (verbal group) received a verbal (written) statement of the problem, another group (picture group) received a verbal (written) statement of the problem plus an illustration of the scene, and the third group (visualisation group) received the verbal (written) statement plus the instructions to visually represent the problem scene in their minds, prior to solving the problem.

The visualisation group achieved the highest number of correct solutions, followed by the picture group. None of the verbal group solved the problem correctly. Thus, in this problem, visual mental images and external images in the form of pictures helped problem-solvers avoid the tendency to resort to familiar but inappropriate strategies, and thereby improved performance on the problem-solving task.

More generally, the results of the experiments examining the role of visual mental images in reducing mechanisation bias and functional fixedness demonstrate that imagery can be employed in complex problem-solving to remove or reduce the effects of cognitive phenomena that inhibit problem-solving. In doing so, they can improve the problem-solver's ability to solve complex problems where unusual or creative strategies may be required.

PROBLEM-SOLVING

Explanations of the ways people solve problems have a long history, with two general theories emerging. The first is *associationism* and the second is *restructuring* (often called Gestalt thinking). Aristotle is regarded as the father of associationism. He attempted to explain all forms of thinking and argued that thinking (and problem-solving) could be explained in terms of two basic components: ideas and the associations between those ideas. In Aristotle's theory, thinking and problem-solving are governed by three laws. The first is the *doctrine of association by contiguity*, which states that events that occur in the same space and at the same time will be associated in memory and retrieval. If one thinks of one idea, one will be prompted to think of the other. The second law is the *doctrine of association by similarity*, which states that events that are similar will be associated. The third is *the doctrine of association by contrast*, which states that objects or events that are opposites tend to be associated.

Gestalt or restructuring explanations of problem-solving (Duncker 1945; Katona 1940) are based on the premise that solutions can be found by gaining a greater understanding of all of the elements of a problem. Once this has been achieved, the elements can be reorganised in such a way that they represent a solution. Gestalt explanations of problem-solving have been criticised for lack of precision and empirical support (Mayer 1991). Furthermore, gestalt theory has always been restricted to explanations of certain kinds of problem-solving. These have generally comprised problems which required a creative response to achieve a resolution. However, there appears to be a growing recognition that many problems which were previously thought to be routine and simple do in fact contain degrees of complexity. Perkins' work on problem types, mentioned earlier, supports such ideas.

Cognitive strategies based on the problem space model advanced earlier suggest that, for complex problems, achieving a representation of the problem that appears to facilitate resolution is a key stage of the problem-solving process. One needs to recognise that the problem as given may not be the final representation of the problem, and that the problem-finding strategies mentioned earlier will need to be employed. In a similar manner, the traversal of the search and construction space of complex problems may employ steps found through search, but may also require creative steps that need to be constructed. Finally, strategies for determining an appropriate solution for complex problems require that the problem-solver investigate the nexus between desirable and possible solutions in establishing a satisficing solution.

Using activity theory, Engeström (1987) argues that strategies for achieving solutions to complex problems require that the problem-solver view the act of problem-solving not simply as an individual applying cognitive processes in response to the problem demands. Engeström argues that problems can only be addressed once they are represented as part of an activity system. The activity system involves consideration of the rules and meaning within a setting and the tensions that are a function of the history between the tools and processes of the activity system within which the complex problem resides.

Problem-solving as a context-specific activity

Problem-solving in workplaces often takes place within the particular social or cultural context of that workplace—or , as Rogoff suggests, *'thinking is intricately interwoven with the context of the problem to be solved'* (Rogoff 1984, p. 2). Workplace problem-solving is sometimes referred to as everyday problem-solving, to distinguish it from problem-solving undertaken within a school setting or research laboratory. There can be an inference that everyday problem-solving is somehow less important than the formal problem-solving undertaken in schools and laboratories. However, it may be more useful to think of formal and informal problem-solving as problem-solving occurring in two different contexts. Thought about in this way, formal problem-solving in school simply involves another context rather than a context where general principles will be learnt that can be applied to problems in any context.

Expert problem-solving

Expert problem-solvers have a number of things in common. Their expertise is connected to a domain, occupation or context. In this sense, there is no such person as a general expert. Even within domains, expertise is tied to the particularities of the domain. For example, in a study of chess experts, Chase and Simon (1973) found that chess masters could recall board arrangements to a higher degree of accuracy than novices if the arrangements were ones they would meet in a real game of chess. If the arrangement was random, however, the chess expert was no better than the novice chess players. Similarly, then, an airline booking officer who is expert on the computer system of one airline may not be an expert at performing similar tasks on the computer system of another airline.

The ways in which experts represent problems vary across occupations. In a study of architects, Middleton (1998) found that expert architects had a large store of domain-specific knowledge that they could apply to solve architectural problems. This included both knowledge of architectural components and knowledge of the relations between different aspects of the knowledge that was being applied to solve the problem. In itself, this is no different to findings from studies of expertise in other areas; however, the knowledge did not appear to be in the form of abstract principles, but manifested as templates of possible solutions or solution elements. These templates appeared to be represented in memory as visual mental images.

Expert problem-solvers in a domain are able to analyse problems at multiple levels of abstraction, and to extract principles from the problem as given. These principles are then used to work in a forward direction through the search space to solve a problem efficiently.

One component of expertise in many settings, including workplace settings, is *tacit knowledge*. Experts in many areas are not able to articulate what it is that makes them expert. That is, they can describe the procedures they go through to solve a problem, but are unable to say why their solutions are better than that of another practitioner who is deemed proficient but not expert. For example, a world champion Formula 1 racing car driver cannot describe what it is they do that is different from other Formula 1 drivers who have not achieved a world championship. The difference is superior tacit knowledge. This is sometimes referred to as *knowledge in action*, or *action as knowledge*.

DEVELOPING PROBLEM-SOLVING SKILLS: IMPLICATIONS FOR TEACHING AND LEARNING

Complex problems occur within particular settings and contexts. The nature of the setting and context will shape the nature of the problem and possible problem-solving strategies. One aspect of the context for any problem is the skills and attitudes a problem-solver brings to the task. These skills and attitudes constitute part of the individual search and construction space of every problem-solver. Instructional practice should take into account the complex of learners' histories and their problem-solving abilities. In developing learning activities care should be taken to build on existing problem-solving abilities in moving to more complex problem-solving. This may involve starting with problems where only one of the three elements of the problem space is considered complex, to problems where all three elements are complex.

Problems have meaning in the situation in which they occur. Programs need to draw on real contexts for useful problem-solving skills to develop. That is, learners need to encounter a range of problems that represent the richness and diversity of problems that they could expect to encounter within an enterprise.

Learning experiences that develop problem-solving skills need to engage learners in problem-finding—in attempting to represent problems in ways other than the representation initially encountered. The way in which problems are encountered by a problem-solver represents the givens of the problem; however, the givens may need to be explored in depth before problem-solving commences.

Problem-solving is often a shared activity. An important aspect of developing problem-solving skill is to understand that different people bring different skills and perspectives to the problem-solving activity. Making these skills and perspectives explicit is an extension of problem-finding and increases the richness of the learning experience of all participants.

Finally, developing expertise in solving complex problems involves two general areas of learning. The first is the development of problem-solving skills through engaging in a range of authentic problem-solving activities. The second is concerned with developing an understanding of the relationships among elements within problems and relationships across problems.

REFERENCES

Anderson, J.R. 1982, 'Acquisition of cognitive skills', *Psychological Review*, vol. 89, no. 4, pp. 369–406
—— 1990, *Cognitive Psychology and Its Implications*, W.H. Freeman & Co., New York
Antonietti, A. 1991, 'Why does mental visualisation facilitate problem-solving?' In *Mental Images in Human Cognition*, eds R.H. Logie & M. Denis, North Holland, Amsterdam, pp. 211–39
Chase, W.G. & Simon, H.A. 1973, 'Perception in chess', *Cognitive Psychology*, vol. 4, pp. 55–81
Duncker, K. 1945, 'On problem solving', *Psychological Monographs*, vol. 5 (All no. 270)
Engeström, Y. 1987, *Learning by Expanding: An Activity-Theoretical Approach to Developmental Research*, Orienta-Konsultit, Helsinki
—— 1999, 'Expansive learning at work: towards an activity-theoretical reconceptualisation', keynote address, *Changing Practice Through Research: Changing Research Through Practice*, 7th Annual International Conference on Post-Compulsory Education and Training, Centre for Learning and Work Research, Griffith University, Brisbane
Getzels, J. & Csikszentmihalyi, M. 1976, *The Creative Vision: A Longitudinal Study of Problem Finding in Art*, Wiley, New York

Greeno, J.G. 1978, 'Natures of problem-solving abilities', in *Handbook of Learning and Cognitive Processing*, Vol. 5, ed. W.K. Estes, Lawrence Erlbaum, Hillsdale, NJ, pp. 239–70

Greeno, J.G. & Simon, H.A. 1988, 'Problem solving and reasoning', in *Stevens Handbook of Experimental Psychology*, 2nd edn, vol. 2, eds R.C. Atkinson, R.J. Herrnstein, G. Lindzey & R.D. Luce, Wiley Interscience, New York, pp. 589–672

Katona, G. 1940, *Psychological Economics*, Elsevier, New York

Kosslyn, S.M. 1994, *Image and Brain: The Resolution of the Imagery Debate*, Bradford Books, Cambridge, MA

Kotovsky, K. & Fallside, D. 1989, 'Representation and transfer in problem solving', in *Complex Information Processing: The Impact of Herbert Simon*, eds D. Klahr & K. Kotovsky, Lawrence Erlbaum, Hillsdale, NJ, pp. 69–108

Kotovsky, K., Hayes, J.R. & Simon, H.A. 1985, 'Why are some problems hard? Evidence from the towers of Hanoi', *Cognitive Psychology*, vol. 17, pp. 248–94

Larkin, J.H. 1989, 'Display-based problem-solving', in *Complex Information Processing: The Impact of Herbert Simon*, eds D. Klahr & K. Kotovsky, Lawrence Erlbaum, Hillsdale, NJ, pp. 319–41

Maier, N.R.F. 1930, 'Reasoning in humans II: the solution of a problem and its appearance in consciousness', *Journal of Comparative Psychology*, vol. 21, pp. 181–94

Mayer, R.E. 1991, *Thinking, Problem Solving, Cognition*, 2nd edn, W.H. Freeman and Co., New York

—— 2001, *Multi-Media Learning*, Cambridge University Press, Cambridge

Middleton, H.E. 1996, 'Solving complex problems', in *Learning in the Workplace: Tourism and Hospitality*, ed. J.C. Stevenson, Centre for Learning and Work Research, Brisbane, pp. 112–22

—— 1997, 'Constructing problem-spaces in Airline customer work sites', in *Learning in the Workplace: Airline Customer Service*, ed. F. Beven, Centre for Learning and Work Research, Brisbane, pp. 104–16

—— 1998, 'The role of visual mental imagery in solving complex problems in design', unpublished PhD thesis, Griffith University, Brisbane

Newell, A. 1980, 'Reasoning, problem-solving and decision processes: the problem space as a fundamental category', in *Attention and Performance Volume VIII*, ed. R. Nickerson, pp. 693–718

Newell, A. & Simon, H.A. 1972, *Human Problem Solving*, Prentice-Hall, Englewood Cliffs, NJ

Perkins, D. 1990, 'Problem theory', in *Varieties of Thinking: Essays from Harvard's Philosophy of Education Research Center*, ed. V.A. Howard, Routledge, New York, pp. 15–46

Polya, G. 1965, *Mathematical Discovery: On Understanding, Learning, and Teaching Problem Solving*, Wiley, New York

Pylyshyn, Z.W. 1973, 'What the mind's eye tells the mind's brain: a critique of mental imagery', *Psychological Bulletin*, vol. 80, no. 1, pp. 1-24

—— 1981, 'The imagery debate: analogue media versus tacit knowledge', *Psychological Review*, vol. 88, no. 1, pp. 16-45

Rausdepp, E. 1980, *More Creative Growth Games*, Putnam, New York

Rogoff, B. 1984, 'Introduction: thinking and learning in social context', in *Everyday Cognition: Its Development in Social Context*, eds B. Rogoff & J. Lave, Harvard University Press, Cambridge, MA, pp. 1-8

Schön, D.A. 1990, 'The design process', in *Varieties of Thinking: Essays from Harvard's Philosophy of Education Research Center*, ed. V.A. Howard, Routledge, New York, pp. 110-41

Simon, H.A. 1981, *The Sciences of the Artificial*, 2nd edn, MIT Press, Cambridge, MA

Sweller, J. & Chandler, P. 1994, 'Why some material is difficult to learn', *Cognition and Instruction*, vol. 12, no. 3, pp. 185-233

Vygotsky, L.S. 1978, *Mind in Society: The Development of Higher Psychological Processes*, Harvard University Press, Cambridge, MA

7

Developing creativity

Irena Yashin-Shaw

INTRODUCTION

This chapter discusses reasons why the development of creative thinking is important in vocational education and training. It presents various definitions and perceptions of creativity before identifying a perspective most relevant to the investigation of this topic within a vocational context. From this perspective, cognitive theory and theories of creative thinking are integrated to present a model which explains cognitive processes involved during creative problem-solving. The model also provides examples of creative thinking cognitive procedures. A case study is used to illustrate the application of this conceptualisation of creative problem-solving within the vocational context of graphic design. This discussion forms the basis for re-examining pedagogy within vocational education.

CREATIVE THINKING IN VOCATIONAL SETTINGS

Many vocational areas require practitioners to engage in design—such occupations include hairdressers, graphic designers, fashion designers, draughtspeople, architects, toolmakers, engineers, silversmiths and Web page designers. Given that original design—which is a creative problem-solving process—is integral to so many vocational fields, it is desirable for educators and practitioners in these fields to develop an understanding of the cognitive basis for the process. Indeed, such an understanding is increasingly relevant in a broader sense to globalising economies where innovation is necessary for international competitiveness. Consequently, creative problem-solving is applicable to an ever-increasing range of occupations.

Original design is by nature an ill-structured domain. Instructional procedures that succeed for well-structured domains may prove to be inadequate for the more complex material and demands found in ill-structured domains (Efland 1995). Furthermore, it is important that instruction in ill-structured domains does not compromise the intrinsic complexity of the cognitive processes involved. Even in well-structured domains such as welding or smithing, there may be aspects which are ill-structured at more advanced levels of operation or inquiry. Thus a model for creative problem-solving in vocational contexts, which preserves flexibility without over-simplifying the complex act of creative thinking, is extremely useful. This chapter presents such a model. However, before examining this model and its applicability in vocational contexts, an orientation to the discussion is provided in the following sections dealing with definitions and earlier models.

WHAT IS CREATIVITY?

The nature and source of creativity has been, and will continue to be, an ongoing subject of speculation and controversy. No single definition is sufficiently encompassing to reflect the myriad of meanings associated with the term, the conception of which changes with the psychosocial context in which it is used. Creativity means something different to a ballet dancer than to a graphic designer or a poet because the evidence of the creativity is expressed in such diverse ways. Indeed, much of the mystique of creativity stems from the difficulty of defining it. Some researchers (e.g. Weisberg 1988) view it as expert problem-solving, while others see it as divergent thinking (e.g. Guilford 1967), the ability to apply heuristics across domains (e.g. de Bono 1970), or the synergistic application of creative resources (e.g. Sternberg & Lubart 1991). Clearly, no one definition would seem to be complete because of the numerous ways in which creativity may be conceptualised.

Researchers have also attributed creativity to a number of sources. For example, Jay and Perkins identify creative dispositions as a primary source. They define dispositions as 'abiding behavioural tendencies in an individual produced by attitudes, values, interests, long-term motives, and like characteristics' (Jay & Perkins 1997, p. 280). They differentiate dispositions from abilities, claiming that for creative behaviour to occur, a person must first be disposed to it and not just have the ability. Reiter-Palmon et al.'s research (1998) showed a correlation between creativity and personality type. They argue that problem construction ability is positively related to the fit of the solution to the personality type. Other researchers (e.g. Hennessey & Amabile 1988; Koestner et al. 1984) have also reported that creative performance is sensitive to external environmental influences affecting intrinsic motivation. Examples of such influences may be expectation of evaluation (Hennessey & Amabile 1988), deadlines (Amabile et al. 1976) and rewards (Lepper et al. 1973), all of which may decrease motivation and creativity. Guastell et al. (1998) identify eight cognitive styles. They found that creative output is highest for people who engage in a wide repertoire of cognitive styles. Similarly, Torrance and Horng (1980) identify two cognitive styles (adaptors and innovators) and conclude that innovators are more likely to produce better and more creative outcomes. Some researchers, such as Cropley (1997), Mumford and Gustafson (1988), Sternberg and Lubart (1991), propose holistic models of creativity, arguing that several factors or dimensions combine to constitute creative outcomes.

The discussion thus far illustrates the diversity of views in relation to creativity. Should it be considered more a product or a process? Both aspects are implicit in the above definitions and attributions. For the purposes of examining creativity from a vocational context, both aspects are important. Inherent in the term *vocational* is an expectation of output; thus creativity in this context must yield a creative product. However, that is unlikely to be achieved without engagement in a creative process. Amabile (1983) provides two definitions of creativity (given below), which together provide a relatively comprehensive definition of this phenomenon and which therefore provide a good starting point for the examination of creativity in vocational contexts.

Amabile (1983) presents a consensual and a conceptual definition of creativity, arguing that one definition in itself is not sufficient for use in a theory of creativity. Her consensual definition caters for the subjective assessment of creativity:

> A product or response is creative to the extent that appropriate observers independently agree it is creative. Appropriate observers are those familiar with the domain in which the product was created or response articulated. Thus creativity can be regarded as the quality of products or responses judged to be creative by appropriate observers, and it can also be regarded as the process by which something is judged is produced (Amabile 1983, p. 31).

Her conceptual definition provides for a more objective approach:

> A product or response will be judged as creative to the extent that (a) it is both a novel and appropriate, useful, correct, or valuable response to the task at hand, and (b) the task is heuristic rather than algorithmic (Amabile 1983, p. 33).

In summary, therefore, a product shall be considered creative if it is a novel and heuristic response and can be judged as creative by experts.

MODELS OF CREATIVE PROBLEM-SOLVING

This section presents a model to explain cognitive activity during the creative and complex task of designing. Antecedents of the model from cognitive theory and theories of creativity are discussed. The field of graphic design is presented as a case study from which sets of cognitive procedures used during creative problem-solving are identified. Until recently, most theories and models of creativity sought to explain the creative process on a gross level in terms of stages of development of creative ideas. Such models commonly have the creative thinker progressing systematically through different stages of idea development or cycling iteratively through various phases, uni-directionally, until completion. The models by Wallas (1926) and Amabile (1983), discussed below, are examples of this process.

In an influential early discussion of creativity in 1926, based on the testimony of creative individuals, Wallas proposed that creative acts proceeded through four stages: preparation, incubation, illumination and verification. In the first stage, *preparation*, individuals acquire relevant knowledge and skills, which may be used as raw materials for subsequent creative activity. In this stage, creative individuals are in the process of constructing rich, complex knowledge structures, which may be manipulated and restructured in the creative act to follow. In the context of modern cognitive theory, Armbruster (1989) suggests that, during this early learning phase, individuals are in the process of acquiring and storing complex knowledge structures called *schemas*. Schemas are active memory structures which aid in the retrieval and acquisition of knowledge (Glaser & Bassok 1989).

The *incubation* stage may be viewed as the gestatory period when the problem is not actively or consciously pursued, but where the subconscious is at work utilising the knowledge acquired during the preparation stage by the 'free working of the unconscious or the partially conscious processes of the mind' (Wallas 1970, p. 95). The third stage of creativity in Wallas's theory is that of *illumination*. It is the point at which 'unconscious' cognitive activity becomes conscious— the 'Ahh' experience, the 'recognition of a mental representation that fulfils, or has the potential of fulfilling, the goal of the creative enterprise' (Armbruster 1989, p. 180). The product of the illumination stage is then typically subjected to the process of *verification*, which is the fourth and final stage. At this point, the individual undertakes the sustained process of revision and refinement of the product.

Wallas's model has been popularly referred to by researchers writing in the field of creativity, being a seminal work for its time. As such, it has provided a basis for stimulating discussion regarding the process of creative thinking on a macro level.

The notion of progressing through steps is also proposed by Amabile (1983). However, she proposes a cycling or looping through five different phases (or stages) repeatedly in order to produce creative outcomes. The stages are explained as follows. After the task is identified in Stage 1, the individual activates a store of information from the existing store of domain relevant skills in Stage 2. This entails the activation of relevant concepts for use in working memory. A response is then generated in Stage 3 and it is at this point that the level of novelty is determined. The response is validated and analysed in Stage 4 to determine the extent to which it is appropriate, useful or valuable. Stage 5, the process may be terminated or it may loop back through the process until success is achieved.

While the notion of creative problem-solving progressing through phases has persisted, current research is further investigating the nature of cognitive activity on a finer-grained level, within each phase. An explanation proposed by Goel (1995) is an example of this. Goel's model characterises the development of the design problem space in four phases: problem structuring, preliminary design, design refinement and detailing, each of which is characterised by particular cognitive activity.

Problem structuring is the process of constructing the problem space through the retrieval of knowledge from various sources, such as long-term memory and external memory, which includes information about people, purposes of the artefact and resources. The *preliminary design* phase sees the generation and exploration of various design solutions, which are abstract and non-specific in nature. This phase is characterised by *lateral transformations* (movement from one idea to a slightly different idea), which widen the problem space. The following phases of *refinement* and *detailing* are characterised by commitment to a particular solution, attention to detail and vertical transformations. *Vertical transformations* deepen the problem space by moving from one idea to a more detailed version of the same idea. This model is an advancement on previous phase models because Goel argues that the phases are not absolute, in that some recurrence of earlier phases may recur periodically as needed.

Finke et al. propose a model of creative problem-solving called the Geneplore model, so named because of its characterisation by two distinct stages of cognitive processes—generation and exploration. During the generative phase, knowledge is retrieved then associated, transformed, synthesised or reduced to create what the authors call 'preinventive structures' (Finke et al. 1992, pp. 17–24), which are internal precursors to the exploration phase. The 'preinventive structures' have various properties (such as novelty, ambiguity, meaningfulness, emergence, incongruity, divergence) which are developed in the exploratory phase. They are also formed without full anticipation of their eventual resultant interpretation.

The exploratory processes differ from the generative ones insofar as they are more organised, systematic, deliberate and controlled. Typical examples would be attribute finding, which identifies emergent features of the developing product; contextual shifting, where an idea is transferred into a different context as a way of gaining insight; and searching for limitations, where the constraints or limitations of an emerging product are identified. These explorations may lead directly to a creative product or may return the developing structure to the generative phase for further modification. The modification may take the form of either focusing or expanding the concept.

Creative thinking, according to Finke et al. (1992), is viewed as the continual cycling or switching—meaning an iterative relocation of cognitive activity—between the phases of generation and exploration. The preinventive structures are therefore able to be continuously regenerated and modified, with product constraints being imposed at any time until a solution emerges. Finke et al. offer the following example to illustrate this process:

> A person may retrieve two mental images and combine them in the generation phase to produce a visually interesting form, and then interpret the form as suggesting a new idea for a product. Further examination of the form may lead to the conclusion that the form is incomplete in some respects. A modified form is then generated by retrieving yet another image and mentally combining it with the already existing one. This process may result in a form that represents an improved or more complete design for the product or may lead to completely new and unanticipated interpretations of the form (Finke et al. 1992, p. 18).

Product constraints are imposed from outside the generation–exploration cycle. They are not part of the loop, but rather inform the cognitive processes at either stage. Products may be constrained for type, category, features, functions, components and resources (materials to be used). The product constraints determine the characteristics, nature and use of the final product.

The Geneplore conceptualisation therefore presents a highly flexible model for creative thinking, having only two stages of operation, each of which may be iteratively applied and each of which is characterised by a number of cognitive processes. It is the identification of these cognitive processes within the global categories of generation and exploration, and the notion of iterative switching between them to build up a solution, which present an advancement on previous models. This model nonetheless has limitations, stemming from the very qualities that provide it with its flexibility—namely, insufficient detail regarding the number and kinds of categories of thinking needed to explain the creative process. Literature from both cognitive psychology and creativity argues for the inclusion of an evaluative process (Goel 1995; Goel & Pirolli 1992; Runco & Chand 1994). Furthermore, any model explaining cognitive activity that is informed by recent advances in cognitive science must also include an executive control process (Anderson 1982; Evans 1991; Scandura 1981; Stevenson 1986). The following model synthesised from the creativity and the cognitive literature (see Figure 7.1) accommodates all these requirements. The model incorporates both a synthesis of theoretically derived features and components, and research-based instantiations drawn from the field of graphic design. The various aspects of the model and their efficacy in explaining creative problem-solving are described systematically after the model.

THE HIERARCHICAL VIEW OF THINKING

Cognitive literature proposes a hierarchical structure of knowledge. The notion of higher-level schemas acting on, or operating on, lower ones is commonly used to explain cognitive structures utilised during problem-solving (Anderson 1982; Stevenson & McKavanagh 1992). Schemas may be defined as 'a complex structure of concepts, propositions, relationships and procedures, which the person has, and which influence expectations and actions in a particular situation' (Evans 1991, p. 54). Without schemas, memory would be a vast collection of isolated facts, which would need to be combed through every time information was needed. This clearly is not the case, as people—especially experts—can retrieve large chunks of information very quickly. This implies some efficient storage and retrieval mechanism which organises memory. The theoretical construct advanced by cognitive psychology to explain this phenomenon is that of schemas. The lowest level of schemas accounts for routine tasks while the highest level of schemas is used to 'identify task or situation requirements, set goals, and monitor progress towards these goals' (Evans 1991, p. 54). Stevenson (1991) refers to these levels as 'knowledge orders'. The highest level of the cognitive hierarchy is referred to as third-order procedures, which act as a control mechanism, while the lowest level is referred to as first-order, or specific-purpose, procedures. The term 'procedures' is taken from Anderson (1982) and refers to knowledge of how to secure a goal. The three levels of the model presented in Figure 7.1 are discussed below.

THE KNOWLEDGE BASE

The knowledge base contains all the knowledge a person holds in long-term memory. It is one's 'stock of knowledge' (Keller & Keller 1996,

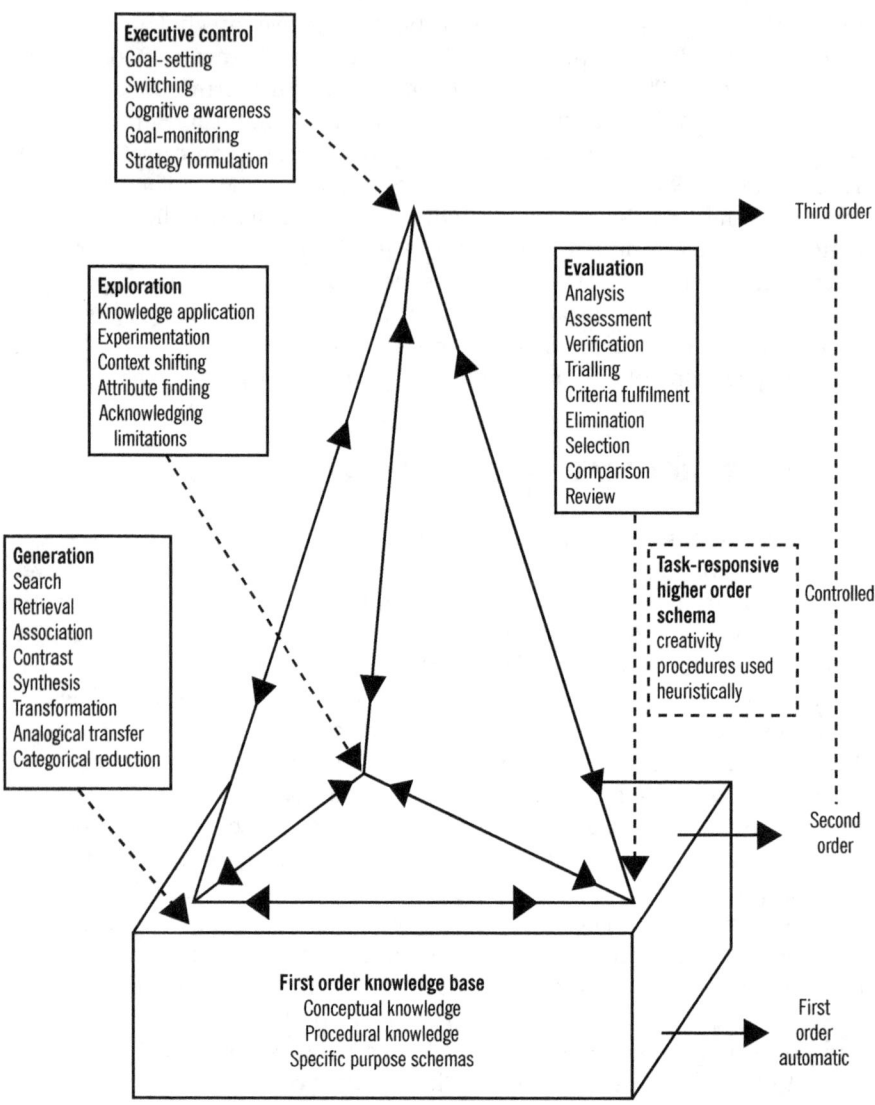

Figure 7.1 The synthesised model for creative problem-solving

p. 119). It includes facts about the world as well as automated knowledge of how to carry out certain fundamental processes in order to achieve a goal. These facts and processes may be operated on by the higher levels of thinking. Ward et al. argue that, in understanding creativity, it is 'just as important to focus on how old knowledge influences new ideas as it is to focus on novelty, per se' (Ward et al. 1997, p. 19). All knowledge in long term memory—that is, both general and domain-specific facts, as well as knowledge of how to perform automated tasks—is available for utilisation by the second-order procedures of generation, exploration and evaluation in the process of creative problem-solving. The knowledge may be accessed by a conscious and systematic search or it may be automatically activated and called into active, working memory by way of its conceptual ties and associations to a concept being consciously utilised. Conceptual ties are the result of schema formation. Knowledge at this first-order level is automatised, as distinct from the second-order controlled (meaning not automatic) cognitive activity of generation, exploration and evaluation. This distinction is clarified in the following section.

SECOND-ORDER PROCEDURES

Second-order thinking is characterised by three categories of thought —generation, exploration and evaluation—each of which is constituted by sets of procedures. Procedures are operators defined by the function they serve in the problem space. The sets of procedures listed in the boxes in the model are meant to be representative only and not definitive, as they vary depending on the nature of the task being undertaken. For example, a problem requiring the construction of a creative artefact would require some different procedures to the solving of a problem that was of a more conceptual nature. Thus procedures involving tactile manipulation, such as transformation, experimentation and testing (which are examples of generative, explorative and evaluative activity respectively), are likely to be employed in the production of a creative artefact, but may well be replaced by other relevant procedures in a different kind of problem. For this reason, the schemas are referred to as 'task-responsive'. Definitions of the second-order procedures and their origins are presented in Tables 7.1, 7.2 and 7.3. Each table is followed by a discussion of the functions of each of the categories of thinking.

Generation

Generative procedures marshal the mental raw materials which promote creative thinking. Finke et al. (1992) explain generation in terms of the construction of mental representations called preinventive

Table 7.1 Generation procedures and definitions

Procedure	Definition
Search (Yashin-Shaw 2001)	A seeking out of possibilities to inform or enrich current thinking
Retrieval (Finke et al. 1992)	A direct transference of specific concepts from the knowledge base into working memory for the purpose of expanding or illuminating the current problem
Association (Finke et al. 1992)	The mental connection of either disparate or related ideas, freed from their normal contexts
Contrast (Yashin-Shaw 2001)	A juxtaposing or setting in opposition of two disparate concepts so as to enhance their differences for artistic or dramatic effect
Synthesis (Finke et al. 1992)	A combination or blending or two or more ideas or concepts
Transformation (Finke et al. 1992)	The manipulation and visualisation of a model so that a new form emerges from the existing one
Analogical transfer (Finke et al. 1992)	A correspondence and mapping between similar features of concepts and principles that are otherwise dissimilar
Categorical reduction (Finke et al. 1992)	Simplifies a concept or image to its fundamental, basic form

structures, which act as internal precursors to the final externalised creative outcomes. As information is retrieved, synthesised, transformed and associated in novel ways, the potential for creative outcomes is enhanced. Generation is therefore responsible for bringing new information into the problem space. As such, it is akin to the commonly used term 'divergent thinking', which is viewed as an essential component of creative thinking (Smith 1995). It may be defined as:

- the ability to make remote associations between topics (Mednick 1962);
- an active search that can free information in memory from the context and cues with which it was remembered so that it can appear as a novel response to the problem (Brown 1989);
- the promotion of unconventional possibilities, associations and interpretations (Guilford 1968);
- the development of tentative possibilities rather than data, speculation rather than conclusions (de Bono 1970).

It is characterised by the tolerance of ambiguity, the ability to hold contradictory ideas simultaneously; the maintenance of flexible constructs; and a preparedness to look far afield for potential solutions. In the proposed model, generative processes may be employed at any stage of engagement in the task of producing creative outcomes; however, initial generative procedures are undertaken without 'full anticipation of their resulting meaning and interpretation' (Finke et al. 1992, p. 22). De Bono (1970) has popularised this process as lateral thinking, which is characterised by such cognitive activity as generating alternative approaches to a problem, even after a promising one may have been found (brainstorming); welcoming chance intrusions; investigating least likely paths; and thinking in non-sequential steps— that is, making mental leaps rather than moving ahead in small sequential and logical steps.

Exploration

Exploration takes place as emergent features worthy of exploitation are identified, extracted and further manipulated. Exploratory activity is differentiated from generative activity insofar as it is more directed and organised, and where possible outcomes are assembled from the information retrieved.

Table 7.2 Exploration procedures and definitions

Procedure	Definition
Knowledge application (Yashin-Saw, 2001)	The application of specific knowledge, procedural or conceptual, to the explorative process in order to develop a particular idea
Experimentation (Yashin-Shaw, 2001)	The consideration of various physical and tactile possibilities in the emerging solution
Context shifting (Finke et al. 1992)	The transference of the idea or concept being considered into a different context as a way of gaining insight
Attribute finding (Finke et al. 1992)	The search for emergent features and recognition of the developing characteristics of the product in progress
Acknowledging limitations (Finke et al. 1992)	Identifying real or possible constraints, shortcomings or difficulties of the emerging product

Evaluation

Evaluation has been described as 'selective retention' by Campbell, who acknowledges the need to apply some form of selective criteria to 'weed out the overwhelming bulk of inadequate trials' (Campbell 1960, pp. 391–2). Guilford (1956) views it as a judgement concerning the extent to which a particular piece of information meets given criteria. Without evaluation, creative problem-solving would be severely frustrated, resulting in inferior solutions. At some point, the value of new

Table 7.3 Evaluation procedures and definitions

Procedure	Definition
Analysis (Perkins 1981)	Critically examining, by focusing attention on a particular aspect of the solution, the strengths and weaknesses of an outcome, proposal or idea
Assessment (Amabile 1983)	To pass a qualified judgement on an idea, concept or outcome by identifying its appropriateness, appeal, usefulness or value.
Verification (Yashin-Shaw 2001)	Confirming and/or justifying a choice
Trialling (Yashin-Shaw 2001)	A mental or physical trial of the product, undertaken to establish its tactile qualities
Criteria fulfilment (Campbell 1960)	The extent to which the product or an idea meets, exhibits or illustrates the characteristics required in the final outcome, through the application of predetermined criteria, characterising acceptable solutions
Elimination (Yashin-Shaw 2001)	The considered rejection of an idea or outcome due to its perceived irrelevance, inappropriateness, uselessness or impracticality
Selection (Yashin-Shaw 2001)	The decision to retain and include particular ideas and concepts
Comparison (Perkins 1981)	The juxtaposition of ideas, concepts or products with the intention of ultimately choosing the most appropriate one or rejecting inappropriate ones
Review (Yashin-Shaw 2001)	A reiteration, enumeration, listing and/or summarising of an idea (or parts thereof) or outcome

ideas must be determined. The functions of evaluation are closely aligned with the popularly used term *convergent thinking*, which is commonly thought of as the opposite or complement of divergent thinking, concerned as it is with conclusions, deductions and assessments (Dowd 1989). De Bono (1970) refers to this kind of thinking as *vertical thinking* because it is selective rather than generative, concerned with practicality rather than possibility and correctness rather than probability.

THIRD-ORDER PROCEDURES

The executive control procedures direct second-order thinking. They allow thinkers to reflect critically on the appropriateness of selected strategies and concepts, employ different ones where necessary and monitor their progress while engaged in tasks (Glaser 1985; Scandura 1981). The executive control procedures are therefore higher-order thinking which directs and guides the entire task by operating upon the second-order procedures in a conscious way. For this reason, executive control is found at the apex of the model because its products are the goals, strategies and dialogue which inform, select and regulate the lower-order categories and procedures (see Table 7.4).

Table 7.4 Executive control procedures and definitions

Procedure	Definition
Goal-setting (Evans 1991)	A statement of the need to achieve some outcome or quality
Switching (Stevenson 1991)	A conscious and intentional change in the direction of the thinker
Cognitive awareness (Yashin-Shaw 2001)	A self-dialogue, which helps to clarify direction by acknowledging the thinker's cognitive position or the various possibilities presenting themselves
Goal-monitoring (Evans 1991)	A conscious intervention to ascertain the extent to which the thinking will lead to the desired outcomes
Strategy formulation (Yashin-Shaw 2001)	A statement used as a forward-looking intermediate stepping stone, which may lead to clearer intentions, goals and directions

OTHER FEATURES OF THE MODEL

Creative products are built up gradually through a process of incremental evolution, as the creative problem-solver continually adjusts the emerging product towards its final form (Jay & Perkins 1997; Perkins 1981). To do this, cognitive components must be able to be combined in various ways to allow this building up to occur. The flexibility to allow the various components to combine in response to task requirements is accommodated in the model by the bidirectional arrows connecting all the higher order categories. In this way, the 'rich interplay of the multiple levels and types of knowledge' (Gott 1989, p. 163) is made possible. The term *interactivity* has been adopted to refer to the phenomenon of frequent switching among the components. Thus to say the categories are interactive means that cognitive activity can shift from one category to another at any time as indicated by the bidirectional arrows linking each category.

Another feature of the model is the direct interface between the higher-order procedures and the knowledge base. This means that any information in memory may be activated and accessed from any category of thinking, enabling each to draw on and utilise knowledge contained within the knowledge base, which provides the concepts and skills and schemas to be used during cognitive activity.

A person may have a number of schemas for solving creative problems and the above model is a general form. Because a creative solution cannot be a standard application of routine procedures, the creativity schemas are heuristic in nature, requiring control rather than being applied automatically. An heuristic is a 'rule-of-thumb' method of solving a problem which does not guarantee a solution, as distinct from an algorithm which is the application of a procedure consisting of specific rules which do guarantee a result. The higher-order, general schemas, which are heuristic in nature, are 'task-responsive' because thinking is likely to vary somewhat depending on the nature of the problem and the domain in which the solver is thinking, as well as the prior knowledge and experience of the problem-solver. The procedures which drive creative problem-solving are likely to be drawn in various combinations in different situations, which is why they have been identified in the model as 'creativity procedures used heuristically'.

CREATIVE PROBLEM-SOLVING IN GRAPHIC DESIGN: A CASE STUDY

Let us now examine how the above model could be useful for illuminating the process of creative problem-solving in the vocational context of graphic design. In a case study, a third-year graphic design student was required to create a catalogue for an avant-garde photography and video exhibition at a small regional art gallery. The theme of the exhibition dealt with the surfing sub-culture in the region. It was stressed that the format and design of the catalogue were not to be a conventional representation as this would be at odds with the intention, philosophy and form of the exhibition. Consequently, the innovation of the exhibition was to be reflected in the form and format of the catalogue. Thus, although the context was an instructional one, the actual task was authentic. Contextualised tasks such as this require students to negotiate the complex requirements of the workplace where problem-solving outcomes must satisfy various criteria and be produced under constraints such as limited budgets and tight time-lines.

The creative problem-solving process was investigated using a method called *protocol analysis* where the problem-solver was required to 'think out loud' during the process of problem-solving. This is one method of capturing cognitive processes in a detailed way as they occur. The protocols (verbal data) were collected in two sessions, recorded, transcribed, segmented (595 utterances over both sessions), numbered and analysed in a detailed way.

During the course of designing, the problem-solver 'built up' the solution through the iterative and differential application of various procedures. That means that no particular category had exclusive association with any particular stage of the problem-solving process. This is exemplified by the set of ten utterances (numbers 26–35 in Table 7.5) taken from near the beginning of the process in Session 1 which, when analysed, shows procedures from all four categories of thought present to some degree.

Although all categories of thinking were present throughout, some categories were deployed with greater relative frequency at different times during the process according to task requirements. For example, executive control and generation procedures were used comparatively more frequently near the beginning of the process, as seen by the block of initial utterances in Table 7.6.

Alternatively, evaluation procedures were used more frequently towards the end of the process, as shown by the extract of protocols in Table 7.7. Utterances 564–87 are provided.

The salient point is that all categories—or kinds of thinking—had a role to play throughout the entire process. Procedures were enacted differentially at various times during the problem-solving process, but they did not occur in a set order; rather, their relative frequencies changed according to task demands. Procedures among and within categories were interactive—that is, the problem-solver switched among them frequently, iteratively and differentially during the entire problem-solving process. The implications of this conceptualisation of creative problem-solving are discussed in the following section.

Table 7.5 Extract of protocols showing presence of all categories of thinking

No.	Utterance	Category & procedure
26	So I am going to come up with an innovative design that's going to have to be just that, not your standard booklet or leaflet because that's boring.	Executive control—goal setting
27	The standard thing I suppose is . . . 12 A4 pages.	Generation—retrieval
28	But . . . the booklet can't be too small.	Exploration—knowledge application
29	So therefore 12 A4 pages roughly folded in half should give us 24 pages. (Participant is physically folding pages in various ways.)	Exploration—experimentation
30	What can you do with that?	Generation—search
31	All I'm doing at the moment is just seeing if anything comes to mind immediately of something creative or innovative that I can do with a standard A4 sheet. (Participant is physically folding pages in various ways.)	Exploration—experimentation
32	Keeping in mind that is one of the formats for printing.	Exploration—knowledge application
33	The first option is quite boring.	Evaluation—analysis
34	If I saw a booklet that was basically just an A4 sheet folded in half that immediately conjures up very conventional methods, very straight and we've been told that it is not what they're after.	Executive control—goal-monitoring
35	It's not innovative in any sense of the word.	Evaluation—assessment

IMPLICATIONS FOR TEACHING AND LEARNING IN VOCATIONAL SETTINGS

This section identifies how instructors within vocational settings may structure the learning experience for students in a way which encourages the kinds of thinking likely to result in creative deployment of

Table 7.6 Extract of protocols showing greater relative frequency of executive control and generation at the beginning of the problem-solving process

No.	Utterance	Category & procedure
1	The first thing I'm going to deal with is format because that is the most detailed, in depth thing he's given us—something we can think about the most.	Executive control—goal-setting
2	I'm just at the moment thinking about formats that first pop into my head—I'll just write this down while I'm thinking about it.	Executive control—cognitive awareness
3	Poster formats, leaflet formats, booklets, fliers.	Generation—retrieval
4	That is all I can think of at the moment so from there I'll probably look at the different formats that I can see for each of those four —as in the poster—the basic two—the horizontal and vertical formats.	Executive control—strategy formulation
5	Yes I'm just trying to structure it out from the most basic ones I know, such as the poster.	Executive control—strategy formulation
6	The flier is the one I'm remembering at the moment.	Generation—retrieval
7	We've seen a few at the school lately that are very innovative and I think that could work in this particular exhibition because the usual structure of a flier—one page one A4 folded in different ways but some of the fliers we've seen lately take on a . . .	Generation—retrieval
8	Well there is a shape which is then repeated and all the information is on those pages and just keeps going on and on and on and wraps round because of the shape—comes round and then forms up with the other side.	Generation—retrieval
9	That adds interest to it I suppose, and that is as I see it, the most important thing at this point is—to gain interest through the innovation of the design.	Executive control—goal-setting
10	I'll just go back to the poster.	Executive control—switching
11	Poster—horizontal format.	Generation—retrieval
12	From there you'd probably have to look at the problems associated with it I suppose and the strong points of the images.	Executive control—strategy formulation

continued

No.	Utterance	Category & procedure
13	Poster—also vertical format.	Generation—retrieval
14	Look at the whole purpose of the poster.	Exploration—knowledge application
15	The first thing you think of is a poster for wall.	Exploration—knowledge application
16	That has got the strength of having a visual impact because you've got more size to work with for a start.	Evaluation—analysis
17	Then you've got more information you can see at one time.	Exploration—knowledge application
18	Then you've got different lateral ideas for a poster that we looked at in second year.	Generation—retrieval
19	A poster can be like a pointed sail, a cardboard cut out, it can have a lot of different variations.	Generation—association
20	But at this point in time a poster wouldn't be an option for me because of the fact it's a catalogue and I see the point of a catalogue as being to explain information about an individual thing at a time.	Evaluation—elimination

cognitive resources, and ultimately creative outputs. Firstly, the cognitive resources needed by creative problem-solvers are identified within a graphic design context, building on the earlier discussion in this chapter of the three different knowledge orders. This is followed by a discussion of how instruction may be sequenced for students in order to develop facility in creative problem-solving. The discussion draws on relevant aspects of the Collins et al. (1989) model of cognitive apprenticeship, showing how a version of the creative problem-solving model presented in Figure 7.1 can be used to help sequence instruction. Finally, the usefulness of the model in Figure 7.1 for 'schema training' (Derry 1990) is discussed, and it is shown that the model may be used as an instructional tool to help develop students' knowledge structures.

What cognitive resources do learners need for creative problem-solving?

In order to be able to solve problems creatively, students need various kinds of knowledge. These include propositional and procedural knowledge, which provides cognitive raw materials with which the

Table 7.7 Extract of protocols showing greater relative frequency of evaluation towards the end of the problem-solving process

No.	Utterance	Category & procedure
564	That's got the strength of having you view only two images at a time.	Evaluation—analysis
565	Those two images will be chosen by me from the set of photographs we were given—as being binary opposites.	Evaluation—selection
566	That way you've got the strength of that opposition coming through—that displacement.	Evaluation—assessment
567	And that is also echoed in the cover graphics.	Generation—association
568	Where that square appears in the top you would have—this white area would be the wave. (physical manipulation of materials)	Exploration—experimentation
569	I think I'm getting to the end of this.	Executive control—goal-monitoring
570	It's got the strengths of all the ideas I've come up with but is also very budget conscious at the same time.	Evaluation—criteria fulfilment
571	I'll just go through the list of things I have to achieve.	Executive control—goal-monitoring
572	I've got the contrast happening, the displacement happening, it's practical—it folds into a small format and folds out to a large format, thereby you can view all the pictures at once.	Evaluation—criteria fulfilment
573	Binary opposites—you've got that happening, the black and white on the cover—economically viable.	Evaluation—criteria fulfilment
574	The interaction happening.	Evaluation—criteria fulfilment
575	Size not a problem, shape not a problem.	Evaluation—criteria fulfilment
576	Transformation—that would be happening to the extent that it folds from a small booklet into a large piece, thereby that would also satisfy the fun element where depending on which way it was folded back together the imagery is in the two front windows.	Evaluation—criteria fulfilment

continued

No.	Utterance	Category & procedure
577	If you've got a poster there are a number of ways it could fold back together—if you fold a poster a different way the image on top is going to change.	Generation—transformation
578	OK, what other criteria?	Evaluation—review
579	Unusual format—no worries.	Evaluation—criteria fulfilment
580	Extreme format—no worries.	Evaluation—criteria fulfilment
581	Something innovative—no worries. Never seen anything before like it. It works. I'm just going to have to make it now. That's the next stage. But as far as I am concerned, that's as economically viable as I'm going to get it. It will be glossy.	Evaluation—criteria fulfulment
582	The gloss stock does not increase the price.	Evaluation—criteria fulfilment
583	The images are black and white.	Evaluation—criteria fulfilment
584	The only problem I can see happening with this is the fact that all the images on this long piece won't be able to be viewed.	Evaluation—analysis
585	For example, no matter which way you fold it back together you may not be able to get one of the segments on top.	Exploration—experimentation
586	Thereby you won't be able to view that image through the front windows on the cover.	Exploration—acknowledging limitations
587	Apart from that, however, it is sound.	Evaluation—assessment

student can work; knowledge of heuristics for combining and developing this raw material in novel ways; and strategic knowledge to monitor the process. These equate to the three knowledge orders presented in Figure 7.1 and will be dealt with in turn in a graphic design context.

Propositional knowledge is referred to as knowledge 'that' (Anderson 1982); it is declarative or conceptual knowledge and is 'knowledge about things, for example information, facts, propositions, assertions, theories, principles' (Stevenson & McKavanagh 1992). Procedural knowledge is referred to by Anderson (1982) as knowledge 'how' and is knowledge about how to employ and execute skills, techniques, algorithms and other problem-solving procedures in order to achieve a goal. For example, in the field of graphic design, propositional knowledge may include facts about drawing techniques, colour mixing, composition, various methods of book, poster or flier construction or formatting, costs of different processes such as dye cutting, or software which may be used in the design process. Knowledge 'how', or procedural knowledge, is the ability to execute the skills of drawing; using the computer and software; performing a dye cut, and so on. The more propositional and procedural knowledge students have, the greater the 'vocabulary' they have at their disposal out of which to construct their creative solutions. Thus, as a precursor to creative problem-solving, students need some domain-specific knowledge. However, because creative thinking is also characterised by a preparedness to look far afield for potential solutions, a good store of non-domain specific knowledge is also useful.

Heuristic knowledge is generally thought of as the ability to apply the 'rule of thumb' method. Such knowledge provides problem-solvers with a way of approaching tasks but does not guarantee a particular outcome. Algorithms, by contrast, yield predetermined results through the application of specific rules. Generally, heuristic strategies are developed through wide experience in a particular field. They are 'tacitly acquired by experts through the practice of solving problems' (Collins et al. 1989, p. 478). For example, a graphic designer who has worked in the industry for some time knows that the first sketches generated for a design are usually simply the preliminary stepping stones to developing ideas and will therefore not spend too much time on including excessive details, as a novice might be tempted to do. Another heuristic strategy employed by more experienced designers may be to analyse the target market at which the design is aiming before proceeding, in order to have a deeper understanding of the salient features required in the design. A more experienced designer undertaking a creative design may also deliberately switch direction of thinking frequently at some stages of the process in order to consciously trigger new ideas and activate different schemas to inform the emerging product. While these skills are acquired over time and with experience, it is possible to aid students in the explicit development of these strategies through the use of conceptual tools such as the model presented in this chapter.

Strategic knowledge refers to how-to-decide-what-to-do-and-when (Gott 1989). Evans (1991) describes it as 'executive schemas' that effect control over the deployment of intellectual resources and the monitoring of progress. In the literature dealing with applied cognition and instructional psychology, this construct is often referred to as *metacognition*, which performs the function of organising, selecting and monitoring cognitive activity (Campione et al. 1989; Jausovec 1994). In the model in Figure 7.1, this kind of thinking is called executive control and helps students to be aware not only of their progress towards their goal but also of how they are arriving there. If students are given the opportunity, and are encouraged, to engage in this highest level of thinking, they are more likely to become autonomous learners, able to self-regulate and develop their skills through reflection. Thus, as with all of these kinds of knowledge, the skills of self-reflection evolve slowly through intensive long-term practice (Derry 1990). The following section examines how these opportunities for engaging in creative thinking may be sequenced for students in order to develop their facility for creative problem-solving.

Designing instruction for developing creativity in students

Collins et al. provide a framework for sequencing instructional material to 'facilitate the development of robust problem-solving skills' (Collins et al. 1989, p. 485). They argue that instructional tasks should provide for increasing complexity, increasing diversity and the development of global before local skills. Each of these will be discussed in turn in relation to creative problem-solving.

Increasing complexity refers to the 'construction of a sequence of tasks and task environments or microworlds where more and more of the skills and concepts necessary for expert performance are required' (Collins et al. 1989, p. 484). In the field of graphic design for example, beginning students need to learn basic skills of composition, colour mixing and facility with various tools, media and technologies embedded in relatively simple applications before progressing to larger integrated projects such as that described in the case study earlier in the chapter. The case study project required the advanced graphic design students to create and construct a catalogue for an avant-garde photography and video exhibition. Projects such as that require a rich and integrated application of all levels of cognitive resources. These include the application of well-known principles and procedures of artefact construction such as dye cutting procedures, binding procedures as well as composition and colour treatment and other domain-specific knowledge. However, as well as that, advanced students were expected to manage the high cognitive load imposed by the search for novelty and originality in design while at the same time being mindful of the context in which the design would be applied.

To help students acquire the skills needed to manage a task of this complexity, students need regular and sustained practice in dealing with the non-routine aspects of their craft. These experiences should be developed incrementally so that students have time to formulate their own heuristic schemas, which will help with managing the high cognitive load associated with creative problem-solving. The model presented in this chapter may be used as a scaffold for this process in a number of ways, as outlined below.

DEVELOPING CREATIVITY

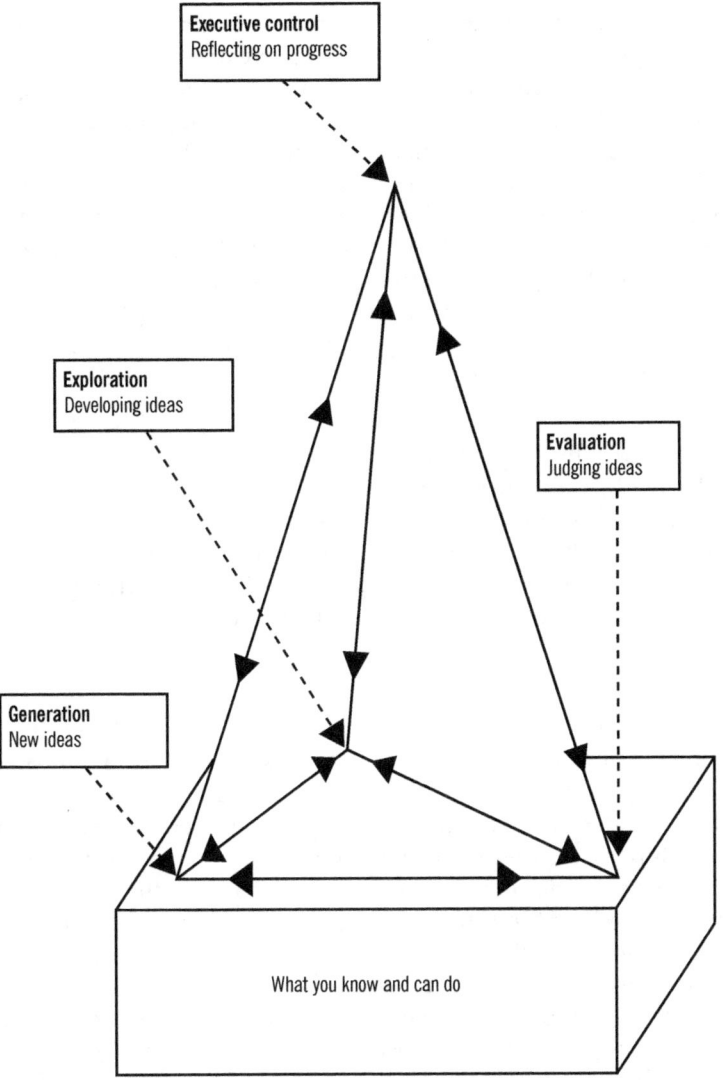

© Irena Yashin-Shaw, 2001

Figure 7.2 Simplified version of the creative problem-solving model

Firstly, students could be presented with a simplified version of the creative problem-solving model as shown in Figure 7.2.

The purpose of this is twofold. Drawing the different kinds of knowledge that may be used in the creative problem-solving process to students' attention can act as a prompt for them to deploy all knowledge types and to shift cognitive activity among the various categories of thinking. Also, the model in this form can begin to provide students with a conceptual framework for thinking creatively; this can be developed further and fleshed out as they acquire experience and expertise. Such a model also helps to make creative problem-solving visible and external for inspection by learners (Collins et al. 1989).

Every time students have the opportunity to apply this framework to a task that requires some novelty, they should be asked to reflect on their cognitive processes with a view to identifying the kinds of steps they employed during the creative problem-solving process. Knowing in advance that they will have to do this will help students to be mindful of their thinking for analysis later. Asking themselves questions may be helpful—for example:

- What was the first thing I did?
- What did I do when I was stuck?
- How did I bring new information to the problem?
- How did I know when I was getting to the end?
- How did I know when I was pleased with an emerging design?
- How did I resist the temptation to do something familiar and routine?

Naming and defining the kinds of steps they used for themselves will allow students to develop heuristic schemas which are highly idiosyncratic and rich in meaning, usefulness and accessibility. For example, a student may refer to a cognitive step similar to the categorical reduction procedure in Figure 7.1 as stylising, or the synthesis procedure as blending, or the retrieval procedure as remembering things. These steps are being referred to here because they are part of the existing model. It is likely students will identify steps which are quite different from those in the model. The term 'categorical reduction' will probably have little meaning for a beginning design student and therefore would only represent a tiny piece of inert, decontextualised knowledge if delivered to them by the teacher—unlike procedures they identify for themselves. Students can then use these highly individualised heuristic schemas for their next creative problem-solving task and add to them any new procedures they find themselves using.

Structuring activities that incrementally increase in complexity will press students into gaining facility with the procedures already identified as well as encouraging them to identify new ones. With developing expertise, students may also consolidate procedures so that they do not end up with sets of procedures that are unnecessarily large and repetitive. Thus, by using the skeleton of the model (Figure 7.2) as a starting point, students can cultivate a creativity heuristic which is genuinely a reflection of their unique thinking style.

Another way of contributing to the development of creativity schemas is by increasing task diversity as well as providing a diverse range of experiences for students. Collins et al. argue that 'as students learn to apply skills to more diverse problems and problem situations, their strategies become freed from their contextual bindings (or perhaps more accurately acquire a richer set of contextual associations) and thus are more readily available for use with unfamiliar or novel problems' (Collins et al. 1989, p. 485). Given that creative problem-solving is exclusively about dealing with unfamiliar or novel problems, this suggestion is highly pertinent. Task diversity for design students may take the form of requiring students to design for different contexts. For example, if students were designing a logo for a new clothing company, how would the logo be different if the company was catering for the teenage market, the surfing sub-culture or leisure wear for retirees? Incorporating diversity into tasks would require students to undertake different kinds of tasks. For example, graphic design students could be required to design across a variety of assignments and contexts including logos, book covers, corporate identities, advertising posters, Websites, and so on. Furthermore, the method of operation should also be varied. Students given the opportunity to work in groups (both small and large) or in pairs on tasks requiring creative outcomes have the opportunity of observing how others employ their individual creativity heuristics. This has the added advantage of pressing students into perhaps explaining to others the rationale for suggestions made and ideas contributed. The process of verbalising one's decisions can help students to clarify their schemas.

The final aspect of sequencing proposed by Collins et al. (1989) advocates global before local skills, which allows students to build a conceptual map of the domain in which they are functioning before attending to the fine details. In designing, this may be a case of students appreciating the interactive nature of the various cognitive components (indicated by the bi-directional arrows in the model) before undertaking the task of actually experimenting with combining the various procedures for creative outcomes.

The sequencing of instruction described above is helpful in a context where the teaching practitioner has the time to develop the strategies through an extended course of study. However, when this ideal situation is not available, the practitioner may use the model in its original form as a short circuit to schema formation in the way described in the following section.

Using the creative thinking model heuristically as a conceptual tool

The categories and procedures characterising creative problem-solving as presented in this chapter provide the practitioner with ready-made sets of cognitive action concepts which may be considered when undertaking creative tasks. These can be used as a conceptual tool, providing a starting point for practitioners teaching students to navigate an ill-structured problem space, the content of which does not allow them the access or time with their students to develop creativity heuristics in the manner described above. Similarly, it may be useful for people such as those in business, who have not had the opportunity to develop individualised creativity schemas over a period of time but find themselves thrust into situations where creative problem-solving is expected. The following discussion, however, continues to relate to design.

The task of producing creative design outcomes may appear less daunting to students if they are provided with ideas about the kinds of cognitive steps they can enact to develop their design. This process is akin to 'schema training', as proposed by Derry. Here 'a student is provided with an abstract prototype representing a hierarchically structured set of concepts, objects, events, questions and so forth' (Derry 1990, p. 356). Schema training can encourage students who have not as yet developed their knowledge structures to become autonomous, active learners. In this way, the model provides a non-prescriptive scaffold for novice and neophyte designers. To this end, students may be provided with the model as it appears in Figure 7.1 with the attendant descriptive tables (Tables 7.1–7.4) which define the various procedures and then apply them to the problem at hand. If a student is having difficulty starting, the teacher may suggest that the student engage in some strategic and then generative thinking by identifying some goals (*goal-setting*) and then beginning to *search* memory for *retrieval* of related concepts. Similarly, if a student has developed a preliminary design but is uncertain about how to proceed, *switching* to a completely different idea may trigger *associations* which provide further possibilities for design development. Alternatively, instead of *switching* to a different idea, the student may choose to translate or shift the emerging design into a completely different context (*context-shifting*) to further explore the emerging solution. The result of this cognitive action may be *analysed* for strengths and weaknesses, ascertained for accordance with the set goals (*goal-monitoring*) or immediately developed further by being distilled into a stylised, simplified form (*categorical reduction*), depending on task requirements. In this way, cognitive activity can shift freely among the categories of thinking with the procedures identified in the model providing a cognitive scaffold as needed.

Creative products are 'built up' as a result of iterative and differential switching of cognition. It is useful for instructors, trainers and supervisors designing instruction in such fields to be aware of the means by which cognitive resources may be deployed. Adopting an interactive approach such as that described above may enhance the quality of output from apprentices and learners in fields requiring creative problem-solving.

CONCLUSION

This chapter has presented a model for creative thinking which preserves flexibility without over-simplifying the complex act of creative problem-solving. Such a model is extremely useful for domains that have traditionally been viewed as ill-structured, such as original design. The model consists of three levels of thinking with higher-order thinking consisting of the categories of executive control, generation, exploration and evaluation, each of which is characterised by particular procedures that may be utilised in any combination according to task requirements. The notion that iterative switching is an inherent—and indeed necessary—part of creative problem-solving requires the teaching practitioner to encourage students to use cognitive resources interactively. Although a particular category may predominate at various stages in a task, frequent incursions of other procedures can occur. The frequency with which such switching of cognitive activity occurs is entirely dependent on the requirements of the emerging solution. It is therefore important for students to realise that all categories of thinking may be found at all stages of creative problem-solving, although their relative frequencies are likely to differ. Thus generation does not have exclusive association with the initial stages of the process, even though it may be more likely to occur with greater frequency at this time as cognitive resources are marshalled and called into working memory. Similarly, evaluative procedures—which often serve to refine an emerging product—are usually associated with the final stage of the creative problem-solving process, but may also be deployed throughout. It is therefore useful for students involved in creative problem-solving to be encouraged to view the process as iterative, interactive and dynamic.

REFERENCES

Amabile, T.M. 1983, *The Social Psychology of Creativity*, Springer-Verlag, New York

Amabile, T.M., de Jong, W. & Lepper, M.R. 1976, 'Effects of externally imposed deadlines on subsequent intrinsic motivation', *Journal of Personality and Social Psychology*, vol. 34, pp. 92–8

Anderson, J.R. 1982, 'Acquisition of cognitive skill', *Psychological Review*, vol. 89, pp. 369–406

Armbruster, B.B. 1989, 'Metacognition in creativity', in *Handbook of Creativity*, eds J. Glover, R. Ronning, & C. Reynolds, Plenum Press, New York, pp. 177–82

Brown, R.T. 1989, 'Creativity: what are we to measure', in *Handbook of Creativity*, eds J. Glover, R. Ronning & C. Reynolds, Plenum Press, New York, pp. 3–32

Campbell, D.T. 1960, 'Blind variation and selective retention in creative thought as in other knowledge processes', *Psychological Review*, vol. 67, pp. 380–400

Campione, J.C., Brown, A.L. & Connell, M.L. 1989, 'Metacognition: on the importance of understanding what you are doing', in *Research Agenda for Mathematics Education: The Teaching and Assessing of Mathematical Problem Solving*, vol. 3, eds R.I. Charles & E.A. Silver, Erlbaum and the National Council of Teachers of Mathematics, Hillsdale, NJ, pp. 93–114

Collins, A., Brown, J.S. & Newman, S.E. 1989, 'Cognitive apprenticeship: teaching the crafts of reading, writing and mathematics', in *Knowledge, Learning and Instruction, Essays in Honor of Robert Glaser*, ed. L.B. Resnick, Erlbaum & Associates, Hillsdale, NJ, pp. 476–94

Cropley, A.J. 1997, 'Fostering creativity in the classroom: general principles', in *The Creativity Research Handbook*, ed. M. Runco, Hampton Press, Cresskill, NJ, pp. 83–114

de Bono, E. 1970, *Lateral Thinking*, Penguin, London

Derry, S. 1990, 'Learning strategies for acquiring useful knowledge', in *Dimensions of Thinking and Cognitive Instruction*, eds B.F. Jones & L. Idol, Lawrence Erlbaum Associates, Hillsdale, NJ, pp. 347–79

Dowd, E.T. 1989, 'The self and creativity: several constructs in search of a theory', in *Handbook of Creativity*, eds J. Glover, R. Ronning, & C. Reynolds, Plenum Press, New York, pp. 233–42

Efland, A.D. 1995, 'The spiral and the lattice: changes in cognitive learning theory with implications for art education', *Studies in Art Education: A Journal of Issues and Research*, vol. 36, pp. 136–56

Evans, G. 1991, 'Student control over learning', in *Teaching for Learning: The View from Cognitive Psychology*, ed. J. Biggs, Australian Council for Educational Research, Melbourne, pp. 51–70

Finke, R., Ward, T. & Smith, S. 1992, *Creative Cognition*, MIT Press, Cambridge, MA

Glaser, R. 1985, 'Thoughts on expertise', ERIC document ED 264 301, version of a talk given at the Social Science Research Council conference on 'The study of expertise as a model for life-span cognitive development'

Glaser, R. & Bassok, M. 1989, 'Learning theory and the study of instruction', *Annual Review of Psychology*, vol. 40, pp. 631–66

Goel, V. 1995, *Sketches of Thought*, MIT Press, London

Goel, V. & Pirolli, P. 1992, 'The structure of design problem spaces', *Cognitive Science*, vol. 16, pp. 395–429

Gott, S. 1989, 'Apprenticeship instruction for real world tasks: the coordination of procedures, mental models, and strategies', *Review of Research in Education*, vol. 15, pp. 97–169

Guastell, S.J., Shissle, J., Driscol, J. & Hyde, T. 1998, 'Are some cognitive styles more productive than others', *Journal of Creative Behaviour*, vol. 32, pp. 77–91

Guilford, J.P. 1956, 'The structure of the intellect', *Psychological Bulletin*, vol. 53, pp. 267–93

—— 1967, *The Nature of Human Intelligence*, McGraw-Hill, New York

—— 1968, *Intelligence, Creativity and their Educational Implications*, Knapp, San Diego

Hennessey, B.A. & Amabile, T.M. 1988, 'The conditions of creativity', in *The Nature of Creativity*, ed. R. Sternberg, Cambridge University Press, Cambridge, pp. 11–38

Jausovec, N. 1994, 'Metacognition in creative problem solving', in *Problem Finding, Problem Solving and Creativity*, ed. M. Runco, Ablex, Norwood, NJ, pp. 77–95

Jay, E.S. & Perkins, D.N. 1997, 'Problem finding: the search for mechanism', in *The Creativity Research Handbook*, ed. M. Runco, Hampton Press, NJ, pp. 257–93

Keller, C.M. & Keller, J.D. 1996, *Cognition and Tool Use: The Blacksmith at Work*, Cambridge University Press, Cambridge

Koestner, R., Ryan, R., Bernieri, F. & Holt, K. 1984, 'Setting limits on children's behaviour: the differential effects of controlling vs. informal styles on intrinsic motivation and creativity', *Journal of Personality*, vol. 52, pp. 233–48

Lepper, M., Greene, D. & Nisbett, R. 1973, 'Undermining children's intrinsic interest with extrinsic rewards: a test of the "overjustification" hypothesis', *Journal of Personality and Social Psychology*, vol. 28, pp. 129–37

Mednick, S.A. 1962, 'The associative basis of the creative process', *Psychological Review*, vol. 69, pp. 220–30

Mumford, M.D. & Gustafson, S.B. 1988, 'Creativity syndrome: integration, application, and innovation', *Psychological Bulletin*, vol. 103, pp. 27–43

Perkins, D.N. 1981, *The Mind's Best Work*, Harvard University Press, Cambridge, MA

Reiter-Palmon, R., Mumford, M.D. & Threlfall, K.V. 1998, 'Solving everyday problems creatively: the role of problem construction and personality type', *Creativity Research Journal*, vol. 11, pp. 187–97

Runco, M.A. & Chand, I. 1994, 'Problem finding, evaluative thinking, and creativity', in *Problem Finding, Problem Solving, and Creativity*, ed. M. Runco, Ablex, Norwood, NJ, pp. 40–77

Scandura, J.M. 1981, 'Problem solving in schools and beyond: transitions from the naive to the neophyte to the master', *Educational Psychologist*, vol. 16, pp. 139–50

Smith, S.M. 1995, 'Fixation, incubation, and insight in memory and creative thinking', in *The Creative Cognition Approach*, eds. S. Smith, T. Ward and R. Finke, MIT Press, Cambridge, MA, pp. 135–56

Sternberg, R.J. & Lubart, T.I. 1991, 'An investment theory of creativity and its development', *Human Development*, vol. 34, pp. 1–31

Stevenson, J. 1986, 'Adaptability: theoretical considerations', *Journal of Structural Learning*, vol. 9, pp. 107–17

—— 1991, 'Cognitive structures for the teaching of adaptability in vocational education', in *Learning and Teaching Cognitive Skills*, ed. G. Evans, Australian Council For Educational Research, Melbourne, pp. 144–84

Stevenson, J. & McKavanagh, C. 1992, 'Skill formation for the work place', in *Work and Education*, ed. M. Poole, Australian Council for Educational Research, Melbourne, pp. 72–90

Torrance, E.P. & Horng, R. 1980, 'Creativity and style of learning and thinking: characteristics of adaptors and innovators', *Creative Child and Adult Quarterly*, vol. 5, pp. 80–5

Wallas, G. 1926, *The Art of Thought*, Harcourt, New York

—— 1970, 'The art of thought', in *Creativity*, ed. P.E. Vernon, Penguin Books, Harmondsworth, pp. 91–7

Ward, T., Smith, S. & Vaid, J. 1997, 'Conceptual structures and processes in creative thought', in *Creative Thought: An Investigation of Conceptual Structures and Processes*, eds. T. Ward, S. Smith and J. Vaid, American Psychological Association, Washington, DC, pp. 1–27

Weisberg, R.W. 1988, 'Problem solving and creativity', in *The Nature of Creativity*, ed. R. Steinberg, Cambridge University Press, Cambridge, pp. 148–76

Yashin-Shaw, I. 2001, 'A cognitive model for understanding creative thinking', PhD thesis, Griffith University, Brisbane

8

Working values

John Stevenson

INTRODUCTION

Being able to perform in the workplace is often called 'competence', usually with a predominant focus on behaviour or overt performance, and sometimes including recognition of the understanding that is involved in that performance. However, seldom do such definitions recognise or expand upon the normative aspects of competence—the values and attitudes that are involved in working.

Yet competence is normative, involving not only the construction of meaning and the execution of technical skill, but also the capacity to make value-laden judgements about what should be done, in that setting, at that time, and for what purpose—'determining what should be done for the best in the realm of conduct' (Carr 1993, p. 263). Values appear to be immanent in any kind of performance in a setting. That is, competence is related not only to personal attitude and values, but also to the historical and cultural aspects of the environment in which it is used—in other words, to what is thought to be appropriate in that workplace setting. The normative activity that takes place in workplaces is the subject of this chapter.

A variety of values operates in all walks of life, including the workplace. In the workplace, these values may come from one's personal upbringing, the ethos of the company, the expectations of one's work colleagues, social institutions such as law, and so on. Values may be in conflict or may be consonant. Moreover, employers place a high value on values and attitudes. On the basis of the National Center on the Educational Quality of the Workforce (1995) data, Stasz (1997) draws attention to the importance of applicants' attitudes in employer hiring decisions. Employers rank an applicant's attitude first (4.6 out of 5) above communication skills (4.2), previous work experience (4.0) and industry-based credentials (certifying applicant's skills) (3.2).

In this chapter, the idea of values and approaches to defining and identifying values are outlined. It is argued that it is difficult to sharply differentiate normative beliefs in terms of attitudes and values; that values are socially derived; and that societal values undergo change over time. The separation of knowledge and values in the psychological literature and the ways in which cognitive psychology treats values as cognitive dispositions are also outlined. It is argued that values in practice extend beyond these dispositions. Theoretical approaches arising from the concepts of settings, communities of practice and activity systems are then discussed. The utility of elements identified in activity systems for examining values as rules; as immanent in technologies; as implicit in objects, outcomes and divisions of labour; and as held in constructions of the objects and outcomes of activity are explained. Because of the wide variety of values that can operate in a workplace setting, it is suggested that individuals find they have to come to a personal reconciliation of the various values which appear to impact on their work. Research on values which appear to operate in various workplace settings is then discussed. Finally, implications of the normative aspect of work are suggested for curriculum development, teaching and learning.

VALUES

Essentially, questions of value are questions of ethics—normative ethics that involve judgements about what kinds of things are ultimately good and how we should decide what actions are right (Singer 1994, p. 10). Values underlying action can be approached in a number of ways. There is a long history of identifying values regarded as important in society. For example, ancient Greek philosophers addressed such values as truth, beauty, knowledge, justice, temperance and honour.

Rokeach differentiates *values*, *attitudes* and *beliefs*. He defines attitudes as:

> an organization of several beliefs focused on a specific object (physical or social, concrete or abstract) or situation, predisposing one to respond to in some preferential manner ... An attitude is thus a package of beliefs consisting of interconnected assertions to the effect that certain things about a specific object or situation are true

or false, and other things about it are desirable or undesirable (Rokeach 1976, p. 159).

> Values, on the other hand, have to do with modes of conduct and end-states of existence ... a value is a single belief that transcendentally guides actions and judgements across specific objects and situations, and beyond immediate goals to more ultimate end-states of existence. Moreover, a value, unlike an attitude, is an imperative to action, not only a belief about the preferable, but also a preference for the preferable. (Rokeach 1976, pp. 159–60).

However, Gaus (1990) disputes this sharp distinction between values and attitudes.

In this chapter, following Rokeach, values are taken to be a desirable mode of behaviour or end-state, guiding actions, attitudes, judgements and comparisons across specific objects and situations. However, the focus here is on discerning the ways in which activity extends beyond knowledge of propositions and procedures, and includes normative aspects. Hence the term 'value' is limited neither to abstract principles, nor to any degree of specificity or generality. Rather, the term is applied to any normative principle that seems to guide actions. Thus, as for Gaus, it is accepted that a sharp distinction is not possible among values, attitudes and beliefs and, in the present chapter, the term *values* is accorded any normative principle which seems to guide actions and judgements about why the goals at which they are directed are taken to be desirable.

SOCIAL ORIGINS OF VALUES

There exist various taxonomies of values. For instance, Rokeach differentiates *instrumental* values (personally and socially preferable in all situations and with respect to all objects) (e.g. broad-minded, clean, forgiving, responsible, honest and courageous) and *terminal* values (an end-state of existence personally and socially worth striving for) (e.g. equality, freedom, a world at peace, a comfortable life, a meaningful life, maturity, national security, respect for others, respect from others, salvation, true friendship and wisdom). He also differentiates between values and *value systems*. Rokeach argues that some values are universally held, but that individuals differ in how they organise them to form values hierarchies or priorities.

Nevertheless, values are socially constructed—that is, various values operate in society and in various groups and settings in society, and these various values have an influence on what individuals see as valuable and desirable and the activity in which they engage. For instance, according to Reed:

Self development is a complex process or appropriation and transformation of some of the values in one's milieu, often under conditions of conflict, either of expediences ('needs') or proprieties ('choices') or both. Under such conditions, individuals do not develop coherent systems of values, but clusters of valuations, some of which may undermine others. Indeed, as I have argued, many individuals will feel considerable ambivalence, even concerning their own core values. Throughout the course of development, these conflicts and ambivalences fuel developmental change (Reed 1996, p. 13).

In society, values undergo change over time. For instance, in a nine-nation Delphi study of the complex global crises that humans will face over the next 25 years, Parker et al. report the value-laden characteristics that individuals will need to handle these crises as follows:

- ability to look at and approach problems as a member of a global society;
- ability to work with others in a cooperative way and to take responsibility for one's roles/duties within society;
- ability to understand, accept, appreciate, and tolerate cultural differences;
- capacity to think in a critical and systemic way;
- willingness to resolve conflict in a non-violent way;
- willingness to change one's lifestyle and consumption habits to protect the environment;
- ability to be sensitive toward and to defend human rights (e.g. rights of women, ethnic minorities) (Parker et al. 1999, p. 125).

Similarly, a contemporary Australian empirical study on desirable future goals for Australia by Campbell et al. (1992) clustered values held by leading thinkers into a normative hierarchy. In the list of learning needs and the goal-value system above, it is apparent that the operating values are related to more than the interests of separate individuals. Rather, they touch on such aspects of life as relationships with others (from an interpersonal level through to local, national and global communities), the economy and the future of the planet itself. At the same time, they incorporate both instrumental and end values, such as responsibility, harmony and respect.

COGNITIVE TREATMENT OF VALUES IN RELATION TO KNOWLEDGE

The ideas of knowledge and values are often treated separately in the cognitive literature. For example, in cognitive psychology there is considerable emphasis on propositional knowledge (knowledge of facts, principles and theories) and procedural knowledge (knowledge of specific routines, methods and algorithms and problem-solving knowledge). In cognitive psychology, there is some recognition of 'dispositions'; however, these are usually restricted to ideas related to tendencies to access and use one's knowledge base and strategies to achieve particular kinds of transfer. Such dispositions as the following are usually identified (Prawat 1989):

- mastery and performance dispositions (goals to increase one's competence versus goals to gain a positive judgement of one's competence, respectively);
- motivational orientation (e.g. attributions of success to effort versus luck or task difficulty);
- action identity (cognitive representation of an action, such as having an identity which consists of actions that focus on 'why' questions as opposed to one which consists of 'how to' actions);
- maintenance difficulty (affected by relative difficulty, complexity, familiarity, enactment time and learning time).

Perkins et al. (1993, p. 75) define dispositions as 'people's tendencies to put their capabilities into action', but confine their examples to 'thinking dispositions'—for example, tendencies of mindfulness (open, alert, flexible processing of information), investment of mental effort, exploration, inquiry, organisation of thinking and risk-taking. Dispositions are seen to affect transfer of existing knowledge to new situations. Transfer attitudes are thought to be affected by self-efficacy, fear of failure, anxiety, intolerance of mistakes and other emotional blocks (Pea 1987).

In this chapter, the idea of values extends beyond that of cognitive dispositions. It involves what individuals and groups at work see and adopt as desirable and preferable activity.

VALUES IN SETTINGS AND COMMUNITIES OF PRACTICE

As Pea (1987) argues, transfers of understanding to everyday tasks are often not taken because of 'appropriacy' and effort, both of which have cultural grounding. Socio-cultural standards affect judgements of whether transfer is appropriate. These may be conventions and mores, even taboos, as well as any cognitive disposition to engage in minimal cognitive effort.

When one considers an individual at work, one needs to recognise that the question of values relates not only to those of the person concerned. Rather, there is also a culture in the community of practice (or setting or activity system) which is constituted by the setting itself, and by those in the setting. Moreover, this culture is historical and is usually undergoing transformation in response to tensions and contradictions which, according to activity theory (Engeström 1999d; Leont'ev 1981), are immanent in such settings.

Workplace environments can be considered as *settings* (Barker 1968, 1978), *communities of practice* (Lave & Wenger 1991), or *activity systems* (Engeström 1999a; Leont'ev 1981 [1959]). The influence of *settings* in pressing individuals to engage in certain kinds of activity is well known (Barker 1978; Lewin 1951; Murray 1938). The ideas of *setting theory* are that:

- behaviour is a function not only of internal cognition, but also the environment in which it takes place and interactions with that environment (Barker 1978; Lewin 1951);
- a press (cf. Murray 1938) arises from characteristics of the environment, which circumscribe the kind of activity that is elicited; and
- individuals shape their (learning) tasks not only on the basis of their internal cognitive representations, but also on their perceptions of the external environment (cf. Doyle 1979; Posner 1982).

The idea of a *community of practice* is 'a set of relations among persons, activity, and the world, over time and in relation with other tangential and overlapping communities of practice' (Lave & Wenger 1991, p. 98). Lave and Wenger argue that the possibilities for learning in such communities of practice are defined by the social structure, power relationships and conditions of legitimacy. These socio-cultural approaches to explaining learning position learners as newcomers who move into and towards the centre of communities of practice as they acquire expertise and identity in that community. The gradual changes in the position of the person influence the kind of learning that takes place (e.g. see Lave & Wenger 1991; Rogoff & Lave 1984). Thus there are normative dimensions of the attendant culture, which affect the activity that takes place.

In *activity theory* (Engeström 1999a, 1999b, 1999c, 1999d), some of the values that operate in the activity system can be identified as 'rules'. The activity system is thought of as a culturally and historically situated collection of individuals (subjects) working together (community), pursuing a shared object (motive). There is a division of labour and there are tools that mediate the work of subjects. An activity system is defined by its shared object, which represents the collective motive to which activity is directed. This object is normative—that is, value-laden. It provides the normative reason for collective activity—for example, the motive to produce a new product with all its various features. Sometimes mission statements are generated to capture such objects. Values are also immanent in the kinds of technology in (or not in) use in the setting, where those technologies have been derived over time from various kinds of human activity directed at various kinds of objects. Various values are also held by those who constitute the community, and are manifested in the ways in which their contributions are organised in a division of labour and directed at the shared object. Such different values lead to different constructions of the object of activity and the desired outcomes. Differences in values can lead to tensions and contradiction in an activity system and can get in the way of successful working for individuals and teams. Engeström (1999d) argues for a process of expansive visibilisation in order to make tensions and contradictions apparent, so that they can be resolved in a way that leads to improved (expanded) practice.

Hence, in this chapter, what is thought to be appropriate by the individual in approaching activity is viewed as a personal reconciliation of values that come from the various sources (elements) that operate in any given workplace. It is assumed that, for a workplace to operate in some kind of effective way, it needs to become an activity system—that is, there needs to be some kind of shared understanding of what is a valued object at which collective activity is to be directed. Hence it is assumed that individuals take on a set of values as guiding principles for their work, where that set of values provides the best reconciliation (for that person) of consonant and competing values that operate in that workplace. That is, from a complex of forces operating in any given workplace, it is assumed that a personal view develops that some normative beliefs and actions are of a higher value than others. These influences may come from personal moral codes, artefacts and technologies in the setting, implicit and explicit rules, manuals, organisation of work, adopted technologies, directions, perceived expectations, and so on. Individuals may find that their own personal goals are or are not consonant with the collective motive.

RECENT RESEARCH ON WORKPLACE VALUES

In the work reviewed above, values have been advanced in relation to various aspects of one's life. However, little has been advanced about the kinds of values that actually seem to operate in workplaces and how such values relate to other kinds of values.

In workplaces, there are manifold normative influences, and the cultural norms of workplaces (including any prevailing and/or conflicting values) influence the ways in which individuals draw upon and utilise their knowledge. Moreover, in workplaces the different kinds of values range from those which are ideological through to expected ways in which classes of tasks are to be undertaken and the character and beliefs of the various individuals who make up the community of practice (Lave & Wenger 1991).

In a study of seven jobs in the United States, Stasz examined explicitly work-related skills and attitudes. Seven jobs were studied: traffic signal technicians, home health aides, licensed vocational nurses, test cell associates, equipment technicians, construction inspectors and survey inspectors. In her analysis of attitude requirements of work, Stasz (1997, p. 213) collected dispositions under three 'somewhat overlapping themes': task/organization (formal job characteristics); practice (the community of practice, which can have different norms from those of management); and quality standards. That is, she recognised that a complex of factors, coming from different sources, affects values in practice.

As discussed above, such attitudes as those found by Stasz can be thought of as reconciled sets of guiding normative principles derived from various origins. Some may originate in the community of practice and may be expectations of one's colleagues or superiors; others may originate with the public with whom one interacts; others may come from wider community expectations; while still others may be expectations that one has of oneself.

From research in the hospitality and airline industries (Stevenson 1996, 1997), values appearing to underlie actions were clustered as shown in Table 8.1. While the headings in the table are arbitrary labels abstracted from actual practice, the table serves to illustrate the variety of normative principles that can be discerned in workplaces, the similarities of value clusters with those found by Stasz, the complex interrelationships and even apparent contradictions that appear among principles, the variety of sources apparent in the set of values, and the apparent isolation of values in these workplace settings from those relating to ideas of a desirable society. The value stances taken in practice appeared to be the result of considering and responding to a mix of obligations and expectations.

IMPLICATIONS FOR CURRICULUM DEVELOPMENT

Curriculum development is a value-laden undertaking which proceeds from a platform of beliefs. According to Walker, a *platform* consists of beliefs (conceptions, theories and aims) that are involved in curriculum development; *conceptions* means 'beliefs about what exists and about what is possible'; *theories* are 'beliefs about what relations hold between entities, that is, beliefs about what is true'; and *aims* are 'beliefs about the good and the beautiful in education' (Walker 1971, p. 56). This platform informs various aspects of curriculum decision-making, including the development of statements of curriculum intent, content, teaching strategies, learning experiences, assessment and evaluation (Laird & Stevenson 1993). Thus the platform determines which teaching and learning concerns are worthwhile considering, what

Table 8.1 Illustrative values found in hospitality and airline work sites

Focus on self	Focus on work		The job		The business		Focus on society
	Interaction with others	Protect oneself	Contribute to the climate	Get job done	Be on the ball	Meet company expectations (profit)	Provide customer service
Be happy/enjoy work	Be responsible						
	Inform others	Assign responsibility	Be friendly/caring	Be flexible	Be vigil/keep up	Get or keep trade	Be friendly
Engage in humour	Assume liability	Blame others	Information/help	Solve/reconcile	Be accurate	Get payments	Help/inform/ feedback
Enjoy people contact	Check with others	Keep others honest	Be courteous	Make sure do all	Be thorough	Normalise	Be courteous
Accept/like variety	Leave office staffed	Lay down rules	Show respect	Find out and clarify	Have plan	Be accountable	Keep customer happy
Have integrity	Use discretion	Hide things	Cooperate/rely	Take initiative	Be efficient	Make profit	Assert but appease
Impute characteristics to others		Acknowledge lack of knowledge	Organise others	Don't waste effort	Do many things		Project professional appearances
Have pride in self			Get information/ help	Persist	Have information backup		Move responsibility to customer
Care about others			Clarify	Keep busy	Be timely		Get salient information
			Reassure		Check		Check bona fides
					Prioritise		Give privilege

Source: Stevenson (1996, 1997).

should be included in the statements of intent and what kinds of practice are legitimate. In terms of activity theory, curriculum development is an activity where the motive can be teased out in terms of a platform of beliefs—including normative beliefs.

In competency-based training, for example, it is clear that for content to be legitimate, it must correspond with a stated industrial standard. However, curriculum documents do not always state the platform of beliefs that is involved. Moreover, statements of intent are often proposed as if they were value-free—assuming competency statements are value-neutral. Moreover, the codes in which curriculum content is expressed can leave little space for codification of values.

Thus, while a workplace can be thought of in terms of a value-laden activity system, curriculum development aimed at preparing people for effective work in that activity system is itself an activity system. In curriculum development activity, those planning and having vocational curricular statements approved may or may not accommodate working values in their own platforms of beliefs and in the curricular statements. Serious dissonance can therefore arise between curriculum planning and working values. Moreover, the implementation of approved curricula depends critically on the beliefs of those undertaking the implementation (Fullan 1982). The clash between the values of policy-makers and those involved in organising teaching and learning is often the cause of differences between curricula as designed and curricula as implemented in practice. Thus further dissonance can occur between values reflected in curriculum plans and teaching practice, with implications for the values with which learners actually engage.

Nevertheless, teaching and learning should not just be a top-down process of knowledge inculcation (Chapters 1 and 2). Rather, learning should develop a facility with normative meanings, rendered in various ways. Thus, some implications for curriculum development that can be advanced are as follows:

- Platforms of beliefs on which curricula are designed need to be explicit so that learners and teachers can access the meaning of content in a normative way.
- Curriculum content should not be portrayed as value-neutral because of the complex of values involved in designing curricula, constructing meaning on curriculum content and drawing upon curricula content in operating in workplace practice.
- Values that operate in workplaces and their relationships with values held in other settings and society more generally warrant recognition and codification in the same way as other content, so that they receive explicit attention in teaching and learning.

- Teaching staff need the opportunity to engage in experiences aimed at interconnecting the values that characterise workplaces, instructional programs and their own beliefs.
- Curricula should contain content aimed at assisting learners to identify values in workplaces and to interconnect these values with their own normative beliefs and with values that operate in various walks of life.
- Curricula should contain content aimed at empowering learners to engage in communication with others about values, so that differences in workplace constructions of objects, and values immanent in technologies and the organisation can be made visible; contradictions and tensions can be unmasked; and practice can be improved.

IMPLICATIONS FOR TEACHING AND LEARNING

Meaning is not value-neutral. The development of values in and for work is not unconnected with the development of meaning from working and other experiences. The principles that can be advanced for teaching and learning in connection with working values are similar to those for the development of any kind of meaning (see Chapters 1 and 2). That is, meaning is best derived from purposeful experience in authentic practice where the functions of the activity are transparent. Specifically, the following principles are advanced to guide teaching and learning.

Use of concrete experience in an authentic area of practice

Like all learning, meaning is best derived from actual concrete situated practice where function and purpose are transparent. Individuals constructing meaning from concrete experience do so in a culture where the appropriateness of various kinds of activity is culturally defined. It is in practice that differences among personally held values, values that appear to be held in wider society and values apparent in working practice come into contrast.

For instance, settings can be analysed by learners (and their teachers) in terms of activity theory elements: subject, object, instruments, division of labour, community, rules and outcomes. Tension and contradictions within elements and between them can be identified—for example, in terms of constructions of the object of the work setting. For instance, some may see the object in terms of salary, prestige and advancement; some in terms of the kinds of products and services generated and their utility to others; some in terms of profit to the company; some in terms of personal challenge and enjoyment of the work; some in terms of contribution to society, and so on.

Thus concrete practice is a rich resource for identifying and considering values and their relationships with other aspects of the setting. Moreover, exploration of values in settings is important because of the ways in which it helps to make transparent the functions and purposes of the setting and the activity within it—an important ingredient in making meaning. At the same time, in authentic practice, values can become meaningful, related to concrete activity in pursuit of vocation.

Making values explicit

The task of teaching involves developing capacities to communicate about values, making connections among different renditions of values (e.g. in actions, in technologies and in words), making connections among values that appear to operate in different walks of life, and making connections among values that appear to be held by different people and groups. However, values may well be hidden or remain tacit in working situations. Thus one of the tasks of teaching and learning is to assist learners to discern values, to unmask them, to identify their sources and to relate them to their own beliefs and to various other kinds of values. For instance, in learning how to change the oil in the sump of a car, lay a course of bricks in the building of a house or install plumbing in a commercial building, various possible values could be reflected in objects related to efficiency, timeliness, thoroughness, expensiveness to the owner, the profit-making capacity of the firm, the effects of disposal on the environment, and so on.

It is possible that this complex of possible object-values may bring into conflict such object-values as achieving technical efficiency, protecting the environment, the efficiency of the end-product, and the profit-making capacity of the firm (for example, see the lists of values identified by Stasz (1997), Stevenson (1996, 1997), Campbell et al. (1992) and Rokeach (1976)). Learners can operate upon these values and any contradictions and tensions among them only if they are alert to them and know their origins. This activity needs to be undertaken explicitly, converting espoused, instantiated and enacted beliefs into a common currency so that inconsistencies become apparent. While verbal renditions of values may be inexact renditions of values personally held, these renditions and their interconnections help in clarifying and communicating about values in practice.

As described above, activity theory is useful in helping to delineate and make visible the values inherent in activity and its various dimensions. The teaching and learning framework of Collins et al. (1989) also has some strength in this regard. Apart from the strengths of making values explicit through modelling, coaching and scaffolding, the techniques of exploiting cooperation and exploiting competition, whereby learners work in groups to develop a consensual view and then to contrast their positions with other groups, may well help in making values explicit and in exploring their relationships. Facilitators would contrast not only differences in the ways in which tasks were approached and problems solved, but the normative reasons for choices and the normative consequences. These could also be related to wider societal goals as appropriate (e.g. global harmony, world peace, a safe and well-protected environment, equity, and so on).

Developing an understanding of societal values and their relationship with working values

Given the apparent disconnection of workplace values in practice from considerations of wider society, there appears to be a need to bring the societal context of workplace values more into the open. There needs to be more engagement with such ideas as those of a desirable society, so that workplace values do not remain isolated from socially desirable futures. Various lists of values are available for consideration—for example, those developed by Rokeach (1976), Parker et al. (1999) and Campbell et al. (1992). Such lists can be compared with values empirically found in workplaces and the various ways in which those values operate in those and other workplaces. The ideas of instrumental and end values, universal values and hierarchies of values can also be examined. Views about the historical, cultural and situated relativity of values can be explored. For instance, the idea of *being responsible* is operationalised differently in different work settings, and its relationships with global harmony, justice and environmental responsibility warrant exploration. Such considerations will help individuals to interconnect the meanings that they afford such ideas as that of responsibility and their instantiation in practice.

Making the values underlying curriculum content explicit

The platforms of beliefs underpinning vocational curriculum development need to be explicit so that learners can see how they and their learning are being positioned—complicit with what kinds of societal values (e.g. about certain uses of resources, the engagement of individuals in work, the quality of human interaction, the nature of the natural and built environment and the relationships among people); reinforcing what kinds of workplace practices; and related in what ways to individual goals and aspirations.

Creating opportunities to reconcile normative meanings

Individuals seek to reconcile meanings derived from particular experiences and settings, such as in workplaces, with meanings that they derive from other life pursuits and settings. This connectedness is not only in terms of abstracted concepts and other ways in which meaning is understood; it is also normative. What is appropriate for competent action in work needs to be connected with what is regarded as appropriate at home, in civilian activities and in various other life pursuits. Unmasking and communicating about values assists in seeking reconciliations. The asking of 'what if . . .' questions in teaching and learning, concerning the adoption of certain kinds of wider societal or personal values in the workplace (and vice versa), may help to bring into focus various kinds of tensions and contradictions.

Developing the capacity to engage in assertive action with respect to values

Without direct engagement with values immanent in the ways in which work is currently undertaken, inappropriate industrial practices can be reproduced. In seeking to improve practice, just being able to state a value is not a very useful attribute. Nor, on its own, is being able to identify values operating in various settings. One needs to be able to operate upon values and their interconnections. This capacity requires understanding: understanding of how to recognise values, how to communicate about values, how to engage in assertive action with respect to values, how to develop and change one's own values, and so on. The capacity to engage in activity aimed at improving workplace outcomes requires the capacity to make values visible—through, for example, mirroring values, to others—and to engage in cooperative action aimed at expanding constructions of the object and outcomes of activity in ways that constitute improvement.

CONCLUSION

The capacity to engage in activity in a setting involves values. Values are questions of ethics involving consideration of what should be done for the best outcome in a particular situation. There exist various taxonomies of values, but values are socially derived. Various values operating in contemporary society have already been described. Some of the values which appear to operate in various workplaces have also been identified. These values are context-dependent and can be related to various sources. They also seem to be isolated from values that operate in wider society. While abstract labels can be assigned to these values, the ways in which they influence activity in various settings differ according to characteristics of the setting. Activity theory provides a useful set of elements for examining the nature and operation of values and their development and instantiations over time.

The activity of curriculum development and the various kinds of decision-making that are involved are value-laden. Several principles for addressing the value-laden nature of curriculum development are advanced, including the need for platforms of beliefs underpinning curriculum development to be explicit, for working values to be identified and related to other individual and societal values, for teachers to engage in experiences aimed at the interconnections of values and for learners to engage with content aimed at assisting them also to identify and engage with values.

With regard to teaching and learning, it is suggested that:

- the development of normative meaning should proceed from concrete experience in practice;
- various kinds of values in practice should be made explicit and related to wider societal values;
- learners should consider how curricular content positions them as learners; and
- learners should be involved in experiences aimed at making visible, interconnecting and reconciling normative meanings.

It is also suggested that activity theory is a valuable tool for examining and unmasking values, as well as for making them visible and operating upon differences in value-laden constructions to improve practice.

REFERENCES

Barker, R.G. 1968, *Ecological Psychology*, Stanford University Press, Stanford, CA
—— 1978, 'Theory of behaviour settings' in *Habitats, Environments and Human Behaviour*, eds R.G. Barker & Associates, Jossey Bass, San Francisco
Campbell, W.J., McMeniman, M.M. & Baikaloff, N. 1992, 'Visions of a desirable future Australian society', *New Horizons in Education*, vol. 87, pp. 17–39
Carr, D. 1993, 'Questions of competence', *British Journal of Educational Studies*, vol. 41, no. 3, pp. 253–71
Collins, A., Brown, J.S. & Newman, S.E. 1989, 'Cognitive apprenticeship: teaching the crafts of reading, writing, and mathematics', in *Knowing, Learning, and Instruction. Essays in Honor of Robert Glaser*, ed. L. Resnick, Lawrence Erlbaum Associates, Hillsdale, NJ, pp. 453–94
Dewey, J. 1916, *Democracy and Education*, Macmillan, New York
Doyle, W. 1979, 'Classroom effects', *Theory into Practice*, vol. 18, no. 3, pp. 138–44
Engeström, Y. 1999a, 'Activity theory and individual and social transformation', in *Perspectives on Activity Theory*, eds Y. Engeström, R. Miettinen & R.-L. Punamäki, Cambridge University Press, Cambridge

—— 1999b, 'Expansive visibilization of work: an activity-theoretical perspective', *Computer Supported Cooperative Work*, vol. 8, pp. 63–93

—— 1999c, 'Innovative learning in work teams: analysing cycles of knowledge creation in practice', in *Perspectives on Activity Theory*, eds Y. Engeström, R. Miettinen & R.-L. Punamäki, Cambridge University Press, Cambridge

—— 1999d, 'Expansive learning at work: towards an activity-theoretical reconceptualization', keynote address, *Changing Practice through Research: Changing Research through Practice*, 7th Annual International Conference on Post-Compulsory Education and Training, Centre for Learning and Work Research, Griffith University, Brisbane

Fullan, M. 1982, *The Meaning of Educational Change*, Teachers' College, Columbia University, New York

Gaus, G.F. 1990, *Value and Justification: The Foundations of Liberal Theory*, Cambridge University Press, Cambridge

Laird, D.J. & Stevenson, J.C. 1993, 'A curriculum framework for vocational education', *Australian and New Zealand Journal of Vocational Education Research*, vol. 1, no. 2, pp. 71–92

Lave, J. & Wenger, E. 1991, *Situated Learning: Legitimate Peripheral Participation*, Cambridge University Press, Cambridge

Leont'ev, A.N. 1981 (1959), *Problems of the Development of the Mind*, Progress, Moscow

Lewin, K. 1951, *Field Theory in Social Science*, Harper, New York

Murray, H.A. 1938, *Explorations in Personality*, Oxford University Press, New York

National Center on the Educational Quality of the Workforce 1995, *EQW National Employer Survey EQW-NES*, University of Pennsylvania, Philadelphia

Parker, W.C., Nonomiya, A. & Cogan, J. 1999, 'Educating world citizens: toward multinational curriculum development', *American Educational Research Journal*, vol. 36, no. 2, pp. 117–46

Pea, R. 1987, 'Socializing the knowledge transfer problem', *International Journal of Educational Research*, vol. 11, no. 6, pp. 639–63

Perkins, D., Jay, E. & Tishman, S. 1993, 'New conceptions of thinking: from ontology to education', *Educational Psychologist*, vol. 28, no. 1, pp. 67–85

Posner, G.A. 1982, 'A cognitive science conception of curriculum and instruction', *Journal of Curriculum Studies*, vol. 14, no. 4, pp. 343–351

Prawat, R.S. 1989, 'Promoting access to knowledge, strategy, and disposition in students: a research synthesis', *Review of Educational Research*, vol. 59, no. 1, pp. 1–41

Reed, E.S. 1996, 'Selves, values, cultures', in *Values and Knowledge*, eds E.S. Reed, E. Turiel & T. Brown, Erlbaum, Mahwah, NJ

Rogoff, B. & Lave, J. 1984, *Everyday Cognition: Its Development in Social Context*, Harvard University Press, Cambridge, Mass.

Rokeach, M. 1976, *Beliefs, Attitudes and Values: A Theory of Organization and Change*, Jossey Bass, San Francisco

Singer, P. ed. 1994, *Ethics*, Oxford Readers, Oxford University Press, Oxford

Stasz, C. 1997, 'Do employers need the skills they want? Evidence from technical work', *Journal of Education and Work*, vol. 10, no. 3, pp. 205–23

Stevenson, J.C. ed. 1996, *Learning in the Workplace: Tourism and Hospitality. A Report on an Initial Exploratory Examination of Critical Aspects of Small Businesses in the Tourism and Hospitality Industry*, Centre for Skill Formation Research and Development, Griffith University, Brisbane

—— 1997, 'Values in airline customer service work sites', in *Learning in the Workplace: Airline Customer Service*, ed. F. Beven, Centre for Learning and Work Research, Griffith University, Brisbane

Walker, D.F. 1971, 'A naturalistic model for curriculum development', *School Review*, vol. 80, pp. 51–64

Part III

Emerging challenges in instructional delivery

9

Strategies for developing flexible learning

Clive Kanes

INTRODUCTION

Facilitated by new information and communications media, the last decade has seen the growing convergence of distance education, open learning and face-to-face teaching. Under the rubric of flexible learning, new technologies are being deployed in order to give new meaning to the concept of the learner-centred curriculum. In addition, new technologies have enabled the pace and place of learning to be consciously varied by the student, and this also has generated new kinds of intersections among learning institutions, workplaces and the sites of student learning. The aim of this chapter is twofold. Firstly, it is meant to be read as an exposition outlining the main features of what is known about flexible learning. This is designed to serve as an introduction to readers of the themes and issues engaged by flexible learning practices. Secondly, the chapter aims to present a new model of flexible learning which allows us to present a view about creating flexible learning opportunities. It is only through sketching out the large picture of flexible learning that negotiating its numerous challenges can become a rational and efficient process.

The chapter is organised as follows. In the first two sections, the scope of flexible learning is delineated and a rationale argued. Next, models for flexible learning are presented and assessed. This leads to the presentation of a new activity theoretic model for the development of flexible learning practices. The last sections of the chapter look at implications for curriculum development and for teaching and learning arising from the material developed in earlier sections.

WHAT IS FLEXIBLE LEARNING?

One way to view flexible learning is from the teacher's perspective. In this case, as Caladine puts it, flexible learning:

- *is* a rethinking of traditional teaching practices;
- *takes* the emphasis off 'stand and deliver';
- *has* changes to the traditional arrangement of weekly lecture and tutorials;
- *is* an investigation of distance education techniques and technologies for on-campus teaching and learning;
- *is* not only about technology but rather about the use of techniques that are appropriate to the desired learning outcomes and that give learners greater access to their education, and more control of it;
- *takes* the emphasis off the traditional formula of weekly lectures, tutorials, laboratory classes (Caladine 1999, p.8, [italics added]).

For Caladine, flexible learning—sometimes also called 'flexible delivery'—is about the reorganisation of teaching offerings in the direction of variety and change.

Another way to view flexible learning is from the learner's perspective. In this case, as Collis and Moonen put it, the key idea of flexible learning is '*learner choice* in [the] different aspects of the learning experience' (Collis and Moonen 2001, p. 9). Whereas in traditional learning styles the teacher or institution makes key decisions for the learner about the learning process, in the flexible learning paradigm key curriculum decisions are made by the learner.

When thinking about flexible learning and devising curriculum responses consistent with it, both of these views—the teacher's and the learner's—are of course relevant. Indeed, as Danchak (2001) has argued, flexible learning is really a form of 'blended learning'—the blend revolving around the combination of teacher and student perspectives as well as the range of learning opportunities and methods of teaching.

It is to be noted that, in a sense, flexible learning is not new. Degrees of flexibility have, of course, always been the mark of many teaching and learning arrangements. For instance, learners have been able to choose elective studies, move between full-time and part-time study, select alternative pathways towards professional certification,

Table 9.1 Facets and indicators of flexible learning practice

Facets of flexible learning	Indicators of flexible learning
Access and participation	Recognition of prior learning in formal educational, workplace and informal contexts
	Multiple points of course progression for course entry and exit
Temporal arrangements	Multiple temporal points for course commencement and completion
	Multiple temporal rates for learning
Content	Learners choose course content which best suits their needs
	Learners choose sequence of content which best suits their needs
Mediating information and communications technology	Varieties of traditional and digital information and communications technology: written and printed materials, hard copy postal services, telephone, audio recorder, video recorder, real-time video link, television, stand-alone computer, communications and information software, CD-ROM, multimedia facilities, email, intranet, WWW (Collis 1999, p. 19; OECD 1996, 2001)
Pedagogy and assessment	Varieties of student-focused and teacher-focused learning experiences
	Varieties of social organisation (individual, study group, whole class) in on-campus or off-campus modes
	Varieties of teacher engagement with students and student peer collaboration
	Varieties of synchronous and asynchronous interaction among students and between the teacher and student/s
	Varieties of formative and summative assessment

enrol for face-to-face study, study by correspondence or advance their learning by means of distance education or open learning. Nevertheless, in recent times the range and depth of curriculum choices available to students have become more comprehensive than ever before, and this, supported by new technologies and needs, has led to the refocusing of educational thinking and resources around the concept of student choice. Flexible learning, as it is understood today, is intended to capture this new range of curriculum developments.

Facets and indicators of flexible learning

In order to develop a feel for the elements of flexible learning, it is useful to list the key facets which have come to be typical of flexible learning. These respond to the extent to which greater or lesser degrees of flexibility are shown with respect to *who* may engage in a course, *when* a course is offered, *what* a course will encompass and by *what* technologies it will be mediated, *how* its pedagogy will be handled and, finally, *how* it will be delivered and assessed. Using Collis and Moonen (2001) as a starting point, these suggest that flexible learning consists of a number of *facets* which can be stated as follows: course access and participation requirements; course temporal arrangements; course content; course mediating information and communications technologies; course pedagogies; and assessment practices. Indicators for these might be expressed as shown in Table 9.1.

These facets and indicators of flexible learning practice map out the full spectrum of course flexibility ranging from traditional practice to the most flexible arrangements current (Gillham 1995; Telford 1995).

WHAT IS THE RATIONALE FOR FLEXIBLE LEARNING?

Examining the rationale for flexible learning is an important step in coming to terms with the relationship between flexible learning and the needs of practice in an actual teaching and learning situation (Education Network Australia Vocational Education and Training Advisory Group 2000). Four key areas generate an impetus towards flexible learning: emerging cultural and economic needs; developments in the concepts of learning; demographic questions; and institutional factors.

Economic and cultural needs

Over the last decade, globalisation has been the leading trend within the world economy. Starting as a movement to liberalise trade relations, globalisation has come to be signified by the formation of international markets for a wide range of products such as manufactured items and raw materials, and services such as finance, research and development, information, media, entertainment, education and training. The pace of globalisation is linked to increases in worldwide competition, the high rate of technological advances and the penetration of the Internet and digital communications technologies. As Tinkler et al. (1996) argue, each of these factors is currently influencing major changes in vocational education and training.

Changes in the economy have meant that employers are looking for changes in the skills of their employees. Reich (1992), for example, explains this as the growing proportion of symbolic analytical activity for the production of wealth. By symbolic analysis he means the manipulation of symbols (data words, audio, visual representations) and the development of ideas in order to identify and solve problems and thereby translate these into marketable products and services. Symbolic analysts need to understand and embrace technological developments and respond to the human resource needs of a rapidly changing economy. In addition, workers in the global economy are increasingly expected to create new knowledge by accessing information from broad sources. This means they need to select the kinds of knowledge relevant to work, make choices about how this knowledge can and should be generated and implement strategies to contextualise general knowledge for more specific ends. These changes require new thinking in the workforce and employers look to vocational education and training as one source for this change.

Developments in the forms of learning

Mirroring and supporting changes in the nature of the economy and work, new concepts for learning have also evolved. Tinkler et al. (1996) list these, and descriptions derived from their work are as follows:

- *lifelong learning*—continuous learning across the life cycle in order to 'facilitate flexible career paths' (p. 80);
- *learner-directed learning*—learner taking control of learning with the teacher becoming the facilitator and 'diagnostician to achieve optimum learning outcomes' (p. 83);
- *learning to learn*—learner understanding to 'more effectively plan and realise their own learning' (p. 86);
- *contextualised learning*—locating of learning in different contexts through 'real life learning environments and simulations' (p. 87);
- *customised learning*—meeting different learning needs and preferences of the learner (p. 88).
- *transformative learning*—learners challenge and change belief systems and behaviours in order 'to meet new opportunities and challenges' (p. 89);
- *collaborative/cooperative learning*—individuals learn interactively in the context of groups 'across time and space' (p. 90); and
- *just-in-time learning*—learning made available 'when and where the learner needs to meet their learning needs' (p. 91).

Because flexible learning can be thought of as a tool supporting the practice of these different kinds of learning, it plays a significant role in evolving vocational education and training.

Who needs flexible learning?

Arising from the above, flexible learning finds a clear need among a range of client groups both in, and peripheral to, the paid workforce—especially those who would otherwise not be able to participate in education and training programs. These, for instance, include:

- employees who, in the context of professional development or inservice arrangements, need to keep up with changing technologies and methods of production in their workplace;
- people seeking alternative employment who seek to take advantage of new work or business opportunities in developing industries and enterprises;
- people seeking first-time entry to paid work or who wish to regain entry into paid work, particularly those with family and care-giving responsibilities;
- people with special learning needs (for instance, visual or aural impairments, motor and learning disabilities) (Hodgkinson 1994);
- school-leavers seeking a first-time place in the paid workforce; and
- overseas students or those who study at a distance from the educational site.

Common among these groups is the need for enhanced access to learning and training opportunities. This need arises from a variety of social, economic, cultural and individual circumstances (Hodgkinson 1994).

Institutional factors

As a result of new systems of accountability, qualifications certification, and new kinds of outcomes indicators, education and training institutions have had to develop means of providing more complex learning opportunities to students and clients (Caladine 1999). Thus, as Thomas (1995) and others have argued, apart from the reshaping of education and training methods as indicated above, educational processes have had to respond to the diversification of funding sources, increased competition for funding, the rise of for-profit private education and training institutions, and increased levels of accountability at given levels of funding resource. This means that educational and training institutions need to operate with progressively increasing levels of efficiency. In many cases, therefore, flexible learning strategies—especially those that reduce cost associated with face-to-face teaching—become economically attractive.

Whilst not every flexible learning intervention in every situation will be motivated by all of the kinds of considerations indicated above, over time these factors act to change our working and living environments in such a way that there is a change in perceptions of need and ways of thinking about curriculum. In the next section, therefore, I look at three alternative frameworks for developing flexible learning changes.

THREE FRAMEWORKS FOR DEVELOPING FLEXIBLE LEARNING

The first model examined is that of Collis and Moonen (2001). It consists of the following four components: technology, pedagogy, implementation and institutional framework. Each of these is examined in turn. By *technology*, these authors mean the combination of information and communications technology, particularly digital technologies (software, hardware, networking) used for the following educational purposes:

- publication and dissemination of information;
- communication among teachers, course participants and course managers;
- collaboration among students;
- information and resource managing;
- teaching and learning purposes; and
- course management (Collis & Moonen 2001, p. 19).

By *pedagogy* they refer to knowledge about teaching and approaches to it that teachers bring to their work. Collis and Moonen argue that, in flexible learning, the tendency is to move away from teaching and learning simply as acquisition of knowledge towards teaching as participation in a field of expertise and contribution towards the learning experience of others.

The third component of their model for flexible learning refers to *implementation*. Here the authors make use of the so-called 4-E Model of Collis et al. (2000). In this, the likelihood of an individual making use of a technological innovation is said to be related to four factors: environment (the institutional context); educational effectiveness (perceived or expected); ease of use; and engagement (the person's personal response to technology and to change). In the 4-E Model, the environment factor determines the threshold for the successful implementation of the flexible learning innovation—the more favourable the environment, the less significant the 'sum' of the other factors needs to be in order to bring about change. Conversely, for a less favourable environment, the more significant is the 'sum' of the other factors (educational effectiveness, ease of use, engagement). Collis et al. argue that high-scoring factors can make up for low-scoring factors—for instance, low learner engagement can be compensated for by relatively high ease of use and educational effectiveness, and so on.

The last component of Collis and Moonen's model for flexible learning is concerned with the *institutional framework* of the flexible learning process. Factors needing consideration here include the way the course relates to an institution's profile of educational offering in terms of staff and student expectations, course duration, admission criteria, assessment and evaluation procedures, administration and technical support, library, and so on. Less concrete factors relating to the institutional framework concern the climate of an institution for flexible learning, the management style and leaders' commitment to change. Other components of their model include the implementation of flexible learning processes, pedagogic questions and the choices of technology solutions.

Collis and Moonen see the components of their model as being hierarchically related in the following sense. A bottom-up sequence for the introduction of flexible learning starts with choices made concerning the up-take of technology. This sets parameters for pedagogic choices, and these in turn influence decisions about implementation requirements which, also in turn, shape the institutional framework. Top-down sequencing of flexible learning changes starts with the constraints imposed by the institutional framework and, using these as reference points, moves to devise system-wide implementation strategies for coordinated pedagogic and technology choices.

Whereas Collis and Moonen focus on important components of flexible learning in seeking to understand it, relatively little attention is given to the way teachers, trainers, learners, mentors, technical support staff, administrative staff and managers, and policy-makers communicate with each concerning the object of their endeavours. The next model for flexible learning to be considered, that of Caladine (1999), takes up this theme. Caladine's model concentrates on the kinds of interactions flexibility promotes. These are interactions with materials (taking notes in a lecture, consulting reference sources, utilising video and audio records, accessing the Internet, manipulating computer aided learning package), interactions with the teacher (questions and answers, discussions, face-to-face, phone, email, letters, chat sessions, feedback), interactions between students (formal, informal) and what Caladine calls 'intra-action', which includes reflective engagements of the student such as critical thinking, reflecting, refining ideas, opinions and attitudes, and coming up with conceptions. These constitute four elements of a model for flexible learning. The fifth element is the provision of learning materials. Vehicles for the provision of learning materials include the voice of the teacher (in a lecture, tutorial, laboratory, study group, etc.), visual aids (overhead projection slides, etc.), books and other printed materials, and electronic media (audio and video, Internet and multimedia). Caladine suggests that the model can be used as a guide in the design of teaching activities and as an evaluation device. He suggests that aligning proposed or actual teaching activities with the elements of the model provides an indication of potential teaching effectiveness and efficiency. As Caladine warns, however, the model does not provide an indication of the *best* mix of learning and teaching elements, nor is it sensitive to the special learning needs of students.

Thomas (1995) presents a third model for thinking about flexible learning. Whereas Caladine's model focuses on the interactional elements of the learning process, and Collis and Moonen's focuses on the components of flexible learning from an institutional and resource perspective, Thomas proposes a model which is a blend of these. For her, flexible learning is the 'dynamics of the learning process which takes place between the expert, the learner and the learning resource' (Thomas 1995, p. 5). In other words, Thomas emphasises interactional elements situated around flexible learning concepts. In her model, these consist of the needs and capabilities of the learner, the expert and the learning resource and the interaction of these among each other and with the purpose of learning. Her model thus consists of four mutually interacting variables.

In her learning resource component, Thomas intends to include a myriad of factors within an educational institution or workplace which can be utilised in order to advance learning. These include not only the physical hardware of learning (computers, specialist materials, etc.), but also organisational and infrastructure designed to support learning, learning strategies implemented within the curriculum and the expertise of teachers and more capable student peers.

From Thomas's viewpoint, the strength of this model is that there is no centre position (e.g. the learner, the technology, the teacher) around which the other components are meant to revolve. Of course, the obvious candidate for the centre is the learner. However, Thomas argues that a model skewed in this direction would be unrealistic 'because at many levels at which learning is determined the learner is not even present' (Thomas 1995, p. 6). In other words, the learner's purpose is not necessarily the whole purpose of the flexible learning endeavour. Other purposes, such as solving management problems, drive the movement to flexible learning and, Thomas argues, it would be obfuscation not to recognise this as a legitimate fact of life within institutional settings. For instance, what appears to be a concern for 'learner-centredness' may on inspection be related to interests other than those of the learner. For example, freedom of choice for the learner could be the result of excessive government supervision of the curriculum (through outcomes-based indicators, say); flexibility in meeting a range of learning needs could mask the teacher's insecurity about his or her own expertise; employers' conceptions of what skills are needed by employees may be more indicative of their state of thinking about their industry, and less clearly related to the level of expertise of students. Thus the model Thomas argues for, when translated into a curriculum setting, legitimates and amplifies the various interests of teachers, line managers, mentors and students—all those involved in curriculum work—thus making it *allowable* for [them] to say what they can and cannot do, and for an honest appraisal of availability, development needs and commitment to be included in the equation' (Thomas 1995, p. 6, italics in original). For, as Thomas puts it, the multiplicity of purposes is only suspect when some are withheld, thus distorting the communication among parties.

In conclusion, Collis and Moonen's model is rich in components but downplays interactions among players, whilst Caladine picks up the theme of interaction, but downplays the institutional and pedagogical environment. Neither model grapples with issues surrounding the purposes of those who service flexible learning. Thomas's model represents an advance in that institutional factors, interactions and purposes are brought into active consideration within a single framework. However, Thomas's model leaves technological questions, pedagogic principles and learning theory in the background as far as these impact on the pathway of flexible learning. In the next section, the case for a new model which takes account of these additional factors is advanced.

FLEXIBLE LEARNING AS A LEARNING ACTIVITY

My starting point for constructing this new model is Diana Thomas's remark that the continual change implied by flexible learning 'means we have to live with ambiguity' (Thomas 1995, p. 7). 'Nothing,' she goes on to say, 'stays tidily in its respective corner' (ibid., p. 8). For instance, what may start life as a resource created by an expert teacher in one context may later be used as a learning resource (minus the expert teacher) in another context—but this transfer does not, of course, mean that the teacher's expertise is any less valuable. Similarly, the learner may be the source of expertise for other learners—or indeed become a learning resource, as in the case of learners accessing their own or others' experience in order to contextualise their learning and transform their knowledge.

But what lies at the heart of these tensions? And what role, if any, do they have in leading the flexible learning experience into new stages of development? These questions, not addressed by Thomas's model, are central to the cultural-historical activity theory model for flexible learning I now wish to introduce. In order to set the scene, I need to say a few words about this theory and how it applies to flexible learning. For Leont'ev (1981), activity systems consist of human subjects collectively advancing a common purpose—for instance, obtaining flexible learning and thereby generating desired outcomes (learning attainments). The work of the activity is achieved by actions and operations which are themselves mediated by physical or conceptual tools or artefacts coopted or generated by the activity system in order to advance goals and ultimately accomplish the driving purpose of the system. In the case of flexible learning, this could be tools such as computers, the Internet, information and communications technologies (see mediating information and communication technologies, Table 9.1), but also could include conceptual tools such as learning and teaching principles which help practitioners develop methods and plans for teaching work. These include:

- facets and indicators of flexible learning (see Table 9.1);
- models of flexible learning practice (e.g. models of Caladine (1999), Collis and Moonen (2001) and Thomas (1995));
- flexible learning principles (see section below); and
- flexible teaching and learning methods (see Table 9.2).

In Engeström's (1987) development of this theory, activity is, in addition, mediated by an evolved division of labour, rules and protocols, and the ideas, sentiments and history of a specific community. For instance, in the case of flexible learning, work is divided among different roles—teacher, trainer, 'training officer', learner, student, worker, manager, director, and so on. As we saw in Thomas's remark above, human subjects move among these roles as the work of the activity is advanced. Next, human subjects also regulate their flexible learning activity by following rules and protocols for their work—for instance, teachers have teaching skills and methods, curriculum managers and directors have strategies for implementation of flexible learning schemes, and so on. Lastly, the kinds of interactions characteristic of the flexible learning activity take place within communities, whether these are education or training institutions or workplaces. Figure 9.1 (derived from Engeström 1999b—see Figure 2.1) summarises these components of the model.

An important feature of this model is that tensions, ambiguities and contradictions are considered to be intrinsic to human purpose-driven activity; they are not seen simply as anomalies to be rationalised away, extrinsic to the real aims and purposes of the activity. As we saw in discussion of the work of other theorists above, various themes modulate the purpose of flexible learning. For instance, the learner might be engaged in learning for its own sake or because this will enable a person to solve a particular kind of problem. Learners also wish to obtain qualifications leading to appropriate credentials which then enable them to

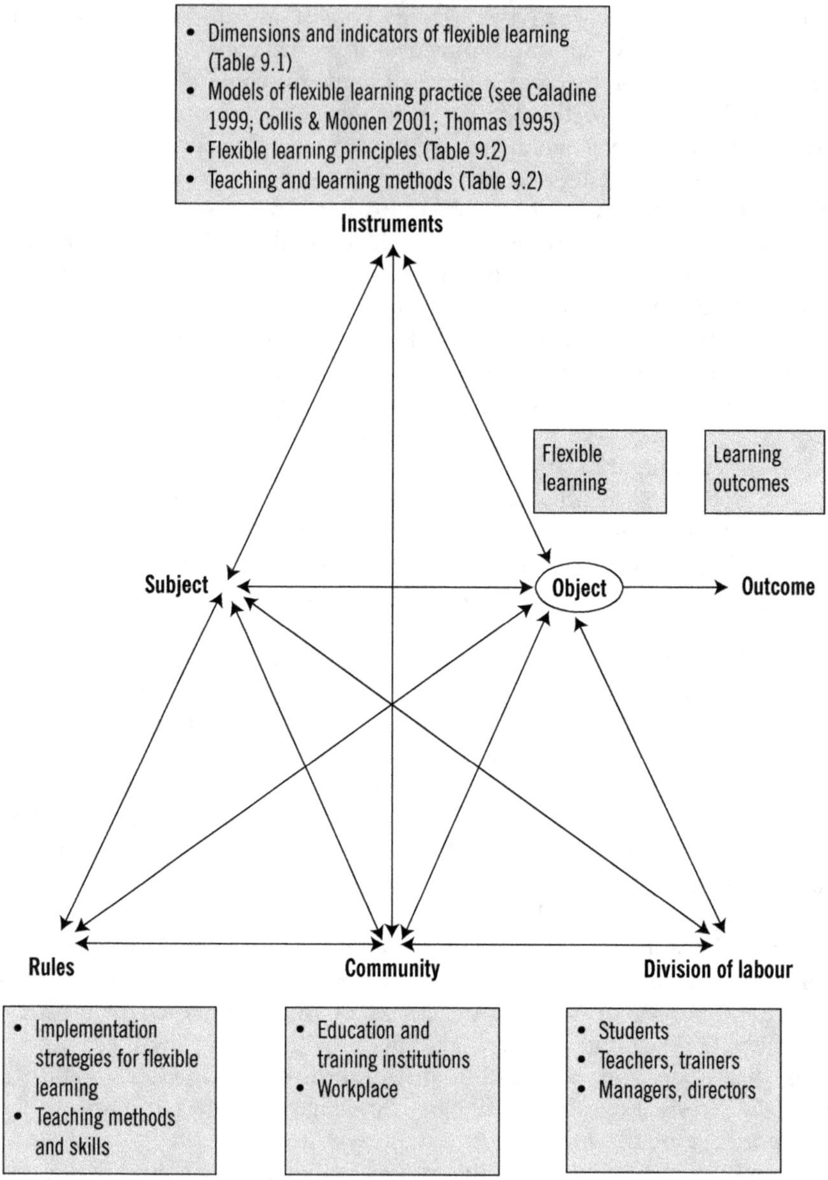

Instruments

- Dimensions and indicators of flexible learning (Table 9.1)
- Models of flexible learning practice (see Caladine 1999; Collis & Moonen 2001; Thomas 1995)
- Flexible learning principles (Table 9.2)
- Teaching and learning methods (Table 9.2)

Flexible learning

Learning outcomes

Subject → Object → Outcome

Rules
- Implementation strategies for flexible learning
- Teaching methods and skills

Community
- Education and training institutions
- Workplace

Division of labour
- Students
- Teachers, trainers
- Managers, directors

Figure 9.1 Model of flexible delivery as a cultural-historical activity system

trade their skills in the labour market. But these different kinds of reasons for undertaking learning—the first revolving around the concept of the use value of learning, and the second around the concept of the exchange value of learning—do not necessarily fit together unproblematically. On the contrary, as learning involves costs, there are tensions and ambiguities between these aspects of the learner's goal, leading to tradeoffs and difficult choices. For example, the learner may not be able to afford the costs of study (the opportunity cost and/or the economic cost) and choose alternative study objectives and goals which substitute for those otherwise preferred; or learning might be cut short or delayed or undertaken using methods and tools not first intended. Likewise, a teacher's goal is seldom the unproblematic goal of student learning. Teaching involves costs, and these must be reckoned against outputs (e.g. course completions, etc.) and competitive bids for service (e.g. tendering for training services). Thus the teacher's work must also drive its way through the competing values of use (facilitating student learning in the broad sense) and exchange (generating accredited outcomes). Likewise, managers and policy-makers also modulate the purpose of flexible learning with their own problems and tensions. In the activity theory jargon, the kinds of tensions described above are referred to as *inner* or *primary* contradictions. These give rise to other levels of tensions, such those between components of an activity system, between the objects at different stages of development and between activity systems.

For instance, the logic of new digital information and communications technologies positions students, the teacher and other experts in a web of distributed knowledge creation and development, and this means that the teacher must surrender control of the learning experience. But not all teachers are comfortable with this or agree that it is desirable. For example, Chambers (1999) found that in the instance of computer conferencing she studied, the potential existed for 'tension between the tutor's aim of encouraging and facilitating discussion among students on one hand and the exercise of their more didactic, academic role on the other' (Chambers 1999, p. 59). This tension illustrates a double-bind conflict between teaching principles and the division of workplace responsibility (the more intensely one enacts the role of facilitator, the less effective one becomes as a representative of the institution in the pedagogic interaction). Thus tension or conflict, sourced to the primary contradiction referred to previously, is created between the components of 'tool' and 'division of labour' within the flexible learning activity system (refer to Figure 9.1). Engeström (1987) refers to this tension as a *secondary* contradiction within the activity system.

In activity theory, the resolution of these conflicts involves the creation of new ways and means to serve the interests of all parties, and so drives flexible learning to a new stage of historical development. For example, Bothams (1995) illustrates how participants in an action learning set generate solutions to their own learning problems and at the same time address management issues. Thus, by finding ways to re-mediate their learning activities, they are able to resolve tensions to the mutual satisfaction of all parties and, at the same time, advance their concept of flexible learning.

The following case study (from Crocker 2001) illustrates tensions arising from flexible learning development in an actual learning context.

Case study: integrating functional skills into Web-based course

In this case, a teacher in Southern Main Technical College, Maine, USA, Lance Crocker, sought to incorporate Web-based instruction in the teaching of a course in Hotel Front Office Operations. The initial problem was that the hospitality industry is considered to involve very 'hands on' kinds of work and is therefore not particularly amenable to Web-mediated learning. Crocker reports, however, he felt that 'there *had to be a way* for me to [do this] but I knew it would take a *totally different approach* than anything I had been doing for the past twenty years' (Crocker 2001, p. 1, [italics added]).

His development of flexible learning proceeded in two stages. In the first, he proposed to replace his lectures with Web instruction. In this, content was arranged within topics such as hotel and organisation types, the guest cycle, industry-specific computerisation, front office accounting and night audit and was transferred to Web format. Supplementing this material, he developed a glossary, case studies and proposed field trips. Functional skills relating to guest service, telephone calls, reservations, registrations, communications and guest settlements were proposed for the off-site internship portion of the course. This internship was undertaken in an actual workplace site.

In the second stage of development, Crocker worked to implement his plans. In two weeks he taught himself the relevant software requirements. He then generated a template for the Website. Next he transported quizzes and exams into the required Web format and identified useful supporting Websites and case studies. Interestingly, he found that all of his courses 'very naturally broke down into the two categories of either conceptual information or functional skill' (Crocker 2001, p. 1), and this prompted him to work on a range of courses simultaneously.

Crocker reports that this new method of teaching has 'worked wonderfully'. He states that 'for the first time in six years, I had a group of first-year students who actually know the vernacular of the industry and I had more time to train and correct behaviours because I was not bogged down with lecture time'. He found that students were able to 'put information into practice almost instantly' (Crocker 2001, p. 2).

Students appreciated being able to go to class when they wanted to, not when he wanted them to.

Unintended consequences of Crocker's new teaching methods followed. A colleague in a sister college within the Maine Technical College system proposed that, because he did not have enough students to run his course in front office in his college, his students be authorised to enrol in Crocker's Web-based component and that credit be transferred across sites. In order to facilitate this plan, new intern arrangements local to the new site were arranged. More radically, the success of Crocker's model for incorporating Web-based instruction led to its adoption in a range of other programs offered by his college. The major requirement for success, Crocker reports, is that instructors must be willing to 'think outside of the box' (Crocker 2001, p. 2).

In terms of the model of flexible learning proposed in this chapter, flexible learning was the purpose driving Crocker's project. In order to advance this purpose, Crocker needed to resolve the central tension, which was the seeming paradox of a hands-on subject being successfully taught with Internet technology. How, for instance, were traditional pedagogies to be resolved in the context of the new demands and possibilities of the proposed Web technologies? In order to achieve resolution, a new conceptual framework was brought to the targeted course. Conceptual material relating to front desk operations was distinguished from skills; new and different pedagogical contexts, methods and tools were proposed for each. Thus lecture time in which students were provided with a step-by-step treatment of concepts relating to the elements of front desk management was replaced by a smorgasbord of learning opportunities, such as quizzes, case studies, glossaries, and so on. Like their instructors, students now became free to make choices about the time and place of learning. Like course administrators, instructors became negotiators: with students; with each other (student load and credit transfer); with industry partners (internships). In the upshot, changes in one course led to changes in many courses, and this in turn led to changes in the way flexible learning was viewed within the institution.

DEVELOPING A FLEXIBLE LEARNING CURRICULUM

Thus far I have used the activity theory model of flexible learning to analyse and illustrate flexible learning ventures. In this approach, the many ways in which flexible learning is engineered in an actual instance are made explicit and explored. However, the model is not limited to retrospective studies such as these: it can also be used prospectively in order to advance flexible learning changes. Engeström (1999a) shows the way forward here with his depiction of the process of 'expansive visibilisation'. This involves the rendition of the flexible learning activity system in its contemporary form and the projection of new forms with a view to identifying prospects and actual pathways for change and development. Stages on the development towards expansive visibilisation, as defined by Engeström (1999a), include:

- *Mirroring and analysing troublesome actions*: In this stage, it is important to collect samples of 'disturbances' (Engeström 1999a, p. 71) relating to the drive towards flexible learning. By this is meant the deliberate unmasking of problems, difficulties, double-binds (Bateson 1972), doubts and aporias (Burbules 2000) within current curriculum practice—for instance, the tension identified above between the didactic aims of the teacher and the pedagogic role of facilitator. Disturbances are made explicit by means of observing, videotaping and interviewing *curriculum workers* such as teachers, students, administrators, technicians and other practitioners concerned with implementing the flexible learning curriculum (Kanes & Stevenson 2001).
- *Modelling flexible learning activity systems*: In this stage, curriculum workers are asked to reflect on their curriculum activities and depict the activity system in which they are currently involved and systems which are in the process of evolution. This task requires that curriculum workers identify artefacts which mediate flexible learning activity, as set out in Figure 9.1. In the course of these deliberations, workers begin to identify inner contradictions working within their activity systems and relate these to the disturbances identified previously. In addition, future flexible learning activity systems are identified and these, together with the model of current activities, become used as tools for ongoing curriculum development deliberations.
- *Designing and implementing new flexible learning actions*: Practical solutions are designed by curriculum workers for new flexible learning practices using the depictions of flexible learning activity systems generated in the previous stage as the points of reference.
- *Following and revising*: Curriculum workers monitor how these redesigned processes work in practice and this leads to the revision of conceptual and procedural components of flexible learning plans, as appropriate.

As indicated in Chapter 4, central to expansive visibilisation is the task of weaving together plans for using new learning technologies with new roles for curriculum workers, new kinds of social interactions, and new rules for supporting the achievement of goals and purposes. As Engeström (1999a) argues, this weaving together is not driven by a 'list of discrete rationally predetermined goals but by a dialectical movement between activity-level visions and action-level concretisations' (1999a, pp. 91–2). That is, curriculum workers must use reflection on their plans for flexible learning as tools for developing and transforming their concrete practice and, equally, reflection on concrete practice must be used as a tool to transform plans for flexible learning. In contrast, the models of Collis and Moonen (2001), Caladine (1999) and Thomas (1995) do not theorise a relationship between the purpose of flexible learning and the synthesis of new tools, procedures and roles for engaging with it. These models, though powerful in a heuristic sense (in that they draw out salient components of flexible learning processes), are limited in that they do not provide conceptual pathways for the rethinking of what flexible learning means in actual experience.

In Figure 9.1, I conceptualised learning principles and teaching methods for flexible learning as tools within the flexible learning activity system. These were largely left implicit within the materials, ideas and perspectives discussed. In the next section, I make these principles and methods explicit.

FLEXIBLE LEARNING PRINCIPLES AND TEACHING METHODS

Related to the changing nature of society, the economy and culture, discussed in an earlier part of this chapter, have been developments in the theory of learning. Two key developments may be singled out. The first is the rise of the *constructivist* view of learning in which learning is characterised other than as information transfer. Rather, knowledge growth is a learner-directed process of developing, extending, modifying and reorganising existing knowledge in order to generate purpose-built knowledge structures (Cobb 1994). A second key development in theories of learning is the new concept of *participatory learning*. In this, learning is accomplished through participation in authentic fields of practice. Learning is construed as an introduction to a community of practice, leading over time to full participation as a legitimate stakeholder (Lave & Wenger 1991). Stepping away from learning as it is experienced in institutions of teaching, this concept emphasises the enculturation of the learner in the concepts, skills, values and dispositions of expert practitioners within a community of practice. Lave and Wenger conceptualise this switch of attention as a movement away from a teaching curriculum towards a new understanding of the learning curriculum. Sfard (1998), however, recognises the need for both these approaches in the planning and implementation of any teaching and learning enterprise. What is central, she argues, is a critical and well-judged relationship between the two. Choices of pedagogy, teaching methods and resources, assessment tools, and so on, will in practice determine what kind of balance is obtained.

Table 9.2 Flexible learning principles and flexible teaching principles and methods

Flexible learning principle (adapted from Donnan's (1999, p. 104) interpretation of Basiel (1999))	Derived flexible teaching principle	Flexible teaching methods
Flexible learning is an active construction based on existing knowledge	Flexible teaching should create opportunities for students to manipulate, extend, modify and develop their existing knowledge	'Problem based learning scenarios, in-text activities, imaginative use of the quiz tools, linking topics with bulletin board and online tutorials' (Donnan 1999 p. 107)
Flexible learning is critically dependent on the learning setting	Flexible teaching should utilise characteristics of settings in which knowledge targeted for growth is located	Use of real-world settings and authentic contexts in the presentation of content. Use of case studies (Donnan 1999 p. 107)
Flexible learning is about solving the problems of adaptation to new settings or new aspects of received settings	Flexible teaching should afford the learner with a challenging environment, but also one in which challenges are appropriately 'scaffolded' or supported	Adopt a 'sense of audience and flag a clear set of cues and clues for active participation' (Heppell & Ramondt 1998, cited in Hart 2001)
Flexible learning involves reflective thinking	Flexible teaching should prompt students to consciously think about their learning and the mastery of skills and concepts	Questioning styles, prompting metacognition, identifying and reflecting on stages in the performance of authentic practice, 'abstracted replay' (Collins et al. 1989), facilitating student–student discussion, mentoring, peer mentoring
Flexible learning is about communication	Flexible teaching should involve methods which encourage students to articulate and share their knowledge with others	The teacher must initiate and maintain a facilitatory tone for social interactions among course participants (Donnan 1999). For example, in reviewing the successful operation of a teaching group,

continued

STRATEGIES FOR DEVELOPING FLEXIBLE LEARNING

Flexible learning principle (adapted from Donnan's (1999, p. 104) interpretation of Basiel (1999))	Derived flexible principles	Flexible teaching methods
		Sherry, (1998, cited Donnan 1999, p. 108) notes that 'the reason this group was successful is because the teacher was successful in setting a good cooperative tone of inquiry for the class, the personalities who participated maintained that tone, and we had something worthwhile to discuss
Flexible learning is multivalent	Flexible teaching should deploy a variety of tools and strategies and thus engage multiple ways of giving meaning to knowledge targeted for growth	See the dimensions and indicators of flexible learning—Table 9.1

Drawing on this literature, together with the models for flexible learning discussed in previous sections, certain principles of flexible learning can be distilled. These are as follows:

- *Flexible learning is an active construction*: Active means that learning requires the learner to become engaged and consciously involved in the processes of learning. Learners are active meaning-makers and resort to their previous experiences when challenged to generate new meanings and methods.
- *Flexible learning is critically dependent on the learning setting*: Learning always requires a context, and the context shapes the kind and quality of learning outcomes achieved.
- *Flexible learning is about solving the problems of adaptation to new settings or new aspects of received settings*: Solving problems means addressing situations which *for the learner* are new or have novel features in order to achieve a resolution deemed workable within the learning context. Workable solutions are those that have legitimacy within the learning context (whether it be in a formal learning situation or workplace). As learners generate a workable solution, they must develop, transform or extend the kinds of meanings they

bring to the problem at hand; by so doing, they display adaptability to the learning context.
- *Flexible learning involves reflective thinking*: When it is most effective, learning requires the learner to become consciously engaged in reflecting on knowledge already acquired (whether concepts or skills). The purpose of such reflection is to modify and extend current knowledge in ways which meet the challenge the learning situation presents to the learner.
- *Flexible learning is about communication*: Conceptual learning is deeply associated with language. Often ideas which subsequently lead to the transformation of learners' understanding first appear in linguistic forms shared in efforts to communicate with another. But spoken language is never without voice—which is the pattern of speech adopted by a person occupying a specific role within a specific context and social setting. By expressing ideas, learners use their own voices and importantly the voices of others who are more knowledgeable in order to generate new meanings and patterns of thinking (Fox et al. 1999).
- *Flexible learning is multivalent*: As indicated above, learning is about the transformation of one way of thinking and behaving into other ways of thinking and behaving. Thus the learning context must provide numerous alternative approaches for the learner's use (Donnelly 2001).

Effective teaching requires that curriculum workers make choices which best facilitate learning. Thus principles of teaching and associated methods should be closely related to the learning principles from which they are derived. Table 9.2 sets out teaching principles and methods against each of the learning principles indicated above. As this table shows, flexible learning is effected by a wide variety of possible teaching methods.

CONCLUSION

This chapter has, firstly, outlined facts of flexible learning and set out indicators for flexible learning in practice. Next a rationale for flexible learning was developed, drawing on economic and cultural needs, associated developments in kinds of learning, the learning needs of particular groups, and institutional factors shaping (especially) the economic realities of life facing vocational education and training providers. Then three models for guiding the development of flexible learning practices were presented and discussed. These were found to emphasise different aspects of the learning curriculum. Arising from these considerations, a new model for developing flexible learning was introduced. Drawing on cultural-historical activity theory, this model supersedes other models, and also provides a set of tools for further development of the flexible learning curriculum. These include: communications and information technologies; facets of flexible learning; indicators of flexibility; heuristic models for flexible learning practice; the expansive visibilisation of the flexible learning curriculum; and learning principles and teaching methods for flexible delivery.

The chapter concluded with a discussion of the learning and teaching principles underpinning the flexible learning model in particular and flexible learning efforts in general. These are conceptualised as tools within the flexible learning development process.

Finally, flexible learning viewed from the perspective of activity theory teaches us that flexible learning needs to be seen as a journey rather than a destination. Instead of thinking about flexible learning as a set of ad hoc solutions to routine problems, the model argued for here encourages us to think of it as an ongoing process of meeting emerging needs by radically transforming present realities.

REFERENCES

Basiel, A. 1999, 'Web-constructivism using Javascript', in *Proceedings of ED-MEDIA 99, World Conference Educational Multimedia, Hypermedia and Telecommunications*, eds B. Collis & R. Oliver, AACE, Seattle, WA, pp. 178–83

Bateson, G. 1972, *Steps to an Ecology of Mind*, Ballantine Books, New York

Bothams, J. 1995, 'Action learning and a means of helping professionals into a new management role', in *Flexible Learning Strategies in Higher and Further Education*, ed. D. Thomas, Cassell, London

Burbules, N. 2000, 'Aporias, webs, and passages: doubt as an opportunity to learn', *Curriculum Inquiry*, vol. 30, no. 2, pp. 171–87.

Caladine, R. 1999, *Teaching for Flexible Learning: Learning to Apply Technology MOLTA*, Antony Rowe, Gilwern

Chambers, D. 1999, 'Shifting paradigms: international computer conferencing in Europe', in *Open, Flexible and Distance Learning: Challenges of the New Millennium, Collected Papers from the 14th Biennial Forum of the Open and Distance Learning Association of Australia*, pp. 55–9

Cobb, P. 1994, 'Where is the mind? Constructivist and sociocultural perspectives on mathematical development', *Educational Researcher*, vol. 23, no. 7, pp. 13–20

Collins, A., Brown, J., Newman, S. 1989, 'Cognitive apprenticeship: teaching the crafts of reading, writing, and mathematics', in *Knowing, Learning and Instruction: Essays in Honor of Robert Glaser*, ed. L. Resnick, Erlbaum Associates, Hillsdale, NJ

Collis, B. 1999, 'Telematics supported education for traditional universities in Europe', *Performance Improvement Quarterly*, vol. 12, no. 2, pp. 36–65

Collis, B. & Moonen, J. 2001, *Flexible Learning in a Digital World: Experiences and Expectations*, Kogan Page, London

Collis, B., Peters, O. & Pals, N. 2000, 'Influences on the educational use of the WWW, e-mail and videoconferencing', *Innovations in Education and Training International*, vol. 37, no. 2, pp. 108–19

Crocker, L. 2001, 'Don't tell Julia Child—integrating functional skills into web course', *WebCT 3rd Annual Users' Conference*, Vancouver, 23–27 June 2001, http://booboo.webct.com/2001/papers/Crocker.pdf

Danchak, M. 2001, 'Bringing affective behavior to WebCT', *WebCT 3rd Annual Users' Conference*, Vancouver, 23–27 June 2001, http://booboo.webct.com/2001/papers/Danchak.pdf

Donnan, P. 1999, 'Web course development tolls: boom or bust for instructional designers?', in *Open, Flexible and Distance Learning: Challenges of the New Millennium, Collected Papers from the 14th Biennial Forum of the Open and Distance Learning Association of Australia*, pp. 103–10

Donnelly, R. 2001, 'Bringing affective behavior to WebCT', *WebCT 3rd Annual Users' Conference*, Vancouver, 23–27 June 2001, http://booboo.webct.com/2001/papers/Donnelly .pdf

Education Network Australia Vocational Education and Training Advisory Group 2000, *Flexible Learning for the Information Economy: A Framework for National Collaboration in Vocational Education and Training 2000–2004*, Australian National Training Authority, Brisbane

Engeström, Y. 1987, *Learning by Expanding: An Activity-theoretical Approach to Developmental Research*, Orienta-Konsultit Oy, Helsinki

—— 1999a, 'Expansive visibilization of work: an activity-theoretic perspective', *Computer Supported Cooperative Work*, vol. 8, pp. 63–93

—— 1999b, 'Expansive learning at work: toward an activity-theoretical reconceptualization', keynote address, *Changing Practice through Research: Changing Research through Practice*, 7th Annual International Conference of the Centre for Learning and Work Research, Griffith University, Brisbane

Fox, R., Herman, A. & Taylor, P. 1999, 'Breaking the grip of print in distance education', in *Open, Flexible and Distance Learning: Challenges of the New Millennium, Collected Papers from the 14th Biennial Forum of the Open and Distance Learning Association of Australia*, pp. 142–6

Gillham, B. 1995, 'Moving into the open', in *Flexible Learning Strategies in Higher and Further Education*, ed. D. Thomas, Cassell, London

Hart, G. 2001, 'Some perspectives on establishing online learning communities', *WebCT 3rd Annual User's Conference*, Vancouver, 23–27 June 2001, http://booboo.webct.com/2001/papers/Hart.pdf

Heppell, S. & Ramondt, L. 1998, 'Online learning: implications for the university for industry', *Ultralab*, www.ultralab.ac.uk/papers/online_learning/

Hodgkinson, K. 1994, 'Flexible provision for student diversity', in *Flexible Learning in Higher Education*, eds W. Wade, K. Hodgkinson, A. Smith & J. Arfield, Kogan Page, London

Kanes, C. & Stevenson, J. 2001, 'Conceptualising vocational curriculum development as a cultural-historical activity', in *Knowledge Demands for the New Economy*, eds F. Beven, C. Kanes, and R. Roebuck, Australian Academic Press, Brisbane, pp. 305–12

Lave, J. & Wenger, E. 1991, *Situated Learning: Legitimate Peripheral Participation*, Cambridge University Press, Cambridge

Leont'ev, A.N. 1981, *Problems of the Development of the Mind*, Progress, Moscow

Lewis, P. 1994, 'A flexible learning scheme for a first-year mathematics module', in *Flexible Learning in Higher Education*, eds W. Wade, K. Hodgkinson, A. Smith & J. Arfield, Kogan Page, London

OECD 1996, *Information Technology and the Future of Post-Secondary Education*, OECD, Paris

—— 2001, *E-learning: The Partnership Challenge*, OECD, Paris

Reich, R. 1992, *The Work of Nations*, Vintage, New York

Sfard, A. 1998, 'On two metaphors for learning and the dangers of choosing just one', *Educational Researcher*, vol. 27, no. 2, pp. 4–13

Sherry, L. 1998, 'Diffusion of the Internet within a graduate school of education', unpublished dissertation, University of Colorado at Denver, www.cudenver.edu/~lsherry/dissertation/index.html

Telford, A. 1995, 'Mixed-mode delivery: the best of both worlds?', in *Flexible Learning Strategies in Higher and Further Education*, ed. D. Thomas, Cassell, London

Thomas, D. 1995, 'Learning to be flexible', in *Flexible Learning Strategies in Higher and Further Education*, ed. D. Thomas, Cassell, London

Tinkler, D., Lepani, B. & Mitchell, J. 1996, *Education and Technology Convergence, National Board of Employment, Education and Training Commissioned Report No. 43*, Australian Government Publishing Service, Canberra

10

Guiding vocational learning

Stephen Billett

GUIDING LEARNING

This chapter provides a critical discussion of the processes and outcomes of the guided learning of vocational practice. It proposes that the vocational practice individuals have to learn has social origins and that the processes of learning this practice are also social. The vocational knowledge to be learnt has evolved over time with the development of the vocational practice and is manifested in specific ways in particular cultures and communities (e.g. countries and workplaces). Therefore, this knowledge has historical, cultural and situational origins. Because of these origins, vocational knowledge needs to be learnt through engagement with social practices, partnerships and artefacts that provide access to this knowledge. Some of it is easily accessed through observing and listening to others (e.g. other students, teachers, workers) when engaging in activities in classrooms and workplaces, or through reading texts. However, the guidance of a more experienced partner (e.g. teacher or workplace expert) is required to assist learning knowledge that may not be learnt through discovery alone. This includes learning procedures referred to as 'tricks of the trade' and concepts not easily observable or comprehensible without assistance from others who already understand them (e.g. force factors, electrical current and hygiene). Without guidance, this knowledge may remain inaccessible to the learner or be learnt inappropriately. Guidance can also assist in managing the pace and sequence of the learning of a vocational practice that has taken many lifetimes to develop and refine, and whose development continues. Nevertheless, the process of learning through guided engagement in classroom or workplace activities is complex and its outcomes are not wholly predictable. Although social sources and partners play an important role in learning, the process is not one of simple knowledge transmission from the social source to the individual. Nor are its outcomes socialisation or enculturation. Instead, learning is shaped by both the individual's social and cognitive experiences (Valsiner & van de Veer 2000)—how individuals' existing knowledge interacts with what is experienced socially through engagement in the classroom or workplace.

From a constructivist view, we humans are not passive recipients of what we experience (or what others would have us learn). Instead, we are active meaning-makers. What is learnt will in some ways be different for each individual, given our unique personal histories, as these influence what we experience and learn (Billett 1997). Therefore, although the outcomes of learning may be shaped in some ways by the social circumstances in which the learning occurs (e.g. in classrooms and workplaces), that learning is also mediated by individuals' cognitive experiences, which arise from unique personal histories. This interplay between individual agency and social contributions emphasises the significance of the reciprocity between individuals' learning and the social world. Perhaps individuals cannot be taught; they can only learn. However, this learning can benefit from being guided in ways that assist individuals to learn the kinds of proven processes and concepts required for adaptable vocational practice. The key pedagogical goal is to guide the learners' active construction of the knowledge required to secure competent performance in the situations in which they are learning (e.g. classroom or workplace) and extend that learning beyond its initial applications (e.g. to a workplace or another workplace or work task).

The discussion elaborating these issues is structured as follows. Learning as social reproduction is discussed first to establish a basis for evaluating the processes and outcomes of guided learning. Conceptual bases for guiding learning are then discussed in terms of how access to guidance and participation in activities are central to learning vocational practices. Considerations for curriculum are discussed next in terms of goals, enactments and participative experiences, followed by the views of those proposing pedagogical principles from a guided learning perspective. These discussions are of necessity critical for the contributions and limitations of guided learning to be appraised effectively.

INTERSUBJECTIVITY, APPROPRIATION OR MASTERY: OUTCOMES OF GUIDED LEARNING

Guided learning is often associated with the sociocultural theoretical tradition of Vygotsky (1978), and activity theory of his associates (e.g. Leont'ev 1981 [1959]) and recent adherents (e.g. Cole 1998; Rogoff 1995; Wertsch 1998). This tradition emphasises the social origins of knowledge and the social bases of learning. It also tends to privilege social reproduction. That is, it accentuates the reproduction of what is known and accepted over approaches which encourage novelty in responses to emerging tasks. Vocational practices and their transformation over time provide instances of proven practices. While an emphasis on learning proven practices and concepts is important, goals for vocational preparation also need to include being responsive to the changing contexts and requirements for work that will occur throughout individuals' working lives. Therefore, understanding the kinds of learning that may arise through guided learning is essential to appraise its capacity to develop vocational practice that is responsive to some of the diverse and changing requirements for that practice.

Concern about learning as social reproduction is hardly new. Dewey (1938) raised concerns about education as social reproduction, which he encountered in Russia early in the twentieth century. He argued that education needed to be responsive to new circumstances and requirements, to reflect fresh insights and engage individuals' contributions and divergences, rather than being merely socially reproductive (Glassman 2001). Dewey's own ideas were expunged from educational practice in Soviet Russia when uniform and faithful adherence to a particular ideology became valued. Concerns about learning as social reproduction have direct implications for vocational education, as the requirements for vocational practice are founded in proven practices that are constantly evolving. To counter or complicate Dewey's concerns is to acknowledge the interplay between the social structuring of knowledge and individuals' agency. There are differences between what is structured for learners and what learners actually learn. Using curriculum terminology, it is the distinction between what was intended to be learnt and what students actually learnt. So are Dewey's concerns overstated?

In learning theories that accentuate a social basis of cognition, the desired learning outcome is often to achieve shared understanding or intersubjectivity between the more experienced social partner (e.g. co-worker, teacher) and the learner (e.g. co-worker, apprentice or student). Trevarthen (1980, p. 530) defines intersubjectivity as both the recognition and control of cooperative intentions and joint patterns of awareness. It constitutes a shared understanding based on a common focus of attention and some shared presuppositions that form the grounds for communication and action (Newman, et al. 1989; Rogoff

1990). Individuals who have spent lots of time together often enjoy high levels of intersubjectivity. I once observed two carpenters working in tandem. Few words were required to be exchanged as they worked together. There was common understanding, for instance, about when the weight of a piece of timber required assistance from the other to be lifted. Assistance with its lifting, rotation and positioning proceeded without discussion. Such was their shared understanding that their collaborative action proceeded almost in silence. Newman et al. (1989) propose that the key purpose of communication is to develop shared understanding, or intersubjectivity. Because of our unique personal social histories, they hold that we construct meaning initially in quite individual or idiosyncratic ways. They argue that if we all constructed understandings uniformly from what was experienced, there would be little need to communicate, because common understandings would be secured through the same experiences. However, because our understandings are premised on unique personal histories, we need to communicate to clarify meaning and develop shared understanding. Therefore, intersubjectivity arises through shared social interaction. 'An experience is always what it is because of a transaction taking place between the individual and what, at that time, constitutes the environment' (Dewey 1938, p. 43). Interestingly, here Dewey also proposes that the nature and impact of individuals' experience cannot be predetermined because of the inherently subjective nature of the individual having the experience. This proposition emphasises relations between the individual and their social experiences. One implication is that no two people have exactly the same experience, despite being involved in the same event, because of the individual basis for experiences (the cognitive experience) that interacts with the event (the social experience).

It follows that the movement toward intersubjectivity is important for learning the proven vocational practices and concepts that more experienced practitioners have already learnt, and which collectively constitute a cultural practice identifiable as a particular vocation. However, achieving intersubjectivity cannot be guaranteed. Unlike with the two carpenters, it may be resisted when little relatedness exists between the knowledge to be learnt and individuals' interests (Hodges 1998). So learning through engagement in social practice and with social partners should not be seen as merely reproducing what is already known. Although interactions with more expert others are aimed at achieving particular goals, individuals' learning may be directed in ways other than originally intended by those who attempt to organise learning. For instance, through experiences in schools, colleges and workplaces, individuals learn about power relations, cliques and relations between others—often in ways that were perhaps not intended.

Nevertheless, there is an important role for teachers and co-workers in guiding learners' development of the knowledge to be learnt, including inciting interest in that knowledge. Ultimately, achieving intersubjectivity between a more experienced practitioner and a learner occurs over time and through engagement and negotiation. More experienced partners can assist in guiding the development of understanding and procedures required for effective participation in a vocational practice (Billett 2001a). Through this learning, individuals might come to appropriate these practices—the voluntary acceptance of and commitment to the worth of what is learnt. Individuals become committed to these practices and use them voluntarily because they are consistent with their interests and values. To appropriate these practices, individuals will likely need to experience their successful deployment or enjoy a fittedness between what is to be learnt and their values. Here, it is useful to contrast appropriation with mastery—the superficial learning that arises from the need to comply with a social press, such as the demands of teachers or co-workers, although the learner remains unconvinced and uncommitted (Wertsch 1998). Therefore, given the importance of the exercise of individuals' agency in learning, a key role for guidance is to assist, monitor and guide individuals' appropriation of the kinds of knowledge required for effective vocational practices through supporting successful performance and illuminating bases for that performance.

As it represents outcomes consonant with learners' interests, appropriation is often viewed as desirable (e.g. Wertsch 1998). However, this view warrants critical appraisal. What individuals appropriate may be neither adaptable nor just. Firstly, the particular social practices individuals engage in are likely to shape their learning in some ways. However, appropriating the particular practices of a workplace or educational site may inhibit the wider application of that knowledge. Vocational practice is not enacted uniformly. When you work in a restaurant or training restaurant, you may only access one instance of the vocational practice. The skills required for cooking 'à la carte' food in an upmarket restaurant, for instance, may not be readily applicable to a hospital kitchen or one at a mine site camp. The food may be of a similar cuisine but the requirements for preparing food may be quite different (made to order, choice, purposes). Although valued and supported in a particular social practice and consistent with individuals' beliefs about what constitutes good vocational practice, what is appropriated may not be applicable elsewhere.

Secondly, individuals may appropriate habits and behaviours that are inappropriate. For instance, teasing female apprentices in the classroom or bullying in the workplace might be encouraged and even rewarded by peers, and be consistent with the individual's beliefs about trades not being for females, or that certain individuals are unworthy. Although they are appropriated, these behaviours are hurtful and discriminatory. Equally, other inappropriate practices (e.g. not wearing safety gear, imprudent shortcuts) may be adopted in workplaces or classrooms and appropriated by workers. Yet this does not make them correct. Alternatively, knowledge that should be appropriated might only be mastered because the learners do not understand or value its importance. For instance, when I taught in a vocational college, because of their lack of industry experience, many students had little basis to distinguish between what was more or less important in the course content. Students wishing to become clothing designers often needed convincing of the need to know how garments were cut and constructed in order to design them. Guidance was required to encourage learners to appropriate what they might otherwise only master. So the worth of what is appropriated needs to be viewed in terms of its adaptability as well as broader goals about its worth (e.g. fairness and inclusiveness). Appropriation should not be seen as a good in its own terms, but in terms of what is appropriated.

In sum, the reproductive learning provided through socially guided experiences may be essential for learning proven vocational practices. Nevertheless, individuals also need to be guided to consider fresh solutions and apply their knowledge effectively in situations which differ from those in which it was learnt. For classroom-based learning, for instance, the first adaptation is to situations beyond the educational institution (e.g. workplaces). The direct guidance of more experienced others, such as teachers, can assist the development of robust practice through providing instances of the diversity of vocational practice that students may encounter. So Dewey's concerns about education being directed towards the mere reproduction of knowledge may be quite legitimate. However, the influence of human agency in mediating the demands of social practice should not be under-estimated, thereby creating a need to guide that agency towards developing adaptable vocational practices. So the concern for vocational education is to guide individuals' appropriation of socially derived practices and concepts in ways required to secure effective workplace performance and to extend it to other instances of practice. These represent clear and worthwhile goals for guiding vocational learning.

CONCEPTUAL BASES OF GUIDED LEARNING

The conceptual bases of guided learning are illuminated by four propositions. These are that: (i) learning is a social process based on interactions; (ii) learning arises through engagement in thinking and acting, through activities; (iii) learning through engagement in activities benefits from guidance by social partners; and (iv) particular strategies can be adopted to enhance and extend individuals' learning. The first two of these propositions are discussed together next as they represent interrelated bases for understanding guided learning. The third and fourth are discussed, respectively, in the final sections of the chapter through considerations of curriculum and instruction.

Learning as a social process premised on activities and interactions

As they have historical and social origins, the kinds of procedures and concepts to be learnt for vocational practice do not come from within the individual. Vocational practice develops and transforms over time in response to particular and changing cultural needs (e.g. for cars to be maintained and repaired, for food to be prepared and served, for software to be installed and updated). Moreover, vocational practice is constituted in particular ways in response to specific situational requirements (e.g. the kinds of cars serviced in a particular garage, the needs of learners in a particular course). In order to interact with and learn the knowledge underpinning this practice, engagement is required with the social environment where the knowledge is to be enacted, including that comprising the assistance of others who have learnt that knowledge (e.g. teachers, experts). Learning this knowledge therefore involves interactions with the social world. This process is referred to as being inter-psychological—between individuals and social sources. Inter-psychological processes are held to lead to an intra-psychological outcome—a change within the individual when 'an external activity is reconstructed and begins to occur internally' (Vygotsky 1978, p. 56). The sociologist Bourdieu (1991) noted that when we speak with a particular dialect we have learnt to use our mouth, tongue and palate in ways that have become an unconscious part of behaviour. To speak in a particular dialect, we have appropriated a means of speech (an intra-psychological outcome) that is sourced inter-psychologically through interactions with users of the dialect. The learning process might comprise imitation and practice as modelled in the social environment in which the individual is engaged. However, as discussed, the inter-psychological process is a two-way process, arising interdependently through interactions when individuals are engaged in conscious goal-directed actions and in interactions with the social world. So, although human agency promotes learner independence, it emphasises the need to guide the development of the learning required for vocational practice.

Two kinds of guidance can be seen as characterising inter-psychological interactions. These are, firstly, the close or proximal guidance by others and, secondly, interactions that are less directly interpersonal arising from observing and interacting with others, artefacts and the social world more broadly. The former might comprise direct interactions with more experienced others (e.g. parents, teachers) or peers (co-workers, fellow students) who might also be learning the tasks (e.g. other students or workers). These interactions may provide guidance through an explanation or assistance in task completion or collaboration with a particular procedure. This kind of guidance is particularly useful in easing the demands of learning new knowledge. For instance, when learning to drive a car, a more experienced driver rehearses for the novice the sequence of procedures for gear changes, including the kinds of procedures to become competent in (e.g. 'Let the clutch out slowly until it bites', 'Use the centre of your palm to gently guide the gear change. Don't grab it.'). They can also assist by indicating the sequence of activities, thereby sharing and easing the learning load. Such support can also ease the demand of learning by collaborating in the task and assisting in completing those parts of the task the learner is unable to complete satisfactorily. The more experienced partner can also make accessible knowledge that would not be learnt through trial and error alone (e.g. principles of the operations of an engine or computer). This knowledge might otherwise be inaccessible or unavailable to the learner. Moreover, this kind of guidance can assist the development of performance by organising a pathway of activities through which to learn and by monitoring improvements in performance over time (e.g. organising practice in clutch control then, later, hill starts and then, later still, reverse parking).

Inter-psychological interactions also occur through less interpersonal interactions, such as through observing and listening to others. Accessing knowledge vicariously through observation or listening is a common means of learning and one in which learners take an active role. Observing others performing work tasks, or completing a classroom exercise, are examples of indirect guidance, which can lead to rich and purposeful learning. Episodes of spectacular learning have been identified in children's language and social skill development (Bransford et al. 1985, cited in Pea 1987) where no direct guidance occurs. Similarly, Lave (1990) notes that learning craft skills occurred with little direct instruction. Instead, observation of tasks, other workers, and artefacts in the form of completed and half-completed garments were important means of learning tailoring. It has been consistently found that 'observing and listening' is a key source of the learning to perform work tasks in workplaces (Billett 2001a). Also, through engaging with the tools, tasks and artefacts associated with the practice, the requirements for effective practice become explicit.

The physical context and artefacts play an important intermediate role in building connections between objects and events in the social world, and their symbolic representations (Hiebert 1984, cited in Prawatt 1989). For instance, a warehouse worker used the 'library' of examples in the warehouse to assist in learning how to pack boxes of different shapes; and a worker in a bar commented that when she saw groups of particular customers she was reminded of what they drank (Billett 1994). When shopping in a supermarket, its layout and products guide the grocery shopping. This becomes most evident when we use an unfamiliar supermarket, or the layout changes in the one we use. So guidance can be secured through engaging in an environment that provides clues and cues for task completion and learning. Physical and social environments are not neutral contexts in which activities occur; they can be a highly constituting component of how we think and act. Through interaction, cognitive processes can be displayed, shared and deployed (Newman et al. 1989). This, in turn, permits individuals to evaluate and modify aspects of their cognitive processes (thinking and acting). However, direct guidance may make the knowledge to be appropriated more accessible, including those concepts and procedures that have evolved over time and may not be observable or otherwise easily accessible.

In this way, collaborative engagement in work tasks can also provide support for the learner when they confront new activities and are extending their learning beyond what they currently know. Therefore, guiding individuals' engagement through direct or indirect interactions represents opportunities for interventions to promote their learning (Scribner 1990).

Learning arises through engagement in thinking and acting

Learning arises through thinking and acting. When engaged in conscious intentional goal-directed activity, we deploy our knowledge. However, more than just undertaking or completing a task, learning occurs when engaged in goal-directed activities through the refinement and reinforcement of what we already know or the creation of new knowledge. Refinement arises when we perfect or improve what we are doing. This might be through honing a technique (e.g. becoming faster or more precise). When we complete a task using a particular procedure, it reinforces or refines the effective means of achieving that task's goal. In doing something new, we extend our knowledge. When asked to hammer nails, the apprentice carpenter can do so because she has done this before. Through practice, she is able to perform the task with greater speed and accuracy. She might be asked, and able, to apply her hammering skills to another kind of task, such as strengthening a wooden structure using a nail plate. However, when asked to hammer a nail into hard wood, her existing knowledge may be inadequate. She may need a more experienced carpenter to advise her about drilling a hole prior to attempting to nail hard wood. The first example is the performance of what is to her a routine task; the second is a task of a similar kind applied to another carpentry task. The third kind of task is too difficult because her existing knowledge is insufficient. The first example is of learning by refining and reinforcing something learnt previously. The second example is learning by adapting what is already known to a different but similar application. The third example is learning that the existing knowledge is insufficient. This is where direct guidance is most likely required from a more experienced individual. The novice carpenter may not even consider drilling a hole first, because she sees such an option as unassociated with nailing.

The above examples suggest little separation between everyday thinking and acting, and learning. When we engage in conscious thought or action, we are learning—even if the learning is reinforcing what we already know. This view has long been proposed. Piaget (1966) distinguished between the processes of accommodation and assimilation in everyday thinking and acting. The former process comprises developing new categories of knowledge to respond to novel experiences and the latter involves integrating experiences with what we already know. The former is associated with new learning and the latter with the reinforcement and refinement of what has already been learnt. Therefore, depending on the kind of activities individuals elect to engage in, different kinds of learning will arise. Consequently, the guidance individuals receive in terms of the sequencing, practice and monitoring of progress can be used to assist easing of the demands of new learning. Upon commencing a new task (e.g. using a hammer), the more experienced other can model how the hammer is to be grasped and assist the learner with its use. As the learner gains competency with the hammer, the more experienced collaborator may model and monitor the best posture and hammer swing (e.g. don't crouch over it, use a full swing in the beginning, and smaller swings as the head reaches the surface). Later, the expert might guide the novice in developing strategies for dealing with particular kinds of timbers (e.g. drill a hole in hard woods), use of nails (e.g. galvanised nail for exposed exterior work, special nails for metal sheeting, etc.), how to counter-sink nails and also when other fastenings (e.g. screws) might best be used. So guidance includes the monitoring and sequencing of the activities in order to manage the learning of activities that extend, refine and reinforce what the learner knows.

In sum, as learning occurs through participation in activities, the kinds of activities individuals engage in, their sequencing and learners' progression are all important intervention points for the experienced collaborator to use in guiding learning.

CURRICULUM AND GUIDED LEARNING

The implication for curriculum development arising from guided learning can be considered in terms of the kinds of knowledge to be learnt (*curriculum goals*) and the practices required to guide learners' participation (*participatory practices*).

Curriculum goals

Key curriculum goals have been identified above. These include understanding the situated nature of work performance and the need to develop concepts and practices that are adaptable to situations beyond those in which learning initially occurs. These goals emphasise understanding something of the range of practices that constitute the vocation. The goals for developing vocational practice can be thought of as occurring on two planes: the socio-cultural and the situational. The former is the product of a societal needs and expectations—for instance, there is a societal need for car mechanics, hairdressers and carpenters. There are also societal expectations that, for instance, hairdressers will know how to cut, shape and care for hair, and advise clients on the most appropriate cuts and treatments for them. To do this, hairdressers need to understand the structure of hair, the impact of treatments upon hair structure, how colour can be imparted and changed, how best to communicate with and manage clients, and how hairdressers should conduct themselves. So there are conceptual, procedural and dispositional foundations that can be thought of as the canonical vocational practice, and that reflect a societal or cultural need. However, this canonical practice exists and is abstracted at the societal level. It is only observable and given actual form when enacted in a particular workplace setting. Therefore, the second plane to consider goals for curriculum development is the situational. How vocational practice is constituted in particular workplaces is a product of situational factors that shape what constitutes effective task performance (Billett 2001b).

However, much of the effort in curriculum development in vocational education has been directed to the societal or socio-cultural level with the formation of national curriculum documents and competency standards that aim to represent the abstracted vocational practice as a uniform vocational practice. Such conceptions are driven by beliefs that, if individuals can understand and practise the canonical knowledge of the vocation, they will be able to apply their vocational knowledge to different instances of practice. However, this premise appears flawed, as this kind of deployment often does not occur effectively (Raizen 1994). Canonical vocational practice provides important curriculum goals through an account of the tasks required for the vocational practice and procedures for its enactment. However, this account needs to be augmented by an understanding of some variations in practice and requirements for performance, which constitute its wider enactment. Understanding variations of the vocational practice may be helpful in assisting in the development of adaptable performance. Central to this is understanding which of the various procedures is most appropriate for a particular task and which processes are required to best make that judgement. Making accessible some variations in practice and the bases of those variations can be provided by more experienced partners who are able to elaborate the different requirements and bases for procedures (e.g. 'in this situation you might, however you could also . . .'). A way forward is to view canonical vocational knowledge and its cultural manifestation as being the indispensible content that represents key goals for learning the vocation. However, understanding some of the variations of the vocational practice is just as important in addressing local needs and providing appropriate experiences for learners.

But curriculum is more than intents and content. Ultimately, curriculum is something experienced by learners. They determine what they construct from their experiences. As proposed, for good and bad, individuals do not necessarily appropriate what it is intended that they learn. Therefore, a key concern for vocational curriculum aimed at developing robust practice is guiding the learning of the range of concepts, practices and values associated with the vocation and assisting learners to know something of the range of variations of vocational practice. For instance, vocational students undertaking their studies wholly within vocational colleges reported that the stories and examples provided by their teachers assisted in adapting their college-learnt knowledge to workplaces (Billett et al. 1999). So a key goal for guided learning is the capacity to make accessible both the canonical knowledge of the vocation—its key concepts, practices and values—and some variations of the vocational practice to assist its adaptation across different instances and moments of practice.

Participatory practices as curriculum

Central to a constructivist perspective of curriculum is how individuals are able to participate in the activities from which they will learn. Learners do not experience a syllabus, or a national competency standard. They experience what they encounter through the activities and interactions that constitute the 'enacted curriculum'—what experiences are provided for them in the educational institution or workplace. However, curriculum in vocational education in many western countries has become associated with documents (syllabi) and regulatory frameworks. These conceptions tend to emphasise the 'intended' curriculum—what is proposed to be learnt by sponsors, rather than what is enacted and what is ultimately experienced by learners. Curriculum as enactments and experiences can be conceptualised in terms of reciprocal participatory practices. On the one hand, it is how learners are afforded experiences (i.e. activities and guidance) by the educational institution or workplace (the enactment of the curriculum experience). On the other, it is how learners elect to engage with what they experience. In workplaces, learning has been conceptualised as being enacted through the sequencing of a pathway of activities that progresses from those with lower to higher levels of accountability—that is, commencing with tasks that have limited consequences if mistakes are made to those of greater accountability, where failure carries greater consequences. Lave (1990) referred to this pathway as the 'learning curriculum'. In contemporary workplaces, pathways have been identified in the kinds of experiences extended to hairdressing apprentices (Billett 2001a), airline pilots (Hutchins 1991) and production workers (Darrah 1996). Similarly, in school settings, Posner (1982) advocates a view of curriculum premised on the kinds and sequencing of activities for students. He proposes participation in these activities be premised on a consideration of: (i) the identification of appropriate tasks (e.g. analysis of subject matter, goals undertaken within the task); (ii) student interpretation of those tasks; (iii) student readiness; (iv) student engagement in the task; and (v) the kinds of thinking that are required by the student. In the example of guided learning in the section that follows, many of these considerations are identifiable.

If we consider curriculum as providing pathways of participation to develop adaptive forms of vocational practices, these pathways can be structured to intentionally extend the individual's vocational practice to other circumstances. For instance, in their hospital-based training, nurses are rotated through different work areas in hospitals. This enables them to learn about how nursing is enacted in a range of contexts (e.g. casualty, maternity, oncology, general wards, etc.). These experiences may lead to nurses developing adaptive practices in ways that experience in just one ward would not afford. Similarly, some apprenticeship schemes utilise a structured program of participation in different kinds of workplaces to develop and extend apprentices' learning. So, for instance, the apprentice chef might commence by working in a banquet kitchen for a large hotel; next they might move to a bistro, then 'à la carte' restaurant in the same hotel, before moving on to a small inner-city restaurant and then perhaps to a hospital kitchen. These kinds of experiences afford opportunities to develop adaptive vocational practice. However, the learner may well place different values on the kinds of experiences they encounter. It might lead them to decide to associate only with one area of practice or to disassociate from it entirely (e.g. Hodges 1998). So pathways of participation need to be structured and sequenced, and the learners' experiences and development guided, in order to assist the appropriation of adaptable knowledge. Throughout, there are points at which direct guided learning interventions might usefully be deployed, in order to enrich and guide the learners' experience. These are illustrated and discussed next.

IMPLICATIONS FOR INSTRUCTION

In considering implications for instruction, the following instance of guided learning is relevant.

CASE STUDY

The setting is the consumer advisory call centre of a food manufacturing company. The call centre's role is to respond to consumer requests and complaints through the provision of advice and also to report consumer complaints and requests to the company. Karen, an experienced operator, is assisting Fran to learn how to respond to consumer calls. Prior to this, Fran has worked in this area for some time. She knows the procedures for gathering information to provide to consumers and has been involved in preparing client correspondence. However, this is her first time taking calls from clients and she is a little anxious about the task. The task comprises listening to consumers, expressing concern, being careful not to make any concessions about fault and carefully entering information about each consumer's request into a data base, as the consumer provides the information. So there are multiple tasks that have to be conducted simultaneously when responding to calls. Fran, like others before her, is nervous about taking consumer calls, because the content of each call cannot be predicted. It could be a simple request for information or an irate consumer with a complaint about the product. For some time, she sits and listens through a second pair of headphones and watches the screen as Karen takes calls and enters information into the database. She hears how Karen greets a consumer and responds empathically to a complaint: 'Oh, that's no good.' Then Karen takes a call and, after it is completed, lets Fran enter the information in to the database. This happens over a number of calls. While Fran is placing the information in to the database, Karen explains some of the protocols for placing information into the database. Because Fran has previously been involved in using this database to prepare correspondence to consumers, she understands the importance of accuracy and the need for most of the information. Karen is empathetic and supportive, leaning forward and smiling as she assists Fran.

Karen then selects a request from the previous day, for which she now has the required information. The consumer wanted to know which retail store in their state stocked a particular product. She tells Fran that she can return the call. Fran looks nervous. They swap sets of headphones (as only one has a microphone) and Karen assists Fran to fit them and get her hair off her face. Fran makes the call, while Karen rehearses the standard salutation 'Hello . . . , Fran speaking, . . .', canvasses a few 'what ifs' and reminds her that 'most consumers are nice and easy to talk to'. Fran provides the information to the consumer, who asks a further question that she is able to answer. At the end of the call,

> Karen congratulates Fran who looks relieved. A call comes through. 'It's all yours,' says Karen. Again, Karen rehearses the standard salutation as Fran engages with the consumer. As Fran takes the call, Karen leans forward and, using a pen, indicates on the screen elements of the database that need to be filled out and the best sequence for the data entry. At one point, Fran puts the caller on hold while she asks Karen for some additional information, then goes back to the client. The information is provided to the consumer, with Karen assisting with a written note at one point. The call is concluded satisfactorily. Again, Karen congratulates Fran on her performance as they jointly complete the data entry. Then they have a debrief, with Karen again emphasising that 'most of the callers are really nice people'. Another call comes and Fran, with Karen's assistance, responds to the consumer and completes the data entry.
>
> A few minutes later, there is a break in the flow of phone calls and Karen takes this opportunity to announce to the other workers nearby that Fran has just taken her first call. The other workers gather around Fran, congratulating her. There is physical contact and everybody is smiling. Fran recalls how nervous she was. The others relate their experiences of their first call and continue to congratulate Fran on her achievement. The phones start ringing again. The huddle breaks and Fran takes another call with Karen repeating 'they are mostly really nice people', and lifting her pen to point to the screen to assist the data entry process.

In this example of guided learning, implications for instruction are identifiable. It illustrates how a vocational practice can be learnt through the direct guidance of a more capable partner, assisted by contributions from the social and physical environment and the enactment of the 'learning curriculum' discussed earlier. Some features of the guided learning illustrated above include: (i) the learner's engagement in tasks that are sequenced to manage the direction and demands of her learning; (ii) her prior experience being taken into account, as is the engagement with tasks with less accountability and lower levels of immediate performance requirements; (iii) opportunities to practise the tasks to be learnt; (iv) support in task completion through collaboration; and (v) the provision of support and monitoring by the more experienced other as she progresses with her development. This guidance incrementally transfers responsibility for task completion to the learner as her capacity to manage the task increases through progressive engagement with work tasks. An outcome of this guidance is passage into a work practice shared with her co-workers. The example also illustrates how, beyond the inter-personal engagement between the novice and the more experienced other, interactions with the physical and social environment also occur and these support task completion, and hence learning. Tools and artefacts assist both the task completion and learning, with other workers providing models and support. These contributions include how artefacts, such as the computer screen and the pointer, can assist the thinking and acting required to complete and understand the task.

More than just hints and cues for thinking, these physical tools become active components of the task during these interactions. The learner's previous interactions with some of these artefacts (the database and correspondence) assisted her understanding of the need for precision and consistency when securing information from consumers. The provision of practice is also essential for developing skilled performance to render easier parts of the task completion. Guidance by a more experienced other can assist in making available to the learner an understanding of what constitutes performance and developing the kinds of capacities required for the work practice. The more capable partner identifies and assists the learning of tasks that are difficult or concepts which are opaque. Specific instructional strategies such as modelling, coaching, questioning, analogies and diagrams can be used to assist this difficult learning. Collins et al. (1989) and Billett (2001a) respectively discuss the use of guided learning strategies for classrooms and workplaces. Both accounts refer to extending what is being learnt to circumstances beyond those where the learning occurs. Collins et al. (1989) aim to develop strategic knowledge to assist the wider deployment of what has been learnt. Billett (2001a) proposes illuminating different applications of practice to promote adaptability of practice. Both hold that guided access to practices that has taken many lifetimes to develop, refine and transform can be assisted through instructional encounters with others who have learnt that practice and have the capacities to use instructional strategies to develop further their capacities.

Finally, developing individuals' capacities necessitates a consideration of their readiness to perform particular tasks. Readiness can be seen in terms of the: (i) concepts and procedures (existing knowledge) available to the learner; (ii) learners' well-being (e.g. confidence); and (iii) learners' interpretation of the task. These forms of readiness guide interventions in terms of the learners' prior knowledge, meeting their developmental needs and assisting them to further extend their knowledge in ways commensurate with their level of development. If the demands of task completion are so overwhelming that individuals cannot proceed productively, then the most likely kinds of learning will be that of frustration and failure. Sweller (1989) sensibly proposes reducing the demands of tasks to make them more achievable for the learners, and to enable useful learning to arise. He refers to providing learners with half-worked problems. In the classroom setting, this might mean the teacher completing part of the task or providing a task that is partially completed. In the workplace, as illustrated, there are ways of reducing the demands of a task through the support of an experienced co-worker.

In sum, pedagogical principles are identifiable in the example above. The learning task was broken into component parts to suit the learner's readiness. Fran's previous experience provided an understanding of some of the procedures she now had to use in a more spontaneous, demanding and accountable way. Karen provided a rationale and aids for action (e.g. the salutation and order of data entry) that assisted learning the new tasks by easing their demands. Through previous experience, Fran was aware of the overall task goals (i.e. responding to consumer requests, being empathetic, gathering information and providing a response without acceptance of liability). She also understood the subgoals required to complete the task satisfactorily (i.e. expressing concern and interest, taking all the information required, indicating to the consumer what procedures would be used and then reporting back, either then or later). The supportive and empathetic approach to guiding task completion adopted by Karen was commensurate with the learner's capacity for task completion and her concerns about the task. Based on her readiness, Karen made judgements about how far she could extend the learner into new tasks. An initial goal was to assist her to overcome anxiety about taking the calls. Karen modelled goals and procedures when responding to consumer requests. The support provided by Karen through joint task completion to assist learning eased the demands placed on Fran when learning new tasks. This support included providing assistance with the demanding task of coordinating the actions required for effective task completion. Guided learning in this way can be seen as a collaborative approach to learning that draws on co-workers' expertise, engagement by individuals with the co-worker and also their engagement with tools and artefacts that aid and assist learning.

CONCLUSION

Individuals' learning is shaped by both the immediate social practice they engage in and the legacy of previous social practices that comprise their personal histories and also their cognitive experience. Guidance is required to assist the learning of vocational knowledge in ways that draw upon social contributions. Overall, there is the need to guide the appropriation of proven vocational practices and extend bases of that practice to other circumstances. An initial goal is encouraging shared understanding with a more experienced social partner. However, guided learning needs to extend individuals' development beyond a capacity to respond to present circumstances. While guiding the development of proven practices inter-psychologically, it is necessary to go beyond the social reproduction of one practice—albeit the 'schoolroom' or workplace—and enhance the capacity to adapt to different and changing requirements of the vocational practice.

In summary, the conceptual bases of guided learning have been elaborated through discussions of:

- learning as a social process based on engagement in activities and interactions with social sources of the knowledge to be learnt;
- learning benefiting from guidance provided by experienced social partners; and
- the particular approaches to guided learning, enhancing and extending individuals' learning.

It has been proposed that more experienced partners (e.g. teachers, co-workers) can make particular contributions to learning through organising:

- the kinds of activities individuals engage in;
- their sequencing; and
- learners' progression with those activities.

This guidance by expert partners can make accessible key curriculum goals in the form of:

- the canonical knowledge of the vocation (i.e. its key concepts, practices and values); and
- variations of the vocational practice.

Bases for guiding participation in activities in educational institutions can be premised on a consideration of:

- the identification of appropriate tasks (analysis of subject-matter, goals undertaken within the task);
- students' interpretation of those tasks;
- students' readiness; and
- student engagement in the task (Posner 1982).

Some key goals for guided learning are the:

- organisation of learners' engagement in tasks that are sequenced to manage the direction and demands of learning the proven practices of the vocation;
- use of prior experience with tasks of lesser accountability and lower levels of immediate performance requirements;
- provision of opportunities to practise the tasks to be learnt;

- provision of support in task completion and, in particular, collaboration between the learner and a more experienced other when difficult tasks or hard-to-learn knowledge are encountered;
- use of strategies (e.g. modelling, coaching, questioning, explaining, group discussion) that can assist learning procedures and develop understanding; and
- provision of support and monitoring by the more experienced others as learners progress with their development.

In conclusion, guided learning can be seen as assisting the learning of vocational practice both directly and indirectly through social partnerships. Its key purposes include assisting with the development of socially derived knowledge, yet avoiding the dangers of learning that is restricted to the circumstances of its acquisition. This involves guiding individuals' appropriation of the proven vocational practices and illumination of their application to diverse circumstances. Such guidance necessitates understanding learners' needs and readiness, and sequencing, monitoring and guiding their learning. However, realising the potential of guided learning is far from easy, given the diversity of the work practices to which it might be applied and the complexity of relations between the learner and the social sources of knowledge. However, in prospect, guided learning may provide both bases for, and some ways of, helping individuals learn adaptable practice.

REFERENCES

Billett, S. 1994, 'Authenticity in workplace learning settings', in *Cognition at Work: The Development of Vocational Expertise*, ed. J. Stevenson, NCVER, Adelaide

—— 1997, 'Dispositions, vocational knowledge and development: sources and consequences', *Australian and New Zealand Journal of Vocational Education Research*, vol. 5, no. 1, pp. 1–26

—— 2001a, *Learning in the Workplace: Strategies for Effective Practice*, Allen & Unwin, Sydney

—— 2001b, 'Knowing in practice: re-conceptualising vocational expertise', *Learning and Instruction*, vol. 11, no. 6, pp. 431–52

Billett, S., McKavanagh, C., Beven, F., Angus, L., Seddon, T., Gough, J., Hayes, S. & Robertson, I. 1999, *The CBT Decade: Teaching for Flexibility and Adaptability*, NCVER, Adelaide

Bourdieu, P. 1991, *Language and Symbolic Power*, ed. J.B. Thompson, Polity Press, Cambridge

Cole, M. 1998, 'Can cultural psychology help us think about diversity?', *Mind, Culture and Activity*, vol. 5, no. 4, pp. 291–304

Collins, A., Brown J.S. & Newman, S.E. 1989, 'Cognitive apprenticeship: teaching the crafts of reading, writing and mathematics', in *Knowing, Learning and Instruction: Essays in Honor of Robert Glaser*, ed. L. Resnick, Erlbaum & Associates, Hillsdale, NJ

Darrah, C.N. 1996, *Learning and Work: An Exploration in Industrial Ethnography*, Garland Publishing, New York

Dewey, J. 1938, *Experience and Education*, Collier, New York

Glassman, M. 2001, 'Dewey and Vygotsky: society, experience, and inquiry in educational practice', *Educational Researcher*, vol. 30, no. 4, pp. 3–14

Hodges, D.C. 1998, 'Participation as dis-identification with/in a community of practice' *Mind, Culture and Activity*, vol. 5, no. 4, pp. 272–90

Hutchins, E. 1991, 'The social organization of distributed cognition', in *Perspectives on Socially Shared Cognition*, eds L.B. Resnick, J.M. Levine & S.D. Teasley, American Psychological Association, Washington DC

Lave, J. 1990, 'The culture of acquisition and the practice of understanding' in *Cultural Psychology*, eds J.W. Stigler, R.A. Shweder & G. Herdt, Cambridge University Press, Cambridge

Leont'ev, A.N. 1981 (1959), *Problems of the Development of the Mind*, Progress Publishers, Moscow

Newman, D., Griffin, P. & Cole, M. 1989, *The Construction Zone: Working for Cognitive Change in Schools*, Cambridge University Press, Cambridge

Pea, R.D. 1987, 'Socializing the knowledge transfer problem', *International Journal of Educational Research*, vol. 11, no. 6, pp. 639–63

Piaget, J. 1966, *Psychology of Intelligence*, Adam & Co., Totowa, NJ

Posner, G. 1982, 'A cognitive science conception of curriculum and instruction', *Journal of Curriculum Studies*, vol. 14, no. 4, pp. 343–51

Prawat, R.S. 1989, 'Promoting access to knowledge, strategy, and dispositions in students: a research synthesis', *Review of Educational Research*, vol. 59, no. 1, pp. 141

Raizen, S. 1994, 'Learning and work: the research base', in *Vocational Education and Training for Youth: Towards Coherent Policy and Practice*, OECD, Paris

Rogoff, B. 1990, *Apprenticeship in Thinking—Cognitive Development in Social Context*, Oxford University Press, New York

—— 1995, 'Observing sociocultural activities on three planes: participatory appropriation, guided appropriation and apprenticeship', in *Sociocultural Studies of the Mind*, eds J.V. Wertsch, P. Del Rio & A. Alverez, Cambridge University Press, Cambridge

Scribner, S. 1990, 'Reflections on models', *The Quarterly Newsletter of the Laboratory of Comparative Human Cognition*, vol. 12, no. 2, pp. 90–4

Sweller, J. 1989, 'Should problem solving be used as a learning device in mathematics?', *Journal of Research into Mathematics Education*, vol. 20, no. 3, pp. 321–8

Trevarthen, C. 1980, 'Instincts for human understanding and for cultural cooperation: their development in infancy', in *Acquiring Culture: Cross Cultural Studies in Child Development*, eds G. Jahoda & I.M. Lewis, Croom Helm, London

Valsiner, J. & van der Veer, R. 2000, *The Social Mind: The Construction of an Idea*, Cambridge University Press, Cambridge

Vygotsky, L.S. 1978, *Mind in Society—The Development of Higher Psychological Processes*, Harvard University Press, Cambridge, MA

Wertsch, J.W. ed. 1985, *Culture, Communication and Cognition: Vygotskian Perspectives*, Cambridge University Press, Cambridge

—— 1998, *Mind as Action*, Oxford University Press, New York

11

Integrating approaches to developing vocational expertise

John Stevenson

INTRODUCTION

In Chapter 1, concepts of expertise and the ways in which experts draw upon and interconnect different kinds of meaning were advanced. These ideas were drawn together in Figure 1.1 (see Chapter 1). Based on these ideas, in Chapter 2 a set of principles was generated for vocational teaching and learning in order to build facility with vocational meanings and their interconnections. These were summarised in Figure 2.2 (see Chapter 2). This figure is a simplified framework for thinking about vocational teaching and learning in terms of what constitutes expert action in routine, non-routine and collaborative situations; what kinds of meanings are drawn upon and interconnected in expert action; and what kinds of principles can be used to guide teaching and learning directed at developing vocational expertise.

The purpose of this present chapter is to revisit these principles, and to illuminate them in practice, in the light of the ideas and suggestions advanced in previous chapters. The principles are illustrated in terms of actions that can be taken in teaching and learning, and these are instantiated for various areas of vocational education.

The chapter is structured as follows. Firstly, activity theory is adopted as a basis for conceptualising vocational teaching and learning and for examining the ideas advanced in previous chapters. Then, based on the framework in Figure 2.1, the seven instructional principles are extended into descriptions of sample actions that might be considered when planning and engaging in teaching and learning. Finally, these ideas are instantiated for approaching the teaching and learning of literacy, numeracy, information literacy, creativity, problem-solving and values; and for approaches to flexible teaching and guiding learning.

TEACHING AND LEARNING AS AN ACTIVITY SYSTEM

In order to develop further the framework to guide vocational teaching, and to establish a basis for drawing on Chapters 3–10 in fleshing out the framework, the idea of what constitutes teaching and learning is important. Here teaching and learning are regarded together as a collective activity—one that involves teachers and learners as well as interested others such as those in workplace and learning settings. Those involved in this collective activity are united in their purpose, directing their efforts towards a common end—for instance, the development of learner literacy. As well, teaching and learning are mediated—teachers and learners use instruments (for example, physical and conceptual tools) in teaching and learning activity. As well as mediation by tools, teaching and learning are mediated by the culture of practice—the rules of the work setting or classroom, the taken-for-granted assumptions and regulations and by the way in which responsibilities for teaching and learning are organised. Thus teaching and learning form a dynamic, collective, mediated process; moreover, this activity is usually in a process of transformation, because of advances in instructional technologies, changes in learners' expectations, changes in community needs, and so on.

For these reasons, teaching and learning are conceptualised here as activity in the cultural-historical activity theory sense (Engeström 1987; Leont'ev 1981 [1959]) (see Figure 2.1 in Chapter 2). Teaching and learning as an activity system are depicted in Figure 11.1.

The collective activity is viewed as being directed at developing learners' abilities towards workplace expertise. Thus abilities contributing to workplace expertise are the *object* or motive of the collective activity. In the case of teaching information literacy, the object is information literacy. It is not immediate expertise in information literacy that is targeted, but information literacy abilities that are on the road towards expertise, with expertise being reached after substantial appropriate practical experience and reflection. The *subjects* are those in the activity system working together towards this motive—for example, the learner, the trainer or teacher, others on the job or, in the learning setting, other learners. Together, and with others who

INTEGRATING APPROACHES TO DEVELOPING VOCATIONAL EXPERTISE

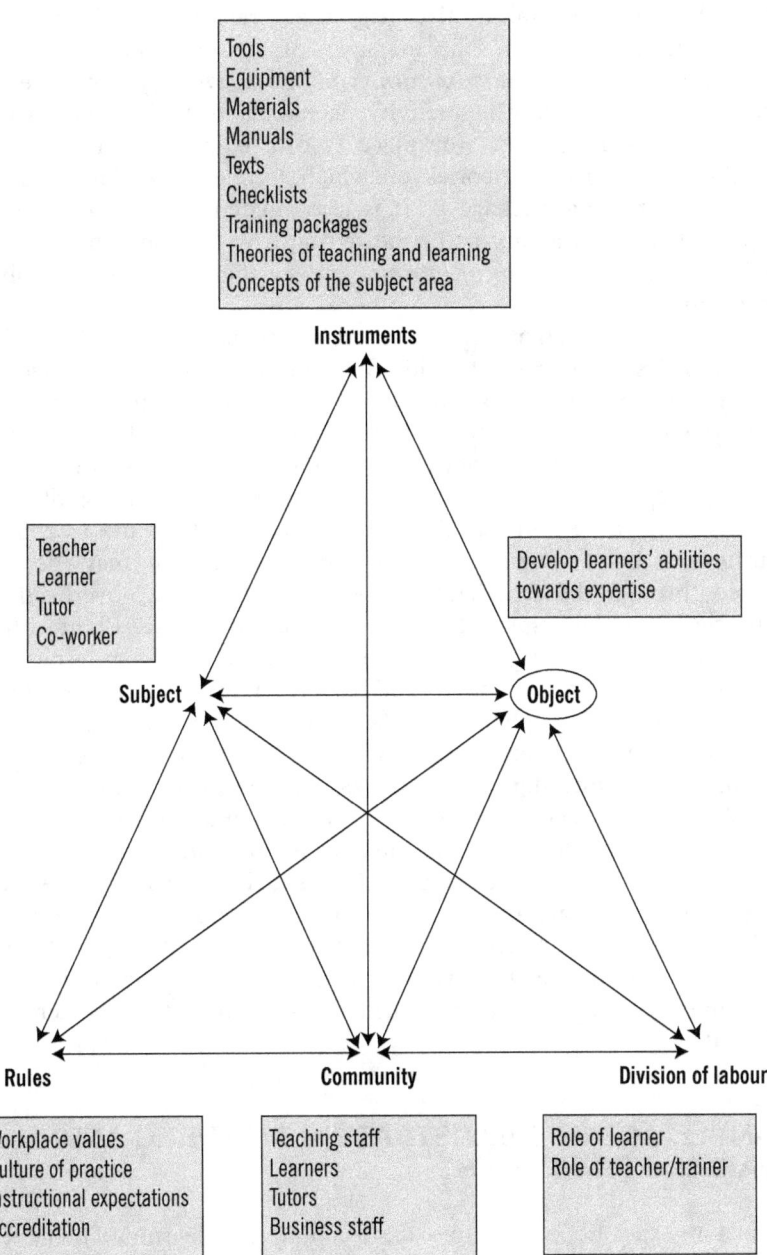

Figure 11.1 Teaching and learning as an activity system

share the same general motive (e.g. the director of a TAFE Institute or training organisation, the manager of an industrial organisation), they would make up the *community* of the activity system. The collective teaching and learning activity is mediated by a large variety of *instruments* (tools) (e.g. workplace tools, equipment and materials; teaching and learning theories on which teachers rely; manuals, texts, checklists, training packages). It is also mediated by *rules* if they are adopted (the cultural norms of the setting), by the ways in which activity is organised (*division of labour*) and by the community involved in the setting.

According to activity theory, these elements (subject, object, instruments, rules, community and division of labour) interact when individuals take action as part of the collective activity of the system. The system shapes activity and the activity is shaped by the system. Moreover, the system is viewed as being in the process of transformation in response to the tensions that emerge in it. Thus, as the teacher designs tools to use in teaching, these tools mediate the teaching and learning activity; however, these tools themselves may be further shaped through the experience of teaching. Tools (e.g. overhead transparencies) may be displaced by newer tools (e.g. PowerPoint software, hypertext, or providing learning opportunities on the Internet) which lead to changes in the activity. Moreover, tensions may develop—for instance, between implicit rules (e.g. keep the learners' attention and keep them on task) and newer versions of tools (e.g. asynchronous instruction, monitoring and feedback), or between newer versions of the object (e.g. teaching learners to be adaptable and innovative) and older versions of elements (e.g. didactic instruction, classroom settings, division of theory and practice). As well, individuals in the activity system may take actions whose purpose does not coincide with the collective object (such actions are said to be directed at *goals*), and tensions may develop between various actions taken by individuals. All of these tensions may lead to transformations in the activity system and its elements.

SAMPLE ACTIONS ILLUSTRATING TEACHING AND LEARNING PRINCIPLES

In making specific suggestions for teaching and learning, then, it must be noted that any generalised principles must be contextualised or situated for a particular setting. That is, such principles must be viewed in relation to the elements of a setting and the relationships among those elements. In the process, such conceptual ideas are likely to undergo transformation in response to the setting—in other words, to be shaped by the setting. Hence any principles can only be guides (e.g. conceptual tools) that can be drawn upon appropriately for the topic area and the given setting. They may need to be modified to become culturally appropriate and situated for the setting and its elements. Thus, if the object is literacy, a particular principle may take a form different from the one it would have if the object were creativity. As well, a principle would take a different form in an industrial workplace setting from the one it would have in a training institution. Further, a principle will need to be considered and applied in the context of considerations about the learners themselves.

With these conditions, the ideas advanced in Chapters 3–10 can be examined for guidance in vocational teaching and learning—a starting point in thinking about what to do when confronted with the challenges of vocational teaching. Taking the seven principles advanced in Chapter 2, the suggestions made in Chapters 3–10 can be considered in terms of how they instantiate these principles in the various topic areas and approaches to facilitating teaching methods. In Tables11.1–11.7, these ideas are collected together as samples of the kinds of actions that are supported in Chapters 3–10.

It needs to be emphasised, however, that the seven principles and the samples of actions that have been illustrated are but one set of instruments available in developing teaching and learning activity. These conceptual tools must be brought into relation with other tools (e.g. material tools) and the other elements of the activity system. In addition, it should be recognised that the seven principles and sample actions would not necessarily be known by the terms in which they are expressed in Chapter 2 and here. Rather, they would take their form

Table 11.1   Sample actions flowing from the principle:
Proceeding from learners' sense of vocation

Principle
Learning should proceed from the learner's sense of vocation—needs, aspirations and intentions, previous experiences and the meanings extracted from them, existing capacities-to-do, relationships among the learner's work and non-work goals and meanings.

Sample actions
1 Assess/self-assess learners' abilities
2 Take account of learner readiness and needs
3 Provide a cognitively challenging, but adequately supported environment
4 Develop competence holistically, so that the learning in topic areas is integrated into the learning of other abilities
5 Select learning tasks that are appropriate to learners' goals
6 Develop meanings in an ordered sequence, e.g. learners should:
   • increase diversity as learning progresses
   • provide adequate practice on simple tasks before moving on to more complex tasks with suitable strategies
   • learn global before local skills
7 Provide opportunities to manipulate, extend, modify and develop existing knowledge

Table 11.2 Sample actions flowing from the principle: *Contextualising learning and making functions and purposes explicit*

Principle

Learning should occur in settings or activity systems where the function and purposes of the learning are clear and explicit, related to vocation; and collective motives and personal goals should be related. The tasks in which learners engage should be tasks that have an explicit relationship with tasks that constitute current or future work or other vocations.

Sample actions
1. Ensure instructors and learners have an in-depth knowledge of site-specific workplace tasks
2. Ensure instructors and learners have an in-depth knowledge of site-specific organisational systems, social literacies and values
3. Simulate work conditions and use scenarios
4. Use authentic texts and tasks, simulations and role plays, transforming learning spaces as necessary
5. Use setting characteristics as opportunities for learning
6. Include non-explicit social literacies in learning
7. Make functions and purposes explicit when engaging learners in tasks
8. Use language and processes for teaching and assessment that are appropriate for the target workplace setting
9. Engage learners in multiple experiences on authentic tasks in authentic situations
10. Engage learners in actively solving the problems of adaptation to new settings
11. Engage learners with multiple perspectives and resources
12. Empower learners to take assertive action in target settings
13. Assess holistically

Table 11.3 Sample actions flowing from the principle: *Focusing learning primarily on the capacity-to-do*

Principle

Learning should focus primarily on developing the capacity-to-do; where learners seek to accomplish goals.

Sample actions
1. Organise learning in relation to the practices of the vocation, applying less developed abilities to lower accountability tasks
2. Engage learners with people and resources
3. Engage learners in a range of familiar and new contextualised practices
4. Ensure learners encounter and operate upon manuals and texts found in the workplace
5. Provide opportunities to manipulate, extend, modify and develop existing concepts and skills
6. Ensure learners explore alternative methods to perform tasks
7. Engage learners in regular and sustained practice in dealing with the non-routine
8. Ensure learning focuses on developing the capacity for informed normative action
9. Have learners actively solve problems of new and received settings
10. Teach strategies for action explicitly
11. Engage learners in reflection, generating new concepts and skills and improving their learning approaches

Table 11.4 Sample actions flowing from the principle: *Making setting element relationships clear*

Principle
The relationships among elements of the learning activity system should be made clear—the implicit and explicit rules and the normative nature of meaning in the setting; the tools, technologies, processes, equipment and materials and tensions in their histories; the ways in which subjects share objects in achieving outcomes and how these are represented in the setting; who constitutes the community and the nature of the division of responsibilities. This includes power relationships in the setting and how the learner is positioned with respect to them.

Sample actions
1   Ensure instructors and learners develop an in-depth knowledge of site-specific organisational systems, work practices and values
2   Ensure learners understand competing discourses in workplaces, gaining access to insider terminology and documents while still being socialised into the workplace and its canonical knowledge
3   Analyse workplaces in terms of their elements, relationships among them and tensions and contradictions
4   Base learning on activities and interactions with social sources of knowledge
5   Ensure meanings are consistent with legitimate and workable solutions in the setting
6   Ensure learners have access to nuances and conditional aspects of activity
7   Use setting features to develop knowledge

Table 11.5 Sample actions flowing from the principle: *Sharing meanings*

Principle
Learning should involve sharing meaning. This involves making aspects of the activity system visible for inspection; showing and demonstrating, discussing and sharing alternative different ways of reading tasks, the setting, problems and various ways forward; and finding ways of cooperating that improve practice. It also involves reconciling capacities-to-do; other intuitive and tacit meanings; theories; principles; other symbolic representations of meaning; and other relevant realms of meaning. Such learning should proceed from direct concrete experience rather than verbalised propositional statements. It also involves building connections with manuals, instructions and texts.

Sample actions
1   Ensure learners have access to competing discourses in the workplace and opportunities to observe and work with experienced workers in a mentoring situation
2   Ensure learners engage with multiple resources and perspectives
3   Provide opportunities for interactions with, guidance and support from, and collaboration with, experienced practitioners
4   Have learners explore the modes of rendition of workplace beliefs and their interconnections
5   Encourage learners to articulate and share their knowledge with others
6   Use group work to identify and clarify workplace values and explore similarities and differences in views
7   Make explicit the espoused, instantiated and enacted beliefs of the setting
8   Ensure learners understand why some methods are chosen over others
9   Give learners access to heuristic and strategic knowledge, which is tacitly known by experts
10   Share schematic representations of particular kinds of knowledge with learners as a reference for their own progressive development of their own meanings and ways of proceeding
11   Teach the implicit strategic knowledge of experts, explicitly and in combination with more specific knowledge

Table 11.6 Sample actions flowing from the principle: *Relating one learning setting meanings with those of other settings*

Principle

The relationships among the learning activity system, other activity systems in which the learner is involved and the wider community should be explored, so that the learner can seek to connect meanings across systems and tensions and contradictions among them. This will involve discussion, reading, formulation of views, and reconciling tensions and contradictions. It will also involve reconciling the individual's plural vocations in work, personal life and society. Learners will have the opportunity to discern the inter-relationships among society, its economy and personal and community welfare and quality of life; the forces and pressures involved; and their own position and responsibilities in relation to them.

Sample actions

1. Provide multiple, diverse contextualised experiences, including problem-solving, and ensure learners work out connections among routine and non-routine procedures and their contexts of use
2. Ensure learners work across domains, assignments and contexts; work alone and in groups; and engage in working as well as observing in order to derive meanings from plural ways of thinking and acting
3. Ensure learners engage with multiple perspectives and resources
4. Ensure learning includes access to variations in vocational practice
5. Provide opportunities for generating new skills and concepts by extending, modifying, developing and transforming existing meanings
6. Ensure learners understand the societal context of workplace values
7. Ensure learners compare workplace and societal values
8. Ensure learners explore the historical, cultural and situated relativity of workplace values
9. Make explicit the platform of beliefs underpinning vocational curricula
10. Use strategies such a modelling, coaching, questioning, explaining and group discussion

---

from the activity systems where they are drawn upon to mediate teaching and learning activity. Moreover, they may be in the process of evolving into rules of practice for that setting, as the teaching and learning activity is transformed over time—for instance, where they may have been taken to underpin formal processes of curriculum development. The instantiation of these principles and actions is illustrated in the next section.

INSTANTIATIONS OF PRINCIPLES AND SAMPLE ACTIONS IN APPROACHING VOCATIONAL TEACHING AND LEARNING

Here, the suggestions made in Chapters 3–8 on teaching literacy, numeracy, information literacy, creativity, problem-solving and workplace

Table 11.7 Sample actions flowing from the principle: *Building connections among different meanings and their renditions*

Principle

Learning should involve building connection among meanings and different renditions of meaning. This involves making explicit the connections outlined in other points here—meaning and doing; others' meanings; knowledge codified in manuals, instructions and texts; connections within and among elements and systems, and with broader society; meanings across plural vocational pursuits; old and new meanings; old and new work, technologies, tools, equipment and materials. It involves experiences in discerning the connections among different renditions of meaning in words, diagrams, pictures, gestures, action and images. It also involves developing a facility in operating upon such inter-connections as needed in different situations. This involves seeking to understand the qualities of meaning derived from practice and relate them to other qualities that meaning can have, e.g. relating verbal renditions of meaning to imaginal ones; rules to embodied action; step-by-step frameworks for action and planning to automatic action; compiled meaning to verbal propositions. Experiences in connecting the primary sources of meaning (derived from practice) with other renditions involve explicit communication about these meanings.

Sample actions

1. Provide opportunities for learners to manipulate, extend, modify and develop their existing knowledge. Provide opportunities for transforming existing meanings
2. Ensure learners grapple with new problems
3. Focus learners on the construction of new ways of achieving goals
4. Use a variety of tools and strategies to engage multiple ways of giving meaning
5. Ensure learners frame knowledge in a range of different ways, including linguistically, concretely and symbolically
6. Provide opportunities for learners to reconcile normative meanings e.g. through unmasking and identifying values; relating different kinds of values; considering values in practice and abstracted lists of universal, instrumental and end values; and asking 'What if?' questions
7. Ensure learners work out connections among routine and non-routine procedures and their contexts of use; and relate general strategies to the demands and methods of contextualised practice
8. Ensure learners reflect upon strategies and other knowledge used in different contexts, and why they are similar and different
9. Ensure learners think consciously about their learning and mastery of concepts and skills in order to understand the meanings associated with a particular setting and to transform these meanings for other instances and settings
10. Facilitate the incremental transformation of meanings as a result of different experiences and use of targeted concepts and skills
11. Assist learners to synthesise new knowledge as part of their changing conceptual frameworks and as a basis for further thought and action

values, and in Chapters 9 and 10 on flexible learning and guiding learning, are summarised in terms of each of the seven principles above. They illustrate how the various actions summarised in Tables 11.1–11.7 might be instantiated in practice directed at particular topic areas or teaching methods. For each principle, some of the various ways in which

Table 11.8 Instantiations of *proceeding from learners' sense of vocation*

Principle

Learning should proceed from the learner's sense of vocation—needs, aspirations and intentions; previous experiences and the meanings extracted from them; existing capacities-to-do; relationships among the learner's work and non-work goals and meanings.

Instantiations

Literacy

Instructional practices should take account of the language, literacy and numeracy needs of the learner and develop these as part of, not separate from, vocational competence

In the orientation phase of learning, the learners' prior knowledge of the literacies involved could be assessed or learners could self-assess their own facility with the relevant texts

Questions can be used to access the learner's prior knowledge of the topic so that the reading process is likely to be successful

Numeracy

Learning requires an ordered development of numerical meanings

Teaching must not only afford learners a cognitively challenging environment, but also one in which challenges are supported appropriately

Computer literacy

Learners need adequate practice on simple tasks and then to move on to more complex tasks with suitable strategies

Problem-solving

Learners need to engage with less complex problems initially, then move on to more complex problems

Learners should progress to engaging with problems that are complex because they are ill-defined

Creativity

Creative learning should involve increasing complexity, increasing diversity, and global before local skills

Cognitive steps or schema training may assist in learning creativity, especially for those new to creative work

Values

Learners need to engage with content that enables them to identify and engage with values

Flexible delivery

Opportunities are needed for learners to manipulate, extend, modify and develop their existing knowledge

The environment should be challenging but appropriately scaffolded and supported

Guiding learning

Learning tasks should be selected that are appropriate in terms of subject-matter and goals

Participation should take account of learner readiness and learner interpretations of tasks

---

such principles might be instantiated in specialist topic areas (e.g. literacy, numeracy, creativity) and for particular approaches to teaching (e.g. flexible and guided learning) are brought together in Tables 11.8–11.14.

Table 11.9 Instantiations of *contextualising learning and making functions and purposes explicit*

Principle
Learning should occur in settings or activity systems where the function and purposes of the learning are clear and explicit and related to vocation; and collective motives and personal goals should be related. The tasks in which learners engage should be tasks that have an explicit relationship with tasks that constitute current or future work or other vocations.

Instantiations
Literacy
Instructors need an in-depth knowledge of site-specific texts and tasks, as well as site-specific organisational systems, work practices and underpinning values in order to ensure the relevance of the training, to contextualise the training and to build a positive learning environment
Literacies should not be 'bolted-on'; rather, technical literacies need to be taught alongside the technical competence, using the relevant workplace texts
Workers need training for different literacy roles
Training programs need to identify the language, literacy and numeracy competencies essential for work performance, as well as the social literacies of the workplace, which are often not made explicit
Instructional and assessment language and processes should be consistent with those used on the job and appropriate for the learner; and similarly for assessment
In the enhancement phase of learning, the environment should simulate actual work conditions in order that learners experience the need to develop skills in prioritising work, coping with interruptions and developing the social literacies essential for high workplace performance
The enhancement of learning may take place on-site or in a training room using authentic texts and tasks, simulations and role-play. It may require transforming the learning spaces to achieve this
Assessment should be holistic, rather than consisting in performance of discrete often decontextualised skills, preferably over a range of competencies; and using relevant workplace texts and tasks

Numeracy
Learning is shaped by the setting in which it is embedded, and is therefore referenced to the learning setting. The features of the setting provide opportunities for learning. The teacher should use these characteristics of the setting in which the numeracy is to be used
Learning is about actively solving the problems of adaptation to new settings or new aspects of received settings
Meanings must have power in the particular setting in which they arise, being consistent with workable or legitimate solutions within the setting
Meaning-making in numeracy is a social process, requiring engagement with multiple perspectives and resources

Information literacy
Competencies are context-specific and learning needs to involve the development of site-specific concepts and skills in combination with more general strategies
Learning should involve more than paper-based methods, including nuances and conditional aspects of competence
Routine tasks are best served by scenario-based approaches
For transfer, learners need to use strategies in the context of other applications (in order to recognise they are the same strategy)

continued

Problem-solving
Complex problems are complex, in part as a function of the situation in which they occur. Learners need to engage in real problem-solving situations
The situatedness of problems means that learners need to engage in a variety of problem-solving activities

Creativity
Learners should engage in a variety of authentic tasks

Values
Development of normative meaning should proceed from concrete experience in authentic practice, where function and purpose are transparent
Learners need to learn how to engage in assertive action with respect to values and improving workplace outcomes

Flexible delivery
Teaching should utilise characteristics of settings in which the knowledge targeted is utilised
Teaching should afford the learner with a challenging environment for growth

Guiding learning
Engagement should occur in the social environment where the knowledge is to be used
Experienced practitioners should bring important intersubjectivity to learning processes

CONCLUSION

Principles and sample actions have been advanced here to guide vocational teaching and learning. Examples of how these can be instantiated in selected areas of practice have also been summarised.

The basic framework for guiding vocational teaching and learning (Figure 2.2, Chapter 2) has been elaborated in two main ways (see Figure 11.2). Firstly, it has been elaborated, in general terms, by suggesting sample actions for each learning principle (Tables 11.1–11.7). Secondly, it has been illustrated for the teaching of each of the specialist areas of literacy, numeracy, information literacy, creativity, problem-solving and workplace values, as well as for flexible learning and for guiding learning (Tables 11.8–11.14). Together, the figures and tables are advanced as a rich conceptual framework for vocational educators to draw upon in considering practice.

Figure 11.2 represents one possible framework for teaching and learning in vocational education, with particular application to the specialist areas of literacy, numeracy, information literacy, creativity, complex problem-solving and values, and to flexible and guided learning. Other frameworks are also possible. The advantages advanced for this particular framework are that it relates instantiated practice to generalised principles and to a conceptualisation of expertise. It is therefore suggested that it would also be a useful starting point in thinking about teaching and learning for many vocational areas.

INTEGRATING APPROACHES TO DEVELOPING VOCATIONAL EXPERTISE

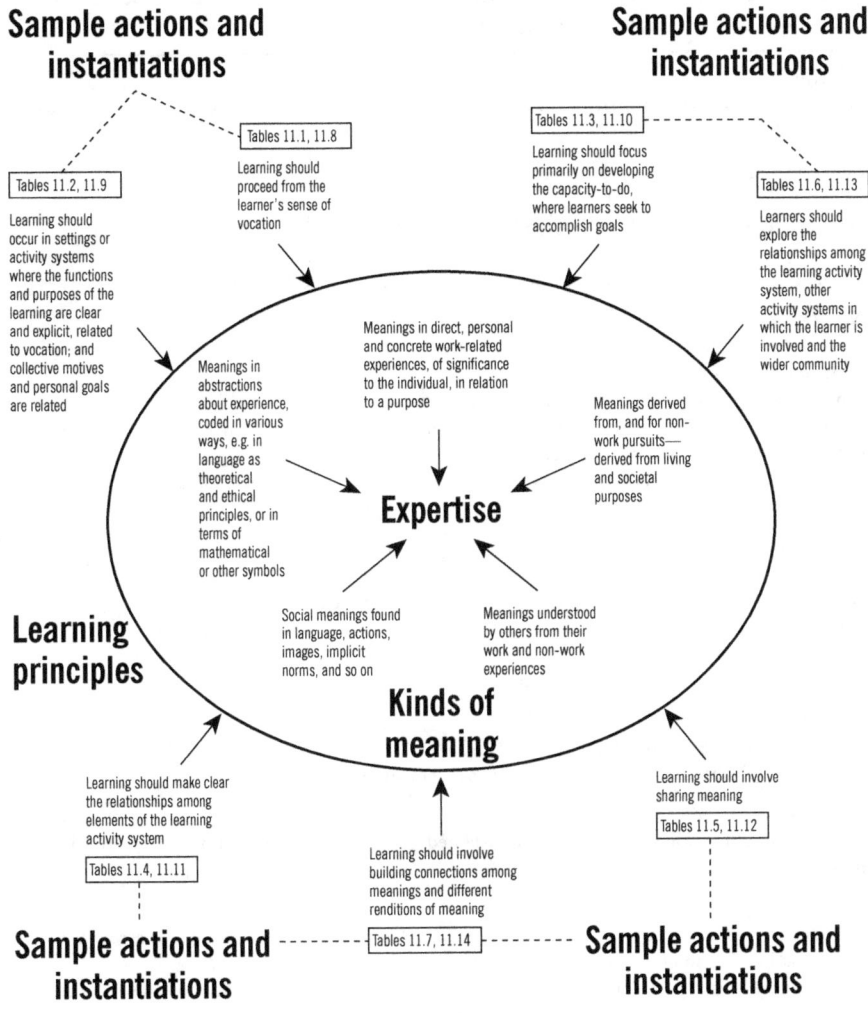

Figure 11.2 Relationships of expertise, meaning, learning principles, sample actions and instantiations

Table 11.10   Instantiations of *focusing learning primarily on the capacity-to-do*

Principle

Learning should focus primarily on developing the capacity-to-do; where learners seek to accomplish goals.

Instantiations

Literacy

Learners need to engage in a range of communicative activities and learn new literacy practices

Learners should encounter and operate upon manuals and texts found in the workplace

Numeracy

Learning numeracy should be about actively solving the problems of adaptation to new settings or new aspects of received settings

Problem-solving requires conscious decisive action

Learning numeracy should involve reflective thinking, generating new concepts and skills

Learning numeracy requires engagement with people and resources

Teaching must provide opportunities for students to manipulate, extend, modify and develop their existing knowledge of numerical concepts and skills

Information literacy

Learners need opportunities for contextualised practice

Learners need opportunities to explore alternative methods to perform a task

For non-routine skills, problem-based action learning approaches (e.g. scenarios) are effective

Instruction should include explicit strategies

Problem-solving

Problem-solving skills are developed through solving real problems

Learners need opportunities to engage in problem-finding

Creativity

Learners should engage in regular and sustained practice in dealing with the non-routine activities of their craft

Values

Learners should learn how to understand, recognise, communicate about and assert values, as well as how to modify their own values

The focus in learning should be on activities which develop the capacity to take informed normative action, and where assertion of better norms is undertaken when appropriate

Flexible delivery

Teaching should prompt learners to think about their learning and the mastery of skills and concepts

Guiding learning

Priority should be given to learner engagement in tasks

Learning should be organised in relation to the practices of the vocation

Prior experience should be applied to lower accountability tasks

Opportunities for practice should be provided

INTEGRATING APPROACHES TO DEVELOPING VOCATIONAL EXPERTISE

Table 11.11   Instantiations of *making setting element relationships clear*

Principle
The relationships among elements of the learning activity system should be made clear—the implicit and explicit rules and the normative nature of meaning in the setting; the tools, technologies, processes, equipment and materials and tensions in their histories; the ways in which subjects share objects in achieving outcomes and how these are represented in the setting; who constitutes the community and the nature of the division of responsibilities. This includes power relationships in the setting and how the learner is positioned with respect to them.

Instantiations

Literacy
Instructors need an in-depth knowledge of site-specific texts and tasks, as well as site-specific organisational systems, work practices and underpinning values in order to ensure the relevance of the training, to contextualise the training and to build a positive learning environment
All workers need to have the skills and understanding to undertake different literacy roles
Learners need to be made aware of the competing discourses apparent in workplaces; and gain access to insider terminology and documents, while still being socialised into the workplace

Numeracy
The meanings developed in a setting need to be consistent with workable or legitimate solutions to problems in that setting
Teaching must prompt learners to consciously think about their learning and mastery of skills and concepts

Information literacy
The learner needs access to the nuances and conditional aspects of the activity
Scenario-based approaches are preferable for learning to deal with non-routine tasks

Problem-solving
Relationships between elements of problems are not always clear and defined. Learners need to develop an understanding of the relationships between elements of a problem

Values
Settings should be analysed in terms of their elements and relationships among them, and tensions and contradictions identified

Flexible delivery
Characteristics of the setting should be used in targeting the knowledge to be developed

Guiding learning
Learning should be a social process based on activities and interactions with social sources of knowledge

Table 11.12   Instantiations of *sharing meanings*

Principle
Learning should involve sharing meaning. This involves making aspects of the activity system visible for inspection; showing and demonstrating, discussing and sharing alternative different ways of reading tasks, the setting, problems and various ways forward; and finding ways of cooperating that improve practice. It also involves reconciling capacities-to-do; other intuitive and tacit meanings; theories; principles; other symbolic representations of meaning; and other relevant realms of meaning. Such learning should proceed from direct concrete experience rather than verbalised propositional statements. It also involves building connections with manuals, instructions and texts.

Instantiations

Literacy
New employees need to have access to competing discourses in the workplace and opportunities to observe and work with experienced workers in a mentoring situation to learn the communication patterns

Numeracy
Meaning-making in numeracy is a socially interactive process and requires that the learner engage with multiple perspectives
Teaching must involve methods that encourage learners to articulate and share their knowledge with others

Information literacy
Strategic knowledge can be explicitly and successfully taught in combination with functional knowledge
Students need to learn why some methods are chosen over others and understand the trade-offs involved

Problem-solving
Problem-solving often involves more than one person. Different people bring different perspectives to the task. Making individual perspectives and approaches to problem-solving explicit and transparent improves the learning of all involved in the problem-solving

Creativity
Learners need explicit instruction in a creativity schema developed from studies of expert creative thinking, so that they can use it in their progressive and incremental development of their own heuristic schemas
Learners need the heuristic and strategic knowledge that is tacitly acquired by experts from experience in working in practice

Values
Espoused, instantiated and enacted beliefs should be made explicit
Normative content should be explored in terms of the mode of rendition and interconnections, to facilitate communication about values and their clarification
Group work can be used in identifying and clarifying values in order to make explicit similarities and differences in views

Flexible delivery
Methods should encourage learners to articulate and share their knowledge with others

Guiding learning
Learning should involve interactions with, and guidance and support from, experienced practitioners
Learning should be promoted by support and collaboration
Learning should include the canonical knowledge of the vocation

Table 11.13 Instantiations of *relating one learning setting meanings with those of other settings*

Principle
The relationships among the learning activity system, other activity systems in which the learner is involved and the wider community should be explored, so that the learner can seek to connect meanings across systems and tensions and contradictions among them. This will involve discussion, reading, formulation of views, and reconciling tensions and contradictions. It will also involve reconciling the individual's plural vocations in work, personal life and society. Learners will have the opportunity to discern the interrelationships among society, its economy and personal and community welfare and quality of life; the forces and pressures involved and their own position and responsibilities in relation to them.

Instantiations

Literacy
Learners need to engage in reflection on what has been learnt
Learners need to choose from a repertoire of skills to suit their interpretation of situations in terms of the context and purpose (reading for meaning in relation to task and social relations)

Numeracy
Learners should engage with multiple perspectives and resources
Learners should generate new skills and concepts by extending, modifying, developing and transforming existing skills and meanings

Information literacy
Learners need multiple diverse experiences, including problem-based scenarios and an understanding that they need to explicitly work out the connections among routine and non-routine procedures and the contexts of use
Learners need to experience and reflect upon strategies used in different contexts, the extent to which they are similar, and the reasons why they are similar or different

Problem-solving
Developing expertise in solving complex problems involves understanding the relations between different problems

Creativity
Learners should work across domains, assignments and contexts, work alone and in groups, and engage in working as well as observing, in order to derive meanings from plural ways of thinking and acting (plural heuristics)

Values
An understanding of the societal context of workplace values should be developed
Workplace norms should be compared with wider societal values
The historical, cultural and situated relativity of values should be explored
The platforms of beliefs underpinning vocational curriculum development should be made explicit for learners

Guiding learning
Learning should include access to variations in vocational practice
Learning should include such strategies as modelling, coaching, questioning, explaining and group discussion

Table 11.14 Instantiations of *building connections among different meanings and their renditions*

Principle

Learning should involve building connections among meanings and different renditions of meaning. This involves making explicit the connections outlined in other points here—meaning and doing; others' meanings; knowledge codified in manuals, instructions and texts; connections within and among elements and systems, and with broader society; meanings across plural vocational pursuits; old and new meanings; old and new work, technologies, tools, equipment and materials.

Instantiations

Literacy

Learners need to synthesise their new knowledge and literacies to form part of their conceptual framework as a basis for further thought and action

Learners need to take different literacy roles: as a text user, text decoder or text analyst to become a critical participant in decision-making

Numeracy

Learners should generate new skills and concepts by extending, modifying, developing and transforming existing skills and meanings

Learning numeracy involves reflective thinking in order to transform meanings associated with a particular setting to other instances and settings. In so doing the learner constructs new concepts and skills

Learners should grapple with new problems

Learners should frame numerical knowledge in a range of different ways including linguistically, concretely and symbolically

Teaching must deploy a variety of tools and strategies and thus engage learners with multiple perspectives and resourses

Information literacy

Learners need multiple diverse experiences, including problem-based scenarios and an understanding that they need to explicitly work out the connections among routine and non-routine procedures and the contexts of use

A focus on the construction of software search algorithms is needed to assist the learner to generalise

Learners need to relate general strategies to the demands and methods of contextualised practice

Problem-solving

Learners need to experience a wide range of problem-solving situations, in various contexts to develop rich interconnected problem-solving skills

Creativity

Learning experiences should facilitate the incremental transformation of meaning as the result of different experiences and targeted facility with the creativity schema

Values

Opportunities should be created to reconcile normative meanings, e.g. through unmasking and identifying values; relating different kinds of values; considering values in practice and abstracted lists of universal, instrumental and end values; and asking 'what if?' questions

Flexible delivery

A variety of tools and strategies should be used to engage multiple ways of giving meaning

Opportunities should be provided for learners to manipulate, extend, modify and develop their existing knowledge

Learners should be prompted to think consciously about their learning and the mastery of skills and concepts

However, while these various suggestions and examples instantiate teaching and learning principles and the kinds of actions that can be considered in developing vocational knowledge, it is emphasised again that they are merely abstracted illustrations. The actual activity and its constituent actions must take their form in relation to the various elements that actually exist in real teaching and learning settings.

REFERENCES

Engeström, Y. 1987, *Learning by expanding: An Activity-Theoretical Approach to Developmental Research*, Orienta-Konsultit Oy, Helsinki

Leont'ev, A.N. 1981 (1959), *Problems of the Development of the Mind*, Progress Publishers, Moscow

Index

activity and expertise 19–20
activity system, teaching and learning 215, 217, 248–50
activity theory 19, 44, 101, 213, 215, 217, 223, 250
    cultural-historical 26–7, 81, 100, 101–4, 105, 140, 212, 214, 248
    and working values 188, 192, 194, 196, 197
aims and curriculum development 190
airline
    customer service 123–7
    industry and literacy 65–7
    work sites and values 191
angling and knowledge 129
assessment 73, 74, 75
attitudes 184–5

behavioural objectives 29, 33
body language 11
brainstorming 163
browsing and hypermedia 129
business services 113

categorical reduction 178
classroom practice 131–2
cluster analysis 98
codifying knowledge 28
cognitive
    objectives 29
    processes 129–30
    psychology 13, 17, 56, 93, 186
    representations of meaning 39
    research literature 18
    resources and creative problem-solving 170–4
    theories 12, 18, 135, 139–40, 147–8, 156, 159, 179, 187
collaborative/cooperative learning 207
communicating meaning 131
competencies 33–4, 35
    workplace 116, 118, 119
competency-based training 32, 34, 61, 116, 117
computer literacy 23
conceptions and curriculum development 190

conceptual knowledge 39
construction industry and literacy 67–71
constructivist view of learning 93, 219
context-dependent knowledge 126
context-specific knowledge 126–7, 130, 131
contextualised learning 207
convergent thinking 165
creative
    problems 140
    thinking in vocational settings 153–4
creative problem-solving 153, 166–8, 170–4
    and cognitive resources 170–4
    Geneplore model 157, 158
    in graphic design 166–8
    and interactivity 165
    models 156–9, 165–6, 175, 177–8, 179
    protocol analysis 167–8, 169–70, 171–2
    synthesised model 160
creativity
    conceptual definition 155
    consensual definition 155
    definition 154–6
    and evaluation 164–5
    and executive control 165, 166
    and expertise 16
    and exploration 163
    generative procedures and generation 161–3
    implications for teaching and learning 168–78
    and knowledge base 159–61
    second-order procedures 161–5
    stages 156
    and students 174–7
    third-order procedures 165
cultural needs and flexible learning 206–7
cultural-historical activity theory 26–7, 81, 100, 101–4, 105, 140, 212, 214, 248

INDEX

curriculum
  content and values 195
  design 71-3
  goals 235-7
  and guided learning 235-8
  participatory practices 235, 237-8
  theories 31-2
curriculum development 28, 30, 31, 43
  implications for 130-1, 190-3
  platform 190, 195
  recommendations for teaching 131-2
customised learning 207

data workers 113
database software and work practice 120-1
decontextualised skills 51
doing and meaning 8-9
domain-specific knowledge 120, 123

economic
  needs and flexible learning 206-7
  policy and employment-related competencies 119
economies, globalising 33, 36, 154
education system 130-1
empirics and meaning 6
enhancing, technical knowledge and literacies 74
esthetics and meaning 6
ethics and meaning 6
evaluation and creative thinking 164-5
expansive visualisation 103-4, 105, 218
expert action 18-19
expertise
  as activity 19-20
  as conceptual change 16-17
  concepts of 4-5
  as creativity/innovation 16
  facility with meaning 5-7
  as judgement and appropriate practice 18-19
  as language 13-15
  and learning 41
  and meaning 22, 41
  as memory and knowledge 12-13
  as performance 13-15
  as problem-solving and transfer 15-16

  psychological concepts of 11-20
  as schemas 17-18
  as shared meaning 19-20
  summary of ideas 20-2
  vocational 247-65
exploration and creative thinking 163
expressive objectives 30

flexible learning *see* learning, flexible
formal problems 140
functional fixedness and problem-solving 145

Geneplore model of creative problem-solving 157, 158
generation and creative thinking 161-3
generic knowledge 120, 123, 124, 126, 127, 130, 131
Getzel thinking 147
global knowledge 131
globalising economies 33, 36, 154
goal
  monitoring 178
  state and problems 136, 137
goalsetting 178
government and information literacy 116-19
grammar 61
graphic design and creative problem-solving 166-8
guided learning *see* learning, guided

heuristic knowledge 172, 173
hierarchical view of thinking 159
higher-order thinking 165
hospitality industry
  and literacy 65-7
  motel front office practice 120-3, 216-17
  and values 191
  Web-based instruction 216-17
human activity system 39
hypermedia 128-30

illiteracy 54
illumination stage of creativity 156
implementation and flexible learning 209
implications and principles
  curriculum development 130-1, 190-3
  developing creativity 168-78

developing literacy 71–5
developing problem-solving skills 149–50
flexible learning 219–22
learning, guided 238–42
numerical practices 93–5, 96–7, 104–5
teaching and learning 40–3, 71–5, 93–5, 96–7, 104–5, 130–1, 149–50, 168–78, 193–6, 219–22, 238–42, 250–9
vocational learning 238–42
working values 193–6
incubation stage of creativity 156
individuals and problem-solving 38
industrial standards 33
information literacy 110–11
  curriculum development 119, 130–1
  definition 114
  and government 116–19
  and knowledge economy 111–13
  research 119–30
  teaching 131–2
  and vocational curriculum 119
  for work 114–19
  in the workplace 119–27
innovation and expertise 16
innovative capacities 36
institutional framework and flexible learning 210
instructional
  objectives 29
  practices 73–4
integrating and knowledge 129
International Adult Literacy Survey (IALS) 54, 64
intersubjectivity 228–31

judgement and expertise 18–19
just-in-time learning 207

knowing 6
knowledge
  academic 36
  angling 129
  base 159–61
  codifying 28
  cognitive treatment of 17, 186–7
  conceptual 39
  construction of 31
  context-dependent 126
  context-specific 126–7, 130, 131
  database 120
  domain-specific 120, 123
  economy 111–13, 115
    and expertise 12–13
  first-order 161
  generic 120, 123, 124, 126, 127, 130, 131
  global 129, 131
  heuristic 172, 173
  integrating 129
  mathematical 92
  nature of 30–1
  procedural 39, 170, 172–3, 187
  propositional 170, 172–3
  scientific 30–1
  second-order 161
  strategic 127–8, 130, 173
  symbolic representation of 143
  tacit 6, 7, 149
  types 39
  and values 186–7
  vocational 30, 34, 226
  workers 113

language 11
  and expertise 13–15
lateral thinking 163
learning
  as an activity system 248–50
  assumptions 28–32
  and cognitive representations of meaning 39
  collaborative/cooperative 207
  constructive/engaging 37–39
  constructivist 219
  contexualised 207
  customised 207
  developments in the forms of 207–8
  engagement in thinking and acting 234–5
  experiences 27
  expertise 41
  implications for 40–3, 71–5, 104–5, 130–1, 149–50, 168–78, 193–6, 238–42
  just-in-time 207
  learner-directed 207
  lifelong 207, 131
  numeracy 93–5, 96–7
  outcomes 33–5
  participatory 219
  planning 37–40

INDEX

principles 40-3, 219-22, 250-9
problem-solving skills 149-50
processes 29
as a social process 232-4
through thinking and action 234-5
transformative 207
in vocational settings 168-78, 226-44
see also vocational teaching and learning
learning, flexible 203-4
  curriculum 217-19
  definition 204-6
  economic and cultural needs 206-7
  facets and indicators 205, 206
  frameworks 209-12
  and implementation 209-9
  institutional factors 208-9
  and institutional framework 210
  and intra-action 210
  as a learning activity 212-17
  models 209-12, 220
  and pedagogy 209
  principles and teaching methods 219-22
  rationale 206-9
  and technology 209
  Web-based instruction 216-17
  who needs 208
learning, guided 226-7
  conceptual bases 231-35
  and curriculum 235-8
  implications for instruction 238-42
  outcomes 228-31
lifelong
  education 131
  learning 207
literacy
  adult 54-5, 58
  and airline industry 65-7
  basic (autonomous) 52, 53, 58-60, 71
  and construction industry 67-71
  critical 53, 62, 63
  definition 23, 51, 52-3, 114-15
  developing 51
  discourses 51, 53-5, 58
  functional 53
  and hospitality industry 65-7
  implications for teaching and learning 71-5

information 110-11, 114-19
  social (ideological model) 53
  as social practice 58, 61-62
  as technology 51, 53, 58, 60-1, 71, 115
  theories, research and practice 55-64
  vocational 53
  in the workplace 53, 64-71
  see also information literacy; multiliteracies

manufacturing 112-13
meaning
  codification of 33-7
  cognitive representations 39
  communicating of 131
  construction of 6
  and doing 8-9
  and expertise 22, 41
  and fields of activity 9
  kinds of 22
  in language 21
  normative 195-6
  and practice 9-10
  and reading 66
  relationships of 7-11, 22
  shared and co-constructed 10-11
  shared, expertise as 19-20
  symbolic 6
  vocation, purpose and function 10
meaning-making 63, 66
mechanisation bias and problem-solving 145
memory and expertise 12-13
metacognition 173
moral meanings 6
motel front office practice 120-3
multiliteracies 51, 53, 58, 62-4, 71
multimedia and problem-solving 144

New Maths movement 86
New Zealand and workplace skills 117, 118
numeracy 23, 81
  cluster analysis 98
  cultural-historical activity system 101-4, 105
  curriculum development 99, 100-5
  dilemmas and conflicts 95-100
  principles of learning and teaching 93-5, 96-7

numerical practices 82–4
   constructing accounts 87–9
   implications for teaching and learning 104–5
   striking rates 89–92
   thematic approach 83–4
   theme of constructibility 83, 92–5, 99
   and theme of useability 83, 86–92, 98, 105
   and theme of visibility 83, 84–6, 98, 105

objectives *see* aims and curriculum development; behavioural objectives; cognitive objectives; competencies; curriculum; expressive objectives; meaning; outcomes; process objectives
orientation 73–4
outcomes 33–5, 38

participatory learning 219
participatory practices as curriculum 235, 237–8
pedagogy 209
performance and expertise 13–15
performance problems 140, 144–5
platform and curriculum development 190
practice and meaning 9–10
preparation stage of creativity 156
principles for teaching and learning *see* implications and principles
probabilistic problems 140
problem space model 136–7, 138, 147, 157
problem state 136
problem structuring 157
problem zone 137–8, 142
problem-finding 141
problem-solving 23, 147–8
   Aristotle's theory 147
   and associationism 147
   as a context-specific activity 148
   creative 153, 156–9, 166–8, 170–4
   and design solutions 139
   difficulty of 141–3, 144
   expert 148–9
   and expertise 15–16
   and functional fixedness 145
   Gestalt explanations 147
   implications for teaching and learning 149–50
   and individuals 37
   knowledge 141
   mathematical 143
   mechanisation bias 145
   and multimedia 144
   and navigating 136, 138
   and redundancy effect 144
   and restructuring 147
   and sacrificing zone 139
   skills 135–50, 149–50
   and spatial contiguity principle 144
   and split-attention effect 144
   verbal 145, 146
   visualisation 145–7
   workplace 112, 148
problems 136–40
   as challenges 140–1
   complexibility of 141–3
   and contradiction 141–2
   creative 140, 142–3
   definition 136
   difficulty of 141–3
   elements 141
   and emergent criteria 142
   formal 140
   and goal state 136, 137
   ill-defined 137–8, 142
   performance 140, 144–5
   probabilistic 140
   representing 143–7
   routine 140, 144, 145
   and search space 136, 137
   strategic 140
procedural knowledge 39, 170, 172–3, 187
process objectives 29
propositional knowledge 170, 172–3
protocol analysis 167–8, 169–70, 171–2
psychological concepts of expertise 11–20

reading 55, 59–60, 66
redundancy effect and problem-solving 144
reflective thinking 220, 221
research and information literacy 119–30
routine problems 140, 144, 145

INDEX

sample actions
   and instantiations 254
   teaching and learning principles 250–5
scaffolding 10, 19
schema training 170, 178
schemas 17–18, 156, 159, 166
search space and problems 136, 137
searching and hypermedia 129
skills
   problem-solving 135–50
   work 112–13, 116–17
social origins of values 185–6
socially situated practices and literacy 51
societal issues and vocational education 30
societal values 195
society 27
software
   database and work practice 120–1
   efficient use of 127–8
spatial contiguity principle and problem-solving 144
split-attention effect and problem-solving 144
strategic knowledge 126–7, 130, 173
strategic problems 140
students and creativity 174–7
subject matter analysis 27
symbolic meaning 6, 7
synoetic meaning 6
synoptics 6–7
synthesising, new knowledge and literacies 74

tacit knowledge 6, 7, 149
teaching
   as an activity system 248–50
   assumptions 28–32
   and cognitive representations of meaning 39
   constructive/engaging 37–9
   and curriculum development 131–2
   and flexible learning 219–22
   implications for 40–3, 71–5, 104–5, 130–1, 149–50, 168–78, 193–6, 238–42
   and information literacy 131–2
   numeracy 93–5, 96–7
   planning 37–40
   principles 40–3, 219–22, 250–9

problem-solving skills 149–50
   in vocational settings 168–78
   see also vocational teaching and learning
technology
   and flexible learning 210
   literacy as 51, 53, 58, 60–1, 71, 115
   using 118–19
   workplace and new 139–40
theories and curriculum development 190
thinking
   convergent 165
   hierarchical view of 159
   higher-order 165
   lateral 163
   reflective 220, 221
   second-order 161–5
   vertical 165
transformative learning 207

values 23, 31, 184–5
   and activity theory 188, 194
   in airline work sites 191
   and assertive action 196
   cognitive treatment of 186–7
   explicit 194–5
   in hospitality work sites 191
   instrumental 185
   and knowledge 186–7
   in settings 187–9
   social origins of 185–6
   societal 195
   systems 185
   terminal 185
   workplace 183, 188, 189–90, 195
verification stage of creativity 156
vertical thinking 165
vocation and meaning 10
vocational education, competency approach 119
vocational expertise, developing 247–65
vocational knowledge 30, 35, 226
vocational practice 226, 228, 230, 232, 238
vocational settings
   creative thinking in 153–4
   teaching and learning 168–78
vocational teaching and learning 26–44, 226–44, 251, 255–259
   curriculum sources 27–8

implications for instruction 238–42
instantiations of principles and sample actions 255–9

Web-based instruction 216–17
work
    changing nature of 64–5
    and information literacy 114–19
    in the knowledge economy 111–13
    practice and database software 120
    skills 112–13, 116–17
workplace
    activities 70
    competencies 116, 118, 119
    implications for teaching and learning 193–6
    information literacy in the 119–27
    literacy 53, 64–71
    and new technology 139
    and problem-solving 112, 148
    values 183, 188, 189–90, 195
writing 55, 59–60

For Product Safety Concerns and Information please contact our EU
representative GPSR@taylorandfrancis.com
Taylor & Francis Verlag GmbH, Kaufingerstraße 24, 80331 München, Germany

www.ingramcontent.com/pod-product-compliance
Lightning Source LLC
Chambersburg PA
CBHW061435300426
44114CB00014B/1694